She hit the brakes that fateful December day in 2017. Some would say she had a flawless course: she received her master's degree in translation studies with high honors and continued on the same route to get an additional diploma in management and a first work experience in an embassy in Brussels.

It was until that day, when she could not get her legs to take her onto the subway, she was 25 and everything was about to change. The "me" person giving voice to the words had tried so hard to be perfect in order to please the "everyones" and "everything" that she completely forgot about herself and got lost.

Livia,
My person.

Alessandra Dubois

ERASABLE

KEEP QUIET; FUEL THE PAIN.

AUSTIN MACAULEY PUBLISHERS™
LONDON • CAMBRIDGE • NEW YORK • SHARJAH

Ordering Information
Quantity sales: Special discounts are available on quantity purchases by corporations, associations, and others. For details, contact the publisher at the address below.

Publisher's Cataloging-in-Publication data
Dubois, Alessandra
Erasable

ISBN 9781647503727 (Paperback)
ISBN 9781647503734 (Hardback)
ISBN 9781647503741 (ePub e-book)

Library of Congress Control Number: 2020921991

www.austinmacauley.com/us

First Published (2021)
Austin Macauley Publishers LLC
40 Wall Street, 33rd Floor, Suite 3302
New York, NY 10005
USA

mail-usa@austinmacauley.com
+1 (646) 5125767

Dear Reader,

Now that you have met me through these lines, perhaps you can imagine the pain that has been ravaging my family for all these years. By the end of the day, emotions such as incomprehension and helplessness were always overcome by love and patience. Time is the key to unlock the silent tears of the soul; time nurses the body, if only you would allow it. Whenever I stopped listening to my inner cries, my parents and my sister were there to echo the voices of benevolence and care. My writing and my being, I owe it to them. They were and still are the northern lights giving me hope to nurture future dreams and to reach for thousand and one stars.

I also wish to thank all the people I have met over the years, for inspiring me and for creating a lasting memory of gratitude and faith. I wish to thank you all for that little *je ne sais quoi* that makes you unique and loved. To all the other souls, lost and found, please listen to your inner voice and do not quiet down your inner light, for it will disappear without you noticing.

Lieve Poppy,
Diep van binnen weet ik dat je het zal halen,
Dat je weer, op een dag, zal stralen...
Knuf en kus,
Mamsie

Poppy darling,
Deep inside I know you'll get through this;
That, one day, you too shall bloom...
Kiss and hug,
Mommy

Dear Reader,
Dear you out there,

I hope you do not mind for me to contact you ('after all these years' might be a little too dramatic an opening, but it has been quite a long time since I have been wanting to write to you). *Avant toute chose*, congratulations are in order, for I am sure that you, as a person out there in the world, have already journeyed up quite a few miles. Oh, I wish I could take a sneak peek inside your atelier, your secret garden, your safe haven, or just your successful life. Perhaps you do not hear (or read) this often, but I wish to remind you that you are, dear Reader, a very talented person, open-minded, with a unique experience in this world, and I have no idea how many further incredible miles you will travel. So what are your future projects? How do you plan to take care of yourself and your soul? Do you have spare time over to read?

For some time now, I have wanted to send you this little piece of writing. I have, however, never pressed the 'send' button. I am wondering if you would be interested in this manuscript I have been writing for a little over a year now. You would be reading about what I have been experiencing lately, and even though this life script is far from finished yet, I would like for you to read me. It is about the burnout reality I am 'stuck into.' I have hit the brakes. The text also introduces some questioning about being too honest and too good a person until you erase yourself and disappear behind a cloak of invisibility. This girl, the 'me,' giving voice to the words, has tried so hard to be perfect in order to please the 'everyones' and 'everythings' until she completely forgot about herself and got lost.

Perhaps you will find this description too foggy, but I wish not to give too many details, for I do not know how these few lines will be received. Also, I do not wish to scare you, dear Reader, but I want this story to be told by myself in order to protect and save the other lost and wandering souls.

I do hope life is treating you well, and please know that I mean it when I say 'take care of yourself.' Please do.

À bientôt, j'espère,

Alessandra

The Lights

Tears running down my cheeks.
Slowly. Silently.
Or are they tears?
Pain in the back of my head. Taking over my legs.
Ignoring the pain.
Pushing through it
I can't feel my legs.
Is this my new routine?
Is this my new normal?
I wonder where the tears go when I keep them from slowly running down my cheeks.
I wonder what my head looks like when the inside is burning.
Whether my legs will hold me up when they've gone numb?
Keep pushing through the pain.
Keep walking on those legs.
Before it all goes blank.
And what remains are ashes in my head.
Numbness taking over my entire body.
The lights just went out.
My light just went out.

Livia Dubois, October 2019

Everyone, save me.

For as long as that inner roar still exists, the little lion will struggle and learn how to become king.

Day One
Sometime in December, 2017

Dear Mou,

I did it. I have finally decided to write down these letters. It is blurry as to how many there will be or what I will put down in each and every one of them, but I do know one thing for sure: we both need this to have closure. To finally start to live without the fear of losing me. Better put, I have finally found a way to convert my inner fears, guilt, and frailty, or so I thought, into a source of energy to write the story of the last couple of years and, most importantly, the last few months. I will not lie, nor will I hide the tough but accurate and relevant facts that have all led to the person I have become, that someone – your little bear – that has changed from one day to the next and that has been blaming herself for too long a time now.

Perhaps we saw it coming but never realized how deep the scar had been clawing its way to my very heart and soul. Perhaps we were not ready to accept it, and I do not believe I still grasp the concept of being 'prison forced' at home, feeling almost like an inmate, with a better view. At the end of this letter-typing process, I hope I can take off the burden that you seem to carry ever since I came back from my Erasmus experience in a city west to the Spanish capital. You saw me. You read through me. I was not happy…and neither am I now. But for the last five years, I came to accept that this was going to last for the rest of my life, that this was it. That there was no more in life to expect, but the thought of being imprisoned in a vicious circle, one that I have drawn myself and have imposed on my body already so weakened by the never-ending self-condemnation process I had unconsciously put in place.

For as long as I can remember, I have always had to struggle with my stressed and anxious self. Over the years, I have constantly been faced with two realities, as if there were this Alessandra girl on the one side, and myself, my real self, on the other. Alessandra has always been a loosy-goosy, warm, and generous person (and I certainly have no intention to brag about it), but, at the same time, she was wearing a mask to hide the most hurtful truth: her struggle with herself, the other self. This is me writing. This is me telling my story and hoping that it will – if not help, then enlighten – some selves like mine on the loose. I hope that it will come with the closure I need and the relief for my dear mom, who has been holding the pieces together for too long now, always making sure her daughter, her *Nja Nja*, would not let herself fall apart.

I still have no idea how I am going to put a long story short, nor do I know how I am going to organize this mess into readable letters. However, I do know for sure it won't be a diary, for I will not be able to keep up writing every day. Maybe a week or more will pass between the letters or sections of this 'brief' summary of my life so far experienced. So, dear Mou, shall we start?

*

I was born on September 16ᵗʰ, 1992, in Belgium (yes, the country breeding terrorists, so we have heard for the last couple of months now by whatever 'intelligent life' is destroying Uncle Sam – thank you, Mr. Obama, for the alien-tweet reference). I have always been different, or at least felt that way. Belgium, being a three-official-language country, does not make it easy for kids; they are socially assimilated to being Dutch, French, or German-speaking (even though we tend to forget about that part of the country, a little to the east, bordering Germany and the Grand-Duchy of Luxembourg). If the United States of America is known for its frontier and all the symbolism behind it, Belgium is known for its linguistic frontier, dividing the country into two communities of people, the Flemish and the Walloons, to put it *clumsily*. So why would I ever say I felt different?

To be honest, the awkward feeling started with the usual 'presentation and please kill me now' minute at school on the first day, that very moment you wish your parents had named you a common name from your country of origin and not an Italian version of it that, even though you find attractive and beautiful, is immediately murdered and killed off with French or Dutch pronunciation in whatever part of Belgium you find yourself in. Yes, my name is Alessandra; you do spell it with double *s* and one *l*, no, not two, and, no, my name is not *Alexandra*. The only exception is Alice, but that nickname has been granted already to my cousin, Gregory, who I may call Greggy Bear (I guess it is a win-win for both of us, a compromise). All these years, from kindergarten to high school, I dreaded that very first day: one, because of the knowledge of the stressful year ahead (homework and examinations); two, because of the Alexandra or pronunciation event that was inevitably going to happen which immediately put me in the spotlight of shame.

Even though I am very grateful and feel blessed that my parents were bold enough to call their first daughter Alessandra, it has been quite an adventure for getting people to pronounce my Christian name properly. Apart from that, I felt different, because my parents were too: one Dutch and the other one French-speaking. Mama and Papa have always been my role models: they have taught (and still do) everything. They were there to listen to all my school presentations before D-Day; when I had to speak in front of the class, they were the shoulder to cry on, they were there when I was all washed out, worn out, stressed, and confused, unhappy and, finally, when I had lost myself, my being.

Yes, dear Mou, you have read the one word that would describe me perfectly right now, that one word that has been haunting me for far too long now: I am lost. And, by that, I mean not lost and unable to get home; the reality is much deeper or worse: I have lost my*self*, my *being*. All my dreams and hopes vanished. The little someone I have come to know over the years, the little girl that grew into a somewhat crazy but generous young lady when heading off for university at age 17, all alone in a student dorm, in a city she had never known. Who would have thought that someday, in October, 2011, when I was told I would go abroad as an exchange student in my third year of my bachelor degree in translation and interpretation, it would be the beginning of a journey to *forgetdom*?

Day Two
Still in December

Dear Mou,

Shall we start the healing process? When you kissed me goodbye early in February, 2011, to see me flying solo to Salamanca, Spain, and begin what we both thought would be the adventure of a lifetime, you already warned me that I needed to be strong and keep face to whatever might happen there. Actually, I was not so much 'flying solo,' since my three best friends were with me. We were young, not so much wild except for one of us, and free, for we had just passed all our exams. We were to start a new chapter; we were about to experience what the Erasmus meant for others. Or so I thought.

The reality was much harder, and if I knew then what I am coming to realize now, I would probably treat myself better than I have done. That year, one of my best friends was at odds with her life and herself, healing from depression and crankiness. She was a mess, and a boy was messing with her head. Two actually. One was her childhood friend, the other one was a hopeless boy madly in love with her and who would not stop sending her text messages (while we were eating – and, oh, I so hate it when people use their cellphones while having dinner, especially since I was the one doing the meal prep). Seeing her like that, I could not let myself be happy. I had to be there for her. I had to stop her sorrow, take whatever negative feeling she could experience away from her. But I did not realize at the time that I was shrinking myself into a deep, down, black hole of forgetdom and that there would be no ticket back home, back to myself. I have lost my real self under the weight of what others might think of me, whether that be society, friends, or family. My mind is a 24-hour-active engine constantly busy, solving the most complicated equations and calculations there are: the human ones.

I seem to experience a constant state of fear and guilt at what others might think of me. Who are they to judge me? Do they know me? Do they really care about me? Looking back, I have found the answer to that last question…no.

No one cares, except for you, Mou, and my bug, my sister, who is only 20 months younger than I am yet feels like my best friend, my everything, my person. She and Mou are the glue that have held the pieces together. They have held and, still are, trying to hold me, to keep me on my feet.

In hindsight, a narcissist best friend who exteriorizes all her negative feelings and moods upon a frail and introvert human being is the perfect recipe to the complete loss of one's self. Myself.

Day Three
You Know It

Dear Mou,

All my life, I have tried to please everyone, to do things right, to help people and support them in any way I could. I too often said yes to prevent others from experiencing any bad feeling, anything at all that could make them unhappy or frail. All the while, I did not realize (at the time) that I was pushing my own self aside, letting it wander even further into obscure and blurry woods I would later have great difficulty coming out of. I would let myself wander there for too long a time, and while saying yes and pleasing everyone, taking care of every possible detail, I developed a sense of responsibility that soon turned into an intense control issue and need of things to be perfect and perfectly organized or done. I would call it *perfectitis*.

There is no such medical term, but the struggle to be perfect and what we believe society expects from us must not be taken lightly. I have fought for the last 25 years to be perfect in any kind of way: the perfect daughter (the one parents are proud of), the perfect sister (the one that takes care of the little sprout), the perfect student (that most of all; arms perfectly crossed and put on the desk, never ever speaking or cheating in class, prioritizing homework over family reunions and life), the perfect friend (the one who listens anyplace, anytime, hiding her own feelings), on the whole, the perfect being or the one who ends up losing her very heart and soul, for she is completely obsessed by what others might think of her doings, her living, and her being.

It took five years to come to this realization, and even though I know now that sometimes saying no is protecting yourself from your darkest shadow, I still cannot help it but feel guilty about it. It is as if my mind were tormented; I could really bite my nails off, but I need my hands to be clean because I love cooking and I simply cannot imagine cooking with rough and damaged hands (crushing the garlic would be too painful, and the onions would hurt the little scars that have found their way in through the lines of my palms).

So, yes, I am still wondering how I am going to come out of this. And by 'this,' I am not even sure what I mean. It took my mother and godmother a whole lot of courage and patience to force me to go see a cognitive-behavioral therapist. I literally cried my way out of it. I did not yet understand the gravity of the situation: my mind was still capable of steering my bottom-hit and crushed body. But that was what made me so dangerous to myself: I was not going to stop. I did not have the intention to just sit around and rest. I would not accept any kind of rest, whether forced or not. After an hour-and-a-half of talking with the therapist, I was a wreck. You know the Titanic? Well, that, but without the privilege of having a beau named DiCaprio. I was alone and lost. I had never really expressed all these suppressed feelings ever since Salamanca; or worse, ever since I started kindergarten. Because, yes, even in kindergarten, I would fold socks and scarfs that did not belong to me so that the teacher would be proud, so that I could feel happy about my good deed. Over the years, in middle school and high school, the negative feeling I experienced of not being good enough – always wanting to prove myself to others and to my dad – evolved into a necessity of controlling everything so as for others not to experience anything bad. I preferred shrinking my life to zero and helping others than trying to figure out how to live my own life and consequently feel guilty about 'abandoning' others. If I could support them and soothe them, lighten them from their burdens or responsibilities, why would I not engage into it?

Several Days Have Passed
As to How Many, I Do Not Know

Dear Mou,

I feel like writing a bit this windy morning. I was watching the Netflix series I actually enjoy most right now, *Grace and Frankie*, and I had a revelation. "I have been denying myself," says Grace aka Jane Fonda in one of the episodes. Well, in fact, she had not had ice cream in nine years and forgot the taste of it. I can't even remember the last time I had a *killer* or the ice cream I made of vanilla, *speculoos* crumbs (the famous Belgian cinnamon cookies) and caramel sauce. It was three years ago when our American family was in town. I remember: I had just finished university, and they were over for dinner, and we all had a *killer*. To cut a long story short, I have been denying myself. From life, from everything. I wish things were different now, for here I am, a 25-year-old, burned-out being, crazy from being imprisoned home. For the last two weeks, I have been busy like usual, grocery shopping, mere shopping, some cooking (you did like that lasagna *al ragù and melanzane*, did you not!?), and some ironing occasionally, well, more on a weekly basis. But what strikes me most is my lack of energy, my headaches (today is almost unbearable), my sense of fatigue…but it is less physical now than spiritual.

Now, I have come to realize that I lack the energy to fight against my father. He does not seem to understand, and like I said, to him, I have now a well-defined period of rest until early February, and this should be comfortable enough so as to get me through. I will be a real electric power ball as from February fifth. If only it were true. If only he would understand…but I certainly do not wish for him to suffer from the same ills as I do. My body is a wreck, a mess, and, now, it is at war with myself. I cannot blame it. I get it; I asked too much of it. And my brain is a hopeless coward, it follows as a sheep now. A frail lamb even. It is tired. Exhausted of this constant drain I put on it; the pressure of always feeling guilty or needed, responsible for everyone and everything. I have been denying my brain, body, and soul until it fell apart…almost fell apart. That is when my godmother intervened and told you to force me to go see the behavioral therapist. I remember that awful night. I remember quite vividly as if it were yesterday.

Throwback to December 14th

I had had a horrible day at work, and, *of course,* the minister had called me in that Thursday night at 5:25 p.m. while I try to leave at 30 sharp and grab the little energy I find in the deepest black corridors of my soul to head for the hour-and-a-half way back home. I had another silly mission: putting a letter into an envelope and writing the address so that it could be sent by the concierge the next day. I could, I guess, have told him that I always arrive early at the office and that there is plenty of time to carry this mission on Friday morning…but I didn't. I never ever leave things for another day. What can be done right here, right now, must certainly not be delayed. It works like a motto for me. And even if, let's say, I *try* to leave it for the next day, my mind would torture me until I do it anyway. Guilt, again. Or the disease of not liking things left undone. Who knows what might happen and delay the task even more? No, better to do things right away. And do them right, most importantly.

That Thursday, December 14th, late in the afternoon when skies were already dark, you and I were waiting on the 6:06 p.m. train…which arrived not on time. Stress level +1000 points. I was crying; I hated you for forcing me to go to that therapist I did not know. I hated the fact that you did not love me enough to get rid of the appointment. What would it be useful for? Certainly not me. At least, that is what I felt at the time. We arrived home, and I swallowed my 'dinner' (two broccoli florets and overcooked fish from the day before). Now I hated you for not letting me have a proper, quiet, and calm dinner, followed by a nice cup of Yogi Tea while vegging out on the couch… Well, more like laying half dead on the sofa, with a burning head and painful, very painful legs. And a huge belly, ready to explode, I almost forgot about that.

So, at 7:43 p.m., we headed off to the therapist's, and after spending 15 minutes having our ears blown off in the waiting room (so loud was the volume of the radio – btw, the worst channel one can listen to in Belgium), the doctor called out my name. I was shocked. Jeans and un-ironed shirt, no tie, and unpolished shoes. The brown hair was cut short, messy even, and I can't say anything good about the beard. On top of that, he drank coke, not the diet can, plain eight lump-of-sugar coke at almost bedtime for me.

I remember I didn't even bother to take off my jacket…a military-green parka I bought half price when in Florence as a day tourist back in the summer of 2012 when I was a DIESEL fan and couldn't think of anything else but fashion and Italian *dolce vita*. I remember, because right after my purchase of which I was over-proud, we went to that little place called Obika Mozzarella Bar in a beautiful Italian patio, welcomed by a pianist wearing a black tie with 40 degrees Celsius. I'm sorry. I'm trailing off. Back to the overheated room with the therapist. How could I not remember the first thing he asked me after writing down my name and birthdate in his pocketbook? "What are you here for?" It felt like a bomb, and I think he saw my surprise because he didn't even wait for me to reply before adding: "Who sent you here?" I told him you did, Mou, and my godmother. When realizing I was almost crying and would not add a thing, he asked why. And then, out of nowhere, I told him: "Because I'm a wreck, that's why. I'm a total wreck and have no life, feel tired all the time, and can't help it but feel guilty about being myself. I'm lost. Completely lost. I have no idea who I am and have no energy to do things normal 25-year-olds do."

I really thought he would start a speech on how stress and anxiety affect the body and soul; that he would theorize the whole concept of stress and how society puts pressure on human beings. He didn't. Instead, he listened very carefully to the years of silent suffering and pain that finally blotted out of my mouth. He didn't laugh, nor did he judge me. I was getting comfortable enough around him and took off the jacket because the tears had made me warm and frail. I didn't dare think of how I must have looked; with blurry eyes, a Rudolph-red nose, and a husky voice. But after one hour, I said it. Well, almost all of it… I left out the part about the eating-control thing and the stress it generates when I have to eat someplace I don't know. I want to know exactly what I'm putting into my body. After one hour, he made some small comments and, Mou, seriously, he seemed to have known me the whole time. What he said was so accurate, yet he didn't know me before! That struck me. I almost fell off my chair. He knew. He knew how deep I felt the pain, how guilt and sorrow were invading my soul, every day, constantly. He knew. And he scared the hell out of me (pardon the language used).

All my life, I have existed *for others*, to please them. I felt a sense of duty, responsibility, so as to make life easier for *others*. I have always worked hard to do things right, to follow the right path, and, now, at 25, I am proud to say I have never ever lit a cigarette (I once inhaled the smoke of the pipe of my father's late uncle, René, when I was a little girl, but that was all), I have never done drugs, nor have I drunk alcohol (except for the small amount there is in tiramisu, well, in those times, I still ate desserts). I'm the good girl, I guess. That's what people would call me. But good girls get lost. And I have been lost most of my life. Whenever there was a family reunion or any kind of social event, I wouldn't attend, for there was homework, exams, a presentation… I had the agenda of a C.E.O. because I never made myself available for these *things* that, for others, seem normal. I always told myself I would attend the next year when I would have more time or when I would have made it through university, the additional diploma, the job seeking… But I never did. So far, I have been 'living' a ghost life. One that doesn't belong to me. I have worked so hard; I was absorbed by my work that I did not make time for anyone or anything. Result: I have no idea who I am and how I am supposed to be and exist on my own. And on top of that, my body has started to get tired of me. It has left me couple of years ago, right after my Erasmus… Again, it all started there.

I came back from Spain on June 16th, 2013, and I remember my sister having her last exam on June 18th. I went with her to Brussels, wandered for a while through unknown, narrow backstreets from the city center, and, afterward, we went to have lunch with our parents. Italian, of course, as it is always my first choice. I had a gigantic *scaloppina alla Milanese* with *spaghetti al pomodoro* on the side. That might have been one of the last times I had a guilt-free meal. I even ate the leftovers out of my sister's plate, for she had a knot in her stomach after relieving pressure and being officially on holidays. The poor lamb wasn't hungry after her exam, and, that year, when she had just finished her first year of law school, she lost quite a few pounds. I was afraid when I saw her for the first time in five months; for that's how pale and skinny she looked. I promised myself I would never leave her alone for so long ever again. True fact is that I myself gained a few extra pounds in Salamanca (there, I said it), but I wasn't that busy with it. At least back then. I had lived by the rules and habits of my so-called best friend for so long a time that I had forgotten about my eating preferences and style. How I hated people checking their phones while having dinner; but I turned mute when she texted her ex-boyfriend while we were sitting at our one-square-meter kitchen table. How I hated being called a princess, for she said I couldn't cook or live by myself. Well, "I don't wanna ruin it, 'Sister,' but sharing our apartment together felt like civil service for me, and I was the cook, cleaning lady, and psychologist of all during these harsh months." So, yeah, I destroyed myself by the ongoing need to prove what I had in my march. You sure knew how to abolish the little self-confidence I have ever had, and, from experience, I can tell how hard it is to recover from it…if possible it be.

That summer of 2013, it really got worse and worse. I was the lucky student who got to do research for a professor I admired. I worked eight to ten hours a day on reading technical books, preparing the study, and doing the research, both July and August. The two first weeks of July, we had taken a family holiday in a medieval village of Tuscany, but I did not set foot in the pool once, for I was always reading or writing for the research, sitting on a wooden chair at the century-old wooden table in the rather-dark dining room of the triplex we had rented. I had my mind set on not deceiving my professor, on doing the best I could, on working as many hours as physically and mentally possible… I ended up being an assistant for the English department, and I got some transcription missions for another professor which was really challenging a task: I wrote the French sentences down on paper while listening to an audio excerpt in Russian and French. The French was to be written between the Russian texts. I loved it. I had to decipher a language I didn't know. And add the minutes or timing in the margin on the left side of the page whenever the French social worker was interviewing the Russian immigrant (or refugee) in Belgium.

I didn't mind having so much work, for I didn't have to think about what I liked or not; I just did what I was asked to do; I continued on my way to believing I would get a Ph.D. and write articles about American foreign policy or interventionism, or anything related to how the U.S. had developed a very peculiar international politics system. But starting that first year of the master's degree, I could clearly feel the competition, the selfishness, and I couldn't bear it. Friends were quickly starting to change; I was the assistant, so, *obviously*, I had a privileged relationship with professors (which wasn't true, I just 'worked my ass off,' and, again, pardon me the expression). But that year, many things started to change for the worse. I most certainly remember the dreadful experience that were the *Skills Labs*, a two-week, intensive, intra-university internship to get us used to the translation environment we would end up working in. Was I really prepared to be isolated and lost?

We were, of course, enrolled in the studying of translation. The whole concept was to imitate the work environment: start at eight and end at five or later, with a one-hour break for lunch, during which we didn't leave the university campus or the very same building we were in, because the translation was not finished on time…and we would (I would) continue when arriving at the *kot* (what we, in Belgium, call our dorms). On top of that, I was all alone in the dorm, a three-story townhouse in Mons, with no roommates because all had gone for two weeks. They were one year older than I was and were abroad, doing their final-year internship. No one was around for these two weeks precisely. Truth be told, this added to the daily (over)doses of stress and pressure of the Skills Labs, the fact of being 'dorm alone' in a city I didn't really like except for supposedly being the best known for translation studies (better, they said, than the ones located in Brussels, which were closer to my real family home and for which I wouldn't have had to go live in a dorm alone at the age of almost 18). Anyways, here I was, 21 and alone, stressed like a chicken, with no real friends; they were all starting to abandon me it seems…especially since I had no best friend anymore…yes, the narcissist one in Salamanca who made my life a living hell for always reminding me I couldn't do anything, couldn't realize how lucky I was to have such wonderful parents, and couldn't be happy in front of her because she had too many problems and couldn't bear the thought of me being a loosy-goosy doll. At the time, that Alessandra I liked. She wasn't too scared of eating a lot, of having seconds of pasta and dessert, of laughing, sometimes irritably, but still. Back in Salamanca, my life changed. I had too many responsibilities at once, and I was acting as a therapist for most of my so-called friends with matters-of-the-heart issues. I was busy solving everyone's problems; I made my very best at helping them, supporting them, healing them…but I ended up forgetting about myself and got lost in the woods.

After the Skills Labs, I was merely the shadow of myself. I had worked so hard; I just couldn't eat anymore. I had forgotten how to enjoy food.

Yet Another Week Has Passed
Still in December

Dear Mou,

It's been over a week now since I've dropped a few lines. Lots of things have happened, and I must say, ever since I've received the encouraging and touching email from the ambassador, a weight has disappeared from my shoulders. I needed his support to finally get some peace with the 'forced-rest' imprisonment. I think I now need to write about the food chapter of my life. I'm ready. At least, I think I am.

You surely remember how I was a big, fat, 3.850-kilo baby when I was born. I've loved food for all my (though little) life, but it is true that for the last couple of years, I've had a fair amount of issues to deal with. With myself and with food.

When I was a little girl, I literally lived for pasta, all kinds of pasta: *al pomodoro* was my favorite, *con vongole veraci e pomodorini di collina, ai frutti di mare, agli scampi, con broccoli, con capesante…* Name them all except for the carbonara, which I still cannot swallow, for it reminds me a little too much of the sick episode after a one-day visit to Disneyland Resort Paris at the age of nine. On the (in the Wallonia) legal holiday, September 27th, 1999, we were heading to the Disney Park at 6 a.m. in the morning, driving from the outskirts of Brussels to Paris. We had a magic day, me and my friend, Caroline, whose parents had invited me. It was not midnight, and we were back at their house after touring the attractions and souvenirs shops. Her father had then decided we needed a proper supper before going to bed and so made some pasta – the Belgian way, it goes without saying, but there was nothing I could do to excuse myself from the table and avoid the culinary disaster that was about to happen in his kitchen. Italians would rather die than know how Belgians ruin classics of their gastronomy. My friend's father merely heated up what seemed to me an astonishing amount of heavy cream and added gruyere cheese and some chopped pieces of industrial, white, labelled ham. I was utterly flabbergasted at first, disgusted right after, but I had to put on my best (or bravest) face and eat the content of the plate, for my parents brought me up with the idea that when you're invited over at someone's place, you ought to be thankful and literally eat your plate till the last crumb. And so I did. As quickly as I could, though, so as to forget the heaviness that came with the creaminess of the 'sauce' and the severe acid reflux that ensued. I think her father must have thought that, apart from being hungry, I had most likely appreciated his cooking skills to such an extent, for I was first to finish it, that he served me another portion, double in size, to my dismay. One knows the feeling when tears invade your eyes, but one has to hold them in, for if he or she is to give in, not drops but torrents of water will fall down onto the rosy and shameful cheeks. I felt like my world would fall apart, and there was little I cared say, for I was even more afraid than sick and, so, again, ate it all without so much as a grunt or a moan. Of course, I felt nauseous the whole night, but the worst part was that I could not even get up and head to the bathroom, since I was not sleeping at home but in Caroline's house. As a child, I was afraid of getting up at night and walking down the black corridors of an unknown house. Instead, I pulled myself together and suffered silently. I now recall this as being my first sleepless night. In a nutshell, please understand that I will never again eat whatever sauce that is prepared with a mix of heavy cream, ham, and cheese. Don't get me started on four-cheese pasta… I think I'll pass out. And last but not least, no, this is not how Romans prepare traditional carbonara.

Apart from that dreadful carbonara episode, I've always been a hearty eater. I used to enjoy every bite, every single dish…except for pure meat dishes, that is true. I liked the ground meat preparations, such as the *tagliatelle al ragù*, but one couldn't seduce me with a 300-gram piece of beef. I used to eat chocolate, whether bars, spread on a loaf of bread, or the vermicelli version from Callebout and Kwatta with vanilla ice cream – seriously, you have to try this – lots of pasta, always *al dente* and following Italian recipes. However, I've never been such a fan of pizza, or maybe just the *calzone*, but, again, it's not a real pizza, it's more a folded pizza with mozzarella and mushrooms (for I would leave out the ham). On weekends and almost on a (sometimes twice) daily basis during the summer days, I had ice cream. I remember having no trouble licking the delicious vanilla and *stracciatella* cones or the occasionally slice of pie or fruit tart when we had no choice at family gatherings, because that is what grownups eat for birthdays or reunions…not ice cream obviously, to my dismay.

So, Mou, you'll probably wonder when exactly change was around the corner… Looking back, I can tell you it all changed when I started high school…third year out of the six it takes in Belgium to finish high school (there is no middle school, just elementary school and secondary school).

I had just met a group of girls that, later on, would dictate our lunch breaks and food habits, for they thought they had to go on a diet 24 hours a day. The strangest part was that one of them weighed no more than 40 kilos (she did synchronized swimming during her leisure time and afterschool hours) and the other one could eat an antelope and not put on weight, ever. These two girls were soon to be friends of mine, at least that's what I thought until I understood that their only concern was to get the boys' attention. It was forbidden to eat next to these girls because they did not want to be tempted by our yummy sandwich. So for a year or so, I ended up eating very quickly, just before classes, hiding somewhere in school so that nobody would spot me. Lunch was made of two slices of bread and ham; a convenient and timesaving option, rather than a delicious or chosen one. It had to be easy-to-swallow-in-no-time sort of sandwiches. I'm not sure I even liked ham at the time. Of course, once at home, at 4:30 p.m., I took advantage of all the food at my disposal and made up for the shortages I experienced at school. It was, as my sister best knows, a real make-up feast.

However, the high-school years cannot and will not explain the origin of my problem with food. Neither will the first years in Mons in my student's room, even though I must admit I did not eat healthy 100% of the time, but let us be honest here, no student really does. Mou, I know you are not going to like what you are about to read, but once more, I need to talk about Salamanca, for it made matters worse.

Three Days Since the Therapist's Meeting His Suggestion, a Letter to My Father

Cher Papa,

Some years have passed, but it seems I finally have the courage to talk to you – or at least, write – about what is happening to me and consequently make my first attempt to deliver my soul. I think I am ready now to tell you that my story came to an abrupt end after Salamanca and the dreadful Skills Labs at university. Looking back, I lost everything, including my inner voice, my being. It started first with my friends, for competition was too fierce in order to get the best internships, and it made us all drive apart from each other at university; it went on with my life, which I lost too, for I was working all day and couldn't think of something to do when I was done with homework, preps, assistant work, or even my thesis. Work never ends, right? We are not in kindergarten anymore or in middle school when we sit doing homework for an incredibly short amount of time a day, and once it is done with, we can go play and ask for cookies and cream. And, finally, I ended up losing my inner self and no longer felt or heard my own voice, my crying out for help. It were as if the story of my life had lost its once so shining star. I used to tell my story to myself, to tell secrets to my soul late at night, just before falling sound asleep; shortly said, I lost my ability to imagine what my life could be after I got the degrees I worked so hard to get.

Starting university back in 2010, I thought I had planned it all out: after five years in Mons and a degree with honors (or could it be more? – the answer was yes, even though I didn't know it yet at the time), I would get another degree in economics, because you, dear Papa, had one from the I.C.H.E.C. Management School, and I thought it could be useful to me as well, not only to prove that *your girl* could do it, but also given the economic circumstances we live in and the great insecurity and lack of confidence I have always felt. Adding to this the fact that I knew I had great difficulty trusting someone and thought I would end up living alone, hence the necessity to control it all myself

(Instead of taking advice from strangers as to how to invest, spend, or save money). Little did I know that at age 25 and a great deal of stress (and pounds) behind, I managed to get both degrees with high honors. However, there was a price to pay: it has left me completely empty and lost. For years, I have worked so hard, striving to get the best grades, to enter and pass the best and most complicated options and classes so that you could be proud, so that I would not feel as if I were inferior or not good enough. Talking of which, I certainly did not want you to give the impression that I was not good enough. I had to work twice as hard as other students, and I always got confused when I didn't get the grades I thought I deserved in math or science classes. The only class I *did* enjoy and in which I was proud to think (not say) that I *was* the best at in school was English and Spanish…but it didn't mean anything in high school, at least not in the Collège Cardinal Mercier, this private catholic school where students are told that only math and science matter in high-school life and where girls beat themselves up, literally and physically, to be the skinniest and most perfect dolls (because, yes, beware of a sweat stain on your shirt it's *gross*, they say). Ironic, isn't it, how a school can destroy a student's confidence and faith and still lay emphasis on Christian values such as respect and love, tolerance, and helpfulness? Isn't the purpose of teaching helping students discover their passion, the path they will follow in life, the meaning they want to give to their own life instead of panicking about their self-portrait through the eyes of *others*?

All these years, I was losing sight of myself, my body, my soul. My dreams were driven further away until they completely vanished into thin air, for I cannot remember now what I wish for, what I really want, nor what I'm supposed to do. I'm all lost in the woods as if wandering for too long a time. Undecided, lost, and torn apart do not bear sufficient meaning to describe my soul's suffering right now.

"It's all in your head," yes, that's a sentence I have heard a lot over the years… Even though people (in general) will never pronounce the very syllables of it, deep down, I just know that is what they are thinking or whispering very low. They are just too afraid or too hypocrite to tell me. At first, I really thought that if my mind were strong enough and my willpower still untouched, I could move mountains and make my body react as such. I thought I could go on and live a normal life. But, what was that like? What was I supposed to think life was about if it weren't for work and deadlines? Was real life supposed to start when I ended university and got a job, found an apartment maybe, met someone and started a family, took care of a place called a *home*?

Deep down, I think there was always this part of me that knew I was different. I was too afraid of losing what I most dreamed of or longed for, so I started to set up other standards. All these years, it was easier for me to focus my attention and energy only on doing things right, finishing school, university, getting another degree, a job…but then, I realized I didn't even know who I was anymore. Or, better said, who I had been and were to be. I didn't know what to do when I had…time If, by magic, I had couple of hours for myself, I had no idea what to do or where to go. I couldn't meet up with friends for 1) I did not have any (at least none I could trust enough to understand what I was going through) and 2) I did not have the energy. I had only existed through the eyes of others; public scrutiny is another word for it. I felt as if I were a failure. I have never been able, throughout the years, to find a balance between life and school/work. I could only do one thing to the fullest. That meant work. I was too weak to have a life of my own, for I was too frail, too worn out, too scared of how people perceived me. I do not even talk about being tired or exhausted, for the hidden meaning behind these terms is too shallow. I physically could not bear my body or mind anymore. I was thinking and overthinking everything as if it were insuperable, almost unconquerable. I was in pain and suffered from the inside; it showed outside.

Papa, in order for you to understand (even though I strongly believe no one understands it completely unless they experience it – but, again, I do not wish this to happen to anyone, not even my worst enemy), let me describe to you the *days of my life*.

I usually get up in the morning after a disrupted sleep (if I get any, sometimes I just lay there and pray to fall fast asleep, but there are nights when even praying has proven useless, and apart from crying and getting up to walk three or four times to the bathroom, there is little I can do but surrender). After showering and getting dressed, I weigh myself, just to make sure how many grams I've won since the previous day. I look in the mirror and see a hurt human being with dark, shadow eyes and a bony body, no butt. I tell myself it won't get any better, so I just leave it to the odds and tell myself that one day, life will be easier on me. I have been waiting for that very day for years now, and I need help to try to find something beautiful about myself, something I like. Blank. I never think of anything… Next thing I know, I am already thinking about going downstairs to have breakfast, even though I know it will be the same as the day before and the day before that. It goes back many years now. I make breakfast, and, yes, I admit it, it takes quite some time, for I treat myself with fresh-cut fruit (I am a heavy consumer of pineapple and grapefruit and can't imagine what footprint I might have when talking about climate change and the direct import of foreign foods in Belgium just to please consumers like me with fruit that is not available in our regions); I weigh my muesli and goji berries, dried prunes, and add some low-fat, reduced yoghurt (plain will only make my belly ache more, as I am almost lactose intolerant). It takes 20 minutes, but I need this time to take care of my body from the inside. I need some 30 additional minutes to finish this feast I have prepared (even though the taste is getting blander and blander with the days… I have no appetite, but I know I must eat, so I try not to think about how the muesli hurts my teeth and will eventually dig some holes in them until they fall out). My reward then is sipping my coffee: black, Americano (which means double the size), and, no, it doesn't get fancier. That's the only thing I still do care about: the control I try to have over my eating habits, for I do not want to go back in time, second year of my master's degree, when I had to eat twice as much calories as you or else I would end up in a hospital for having an eating disorder and not weighing enough. After the Skills Labs back in March, 2014, I lost quite a lot of weight, and I never really had a chance to recover. Friends were scarce, and the pressure of the assistantship and thesis were too much for my body to handle and for me to hold onto. I lost my appetite, I couldn't eat or drink anymore because if I did, I had to cope with unbearable cramps and belly aches. I couldn't skip breakfast, but I was unable to eat more than half a slice of wholegrain bread with low-fat cottage cheese and cucumber. I added lots of pepper to prevent the bland taste. During the summer months, I dared to add some strawberries, but only occasionally. I had a peach, once, perhaps the most flavorsome ever. I was imprisoned in my own world where work came first. Unfortunately, after some years now, my body started to show too many signs of weaknesses I didn't know one could experience, at least not at age 25.

My hair fell off a little too much, too often; it became thinner, and I ended up tying it up in a knot almost all the time. It was the easiest way I could think of to avoid the girly stereotype of spending hours in the bathroom, getting your hair done and finding the proper hairstyle matching your outfit after showering. So, now, every day, I look the same – trust me, I am well aware of that – but at least I do not have to spend too much time doing my hair, and I spare my spaghetti arms of having to carry that Pocahontas hair while brushing it. My skin started to dry out until blood came running out of the cracking craters of my fingertips. Every time I cook, onions rings remind me of the scars I have buried deep inside, for cutting onions or crushing garlic is not a painless process while creating a recipe or organizing and tidying up the kitchen.

My left eye started flickering for no obvious reason while both eyes felt heavier with time, black around the edges, and the time I had saved for not doing my hair proved necessary for arranging my makeup: just some foundation so as not to look like a ghost or…a skeleton. My legs, once so happy and proud to wear high heels, abandoned me in their most fundamental role of holding the weight of my body, as frail as it could be. I felt heavy and couldn't tell anyone without them replying back, "But one hardly sees you standing there, you are so skinny." I am, but – please – it was not as if I was a sumo wrestler back in my 'good healthier days.' Truth be told, I could eat two plates of pasta and then think about what dessert I would choose from (even though I knew I would end up with vanilla ice cream and a melted, dark-chocolate topping and chocolate crumbs while preparing the ice cream), then about the chocolates and the cookies that would come right after with coffee (I used to love the typical Belgian households all-time favorite Delacre or Jules Destrooper collections). I ate it all without ever being overweight ('*je touche du bois*' as I would say in French – hoping it will never happen) and not really minding…at least until the famous, high-school dolls decided over other conventional eating standards in their Ô so exclusive inner circles.

Nonetheless, after losing ten kilos (maybe a little more) in the three months following the skills labs, I felt dizzy, heavy, and could hardly move without my legs aching and my mind ending up giving directions to and striving for these two concrete pillars not to let me down…at least not in public when all eyes were watching your every move. At home, I, at first, believed it was still 'okay' to fall down when trying to get out of the couch or out of bed in the middle of the night; at least no one saw me ending up in tears, as my mind was trying to get my body moving and erasing the shameful episode from my mind. After a while, I always got up on both feet, and I could do daily chores or little trips (to work and back, to the grocer's and back…almost, to the department store and not back, for that felt already like a summit climb of Mount Everest). I just needed some hours more to recover, every single time.

These last few weeks before December, however, I knew and felt deep inside that something was not right. I went too far, and I was afraid I could not go back. I started to realize I would never fully recover, not on my own; I would never be *that girl* again. For the last months, my legs abandoned me *while* at the store, *while* at work, *while* waiting for the subway to end the daily hustle and bustle I could no longer bear by myself. I tried my very best to hide it and bite my lips, but it got harder, and the shrinking, aching, dry, and craved lips had already got used to too much of lip balm that it no longer proved useful. Moreover, the pressure I was putting on my mind almost became unbearable, and the accumulation of tension almost felt like my skull would explode any minute, any second. And, *bam!* Matching time when the headaches started, closely followed by the sleepless half nights, hyperventilation, and panic-attack episodes and other symptoms I would prefer not to recall.

The daily routine got hit pretty hard too as a result of the changes undergone by the screaming, aching body and soul. I needed to go to bed at 9:30 p.m. or else I knew I couldn't sleep. I still believe even my grandmother goes to bed later in the night than I do, even though she eats at five o'clock in the afternoon. At 9:30 p.m., people in Italy go for a healthy after-dinner (and after-*telegiornale*) little *passeggiata*, while French commuters eat out at the local *bistro*, and the Spanish only discover what is on the menu or have just arrived at the tapas bar. I, on the other hand, almost went straight to bed after work, just having taken enough time to have dinner when I got home. If I kept to the go-to-bed-early habit, I could hope to sleep until midnight or 1 a.m. – if I was lucky – even though I knew that the other part of the night, I would be staring at the black ceiling and interrogate *myself*, my *soul*, God, or my late grandfather as to why *this* was happening to me and how come I could not rest and find peace. I couldn't and still can't understand just why. As for the sleeping, I tried it all: counting sheep, creating a recipe, imagining what my life would be like (if I were – ugh – normal), imagining I were at the beach in my great-uncle's holiday house in Lido degli Scacchi, sipping herbal tea or having a spoonful of honey before going to sleep, spraying some essential oils on my cushion…nothing would do.

Some days are better than others, and I even end up thinking I might go back to work and try a first attempt at having a normal life. But let us be honest here, these days are scarce, and reality knocks on the door as soon as I try to imagine my way back to work or when I try to plan a small activity just to be sure I still deserve to live rather than being a plant and slowly dying out. I feel as if every smallest or silliest thing I undertake is insuperable. It often feels humanly and physically impossible and unbearable to accomplish. I find no energy left, and, in the afternoon, more often than not, I break down in tears when I want to tell Mou something I believe is important but do not find the words. Well, it is not entirely true. I see the words in my mind, but I struggle to get them out of my mouth. I stammer and need to close my eyes to concentrate on the sounds that have to come out. I feel nauseous after lunch and dinner, and my chamomile tea no longer helps. I constantly need to heat water in my hot bottle so that I can hold it close to my poor belly. Twice or thrice a day, I boil water to make sure I am warm under the blanket on the couch, laying there half dead and conscious of the shameful sight: not a great one, more like a half-dead heap of bones. Sometimes, when reading one page of a literature classic becomes too painful for the eyes and tiresome for the mind to concentrate, I try to switch on the television, but even changing channels is hurtful…to the spaghetti arms. Plus, I am not able to focus on anything for more than five minutes…maybe ten if it's a cooking show.

As I am writing these lines right now, on a Sunday at 4:13 in the afternoon, I listen to some Zen background music on YouTube, but I know I will be a wreck in just a couple of minutes and will have to stop for today. My belly is already as big as that of a little boy one can see on pictures of famines devastating African countries or anyplace else in the world. I eat, and I eat well enough, but I see in the mirror a belly as big as a pregnant lady, only very much disproportionate when compared to the rest of my body, whether up or down. My bra is giving me a hard time, for the iron wire held in the cups leaves a red mark on my chest, right between both lungs. It hurts, but when Mou asks me why I wear any (since I am home, I can easily go without), I just reply back that I can't stand not wearing a bra, even though I know it irritates my skin and leaves red spots.

These last few days, another thought has been torturing me: my teeth and thighs. The former, for I feel like there are holes in them (or craters, I cannot tell), so much so that I cannot chew properly anymore without jumping from the pain (and I have not told you about the brushing of my teeth part before going to bed; it is like going to war while being totally aware of the minefield you have to cross); the latter, for they are big, aching, and swollen most of the time, while the rest of it, they are just suffering from some sporadic spams. Now and then, I can even spot some little red and white marks around the knees.

However, none of these scratches will reach the importance of my utmost suffering: me losing the appetite for myself; forgetting to feed the matter and the mind. I think I am just too tired to take care of myself and listen to my own inner voice. I find it too difficult alone, and, sometimes, I even wonder if I will ever lead a normal life again. Why is it that I have the impression I move mountains when I only walk from the living room to the kitchen area to take the bottle of water I had forgotten to take with me? Trust me, it is as pathetic as it sounds; just imagine a frail human shadow with panda-shaded eyes cursing herself for having left the only drink she allows herself – water – on the kitchen sink, hence calculating the effort it will cost her to get up from and out of the chair, evaluating the distance in her mind, all the while never losing her sight from the goal and, when finally accomplishing this incredible journey (ironically exaggerated, just a tad), being confronted with the reality of the way back *to the chair*, only, this time, carrying an additional weight in her arms and, thus, given the extra load, trying to keep her balance and reach the long-awaited and well-deserved chair. One could start to believe that the I.C.H.E.C. degree I got in management proved useful when reading about the cost-efficiency analysis my mind has to undergo for these normal human habits.

Considering these low levels of energy, I started very quickly to fuel as much as I could (and with the needed advice from our family doctor who specialized in both acupuncture and nutritional therapy) on high protein and vitamin foods. I cannot help but ask myself why it is exactly that I have to sort out foods and make sure I get enough fish and vegetables to prevent another laughable interlude during which I would end up completely devoid of energy or feeling numb, the worst of it while being in the public's radar? Is it me, or do I complain a little too often, too much? When does one cross the line from complaining to what more feels like…a cry for help? Can you hear me? Can I hear my voice? Why do I keep quiet – *have I kept quiet*, rather – for so long a time, and have I fueled the pain I have first felt inside and which shows now on the outside? The view is not so great, in or out. Ô please, even though *I* might have, do not give up on me, not just yet. Help me understand. Help me in my quest to find confidence and faith, to accept my body, to accept that only time will heal all sufferings. We will never forget, but can somebody help me forgive myself? Sometimes, I just wish someone would tell me it will all be okay and would then hug me and not let go, even though I have developed that self-defense mechanism which stops me whenever I feel too close, too attached to someone or something. Like the old saying, 'you cannot be disappointed if you do not expect anything.' This was it: I shut myself a long time ago from every possible thing I thought would be a negative or unhappy experience.

Moment of Truth: The House Metaphor

To Anyone, and, Maybe, Most Importantly, to an Absent-Minded and Lost I...

Who would have thought that the house you were building from scratch in order to, one day, stand on its own would so soon fall down, tumbling over rocks and potholes, all the while wiping out every single trait de caractère it once proudly possessed?

Listening to Chopin's *Spring Waltz*, I feel like writing about my experience, my safe haven that was little by little broken down into pieces by an inexplicable source – or was it a twist of fate? At first, the surrounding walls – or the body – is under attack, and, for some time, even quite long, it can protect itself from the undesired outsiders. But what if the enemy is no one less than…the spirit inhabiting the house itself? What if the victim is suffering and being ill-treated by its stranger self?

For years now, I have been fighting battles none of the parties at war can either win or lose. How endless it may seem, how far away in distance and time it may be for peace to be found; I believe I still have miles to go. At this point, I am wondering if I really have the strength, the courage, and the needed athletic-trained soldiers of soul to continue fighting. It is tiresome, but above all, it deprives me from the very *traits* that make life bearable for human beings in general: energy, imagination, both body and inner strength, laughter, joy, and, sometimes, even love. Leading the battle upfront, I have started to protect my little haven from outside pain. I am certainly not proud to say that I have become a master in the art of interiorizing all kind of personal emotions. I have closed the doors that one day had enabled access to the fortress I was so sure I was assembling. I had a dream, and I thought I was good at making it come true. But my personal experience, my early life, and the Erasmus, in general, have turned my world upside down; it went from light to darkness, and the most frustrating thing was that I did not see it coming; I did not know it would go that fast. I was not even prepared. There should be a universal law against this. No one, not any single person or being should ever experience such a melodramatic turn of events. I lost everything, but I still think I am blessed, for I can always count on my family to wrap up some bricks and cement and hand it over to me while saying: "Please, try again, we will help you." Building the house again is a one-person work in progress. It is a personal journey, and even though you know their thoughtful expression and support can make it more bearable, at the end of the day, you know that you are the one who can make it happen; you are the one who has to find that inner strength, however deep down it might be buried.

My experience went even further than the falling down and the tearing down of the walls themselves. I went to dig into the past, for no new house can stand on a trembling soil. So I dug, I dug into my lack of confidence issues, my social-relationship issues, my super-developed, self-protecting program, my eating issues, my Cinderella issues. I wish no one had to experience negative or hurtful feelings or events in life, and I made it an ambitious goal to prevent any bad feeling or experience to happen to anyone.

However benevolent my mission sounded, I guess I did not and still have not enough with two shoulders to bear all this. I can't prevent my parents to have a bad day at work; I can't prevent the cashier from being angry while I take too much time to count the coins left in my wallet to pay the exact amount instead of merely pulling out my credit card; I can't prevent my sister to be disappointed by a night out that was canceled last minute. Nevertheless, I can support them all and smile the best I can. I want to be there for others; I wish them all good. I want them to know they can count on me. I want them to know I am not that frail little being you see. Even though, right now, I have to admit, I may not be the ideal person for giving directions for the building of my own house – life – but I sense that, one day, light will appear at the end of the construction plan. It will show me the way. Yes, indeed, everything starts with a plan. I am still digging, further down, and it hurts the most, for I know not for how long a time I will need to pack my shovel on my shoulders. I will certainly not lie to you; there have been lots and tons of tearful moments, and I still feel very sad and disoriented. Especially since the outside walls, or the body, are/is taking so much time in setting themselves up, in lifting itself…just up.

Sometimes, I make myself believe that 'happiness is not for everyone.' Maybe there are people destined to feel this way in order for the universe to find a right balance between the overexcited happy and the utterly desolate ones. I wonder what I am now and who I was then. Oddly (or sadly) enough, I don't seem like I remember who I was before the house tumbled down. Is it fair that these several-year-long changes seemed to have happened just overnight? I most definitely did not see it coming, really, but, again…who would ever expect the crash to be so hurtful, so life-changing, so different?

I have reached such a turning point that, over the years, I came to control every single feeling, emotion. I made sure to hold them within me, to hide them to such an extent that I did not and do not seem able to express them anymore. What if I can no longer find the strength to laugh? One can smile, but smiling is not laughing. Whereas the former is a facial expression one can fake or exaggerate depending on the context or need, the latter is the expression of an emotion or feeling that comes right from the heart or your guts. Unfortunately, I am sorry to tell that I do not remember the last time my laughing gave me abs! Or the last time that I thought my laughing so hard would actually break a rib or two. Nor do I remember the last time I ate an ice cream and *really* or *truly* enjoyed it, even taking some more just for the sake of having frozen vanilla ice cream with hot chocolate on it, or what we have come to call at our house *'muizenstrontjes'* (only the Flemish and childish version of chocolate sprinkles; the brand being Kwatta, the type being dark, obviously). My sister and I used to shower so much chocolate drops on our ice cream that my mother used to tell us we did not have ice cream but chocolate sprinkles with a *drizzle* of vanilla. I no longer remember the last time I had a 'cheat day'; when I allowed myself to eat a *boule de Berlin* in the morning while trying to figure out how I would steal a piece of my sister's chocolate puff pastry, followed by a homemade chocolate-milk drink and Nic Nac cookies (because I had to find something to keep my hands and mouth busy while waiting for the rest of the family to get up, then be out of bed, and, finally, joining me at the breakfast table on weekends). I do not remember the last time it was allowed to eat leftovers from the pasta we had the day earlier and then continue my lunch with two more slices of bread with a store-bought tuna or crab-mayo salad and a hardboiled egg… It has all been neatly erased from my memory record, from me.

Even as terrible as this may appear, I must admit that my body would not be able to cope with such habits anymore. I have let it rot from within. Deep within; so much so that it has gone into lockdown, freezing itself from anything good or bad, whether it would be food or feelings. For months, I was not able to eat or drink much. And the worse part – at what I believed *then* to be the height of the crisis – is that the food *blocage*, the shrinking into 'shadowness,' this 'impersonalization' all happened while we were on a beautiful trip through southern Italy, in Campania, a trip that brought us to Naples, the Cilento region (where you eat Italy's most refined cuisine, trust me), to Amalfi, Positano, and even the beautiful island of Capri (that I do not remember, so sick and nauseous was I because of the boat trip). This holiday had to be one in a lifetime, for we celebrated my parents' 25th wedding anniversary. Out of fright and half realizing the lockdown got a grip on me, I started to count calories just to make sure I had enough to stand on my feet without passing away, even though the true fear that haunted me was the gigantic size of my belly filled with air and anxiety to such an extent that even drinking water turned out to be painful and almost impossible. I could not drink. Nor could I eat. My parents were afraid I might end up with anorexia, but that wasn't it. People started to look at me, to be different around me. They did not understand. I had, truth be told, some binge-eating moments when so sad was I that I ended up eating half a container of frozen, store-bought ice cream. These episodes mostly happened when I would be home alone – obviously – during the holidays, and then, suddenly, when my mother got home from work, I cried my eyes out to let go of the frustration of the traumatic turn of actions. She would always accompany me on a little walk in the little forest near our house, to clear my soul from guilt and sadness, incomprehension, and disbelief. Fortunately enough, I would not let those 'error bursts' happen more than I have fingers on both my hands.

The reason I write all this is because I can no longer fight against myself alone. I can't do it anymore. I can't fight on my own. My soul seems to be disconnected from my body at times, and, right now…honestly, I don't think I see light at the end of the tunnel. It feels like going for a walk without ever knowing when you will reach your peaceful destination. Moreover, I have to carry too much weight of the past, too many painful issues that have left me crawling in the dust. Please, can someone make it stop?

I know I should find the answer within me, but I seriously doubt I can. At least not right now. I feel way too fragile, both physically and mentally. At the end of the day, I feel dehydrated, even though I drink an average of two liters of water (without counting the morning coffee). I sometimes fear that my wish to control so much of my eating habits will lead me into the darker hell of orthorexia… I check restaurants, menus, before going someplace new, just to make sure there is something that I would eat (by this, I mean no meat, no cheese, no cream, for the combination of all would leave me broken from severe stomach pains or cramps). I do not fancy being invited over people's houses because, first, I don't know what I will eat, how they will prepare it, and, two, I get exhausted from all this social talking and networking. At 9:30 p.m., I am already forcing myself to find inner strength to be (or seem) awake for a little more time. Time. Do I have time? Am I allowed to take time out now?

Finally Seeing the Beginning of the Real Fight and What to Expect

Today is April 25th and, again, a couple of weeks have passed since I have last written something down. Never did I promise to put everything on paper, like some might do when keeping a secret diary, but I have always known deep down that I need this time alone to express how I really feel or what I really think. Although, I must admit, one never truly writes everything down, for there is always a secret garden hidden in the long and narrow corridors of a human soul. Access to that safe haven is strictly limited to the mind when healthy or ready.

I guess I have never felt as disconnected as I have been now, for the last couple of months; it is almost as if my body were completely dislocated from my mind. I do want to find the energy to experience greatness and life until I drop dead on the couch at the end of the day, but not the 'exhausted' kind of drop, more a 'happy-I-had-such-a-great-day' kind of vegging out. It was only yesterday when I went to the post office two blocks away from my house, very close indeed, so close actually that a *Mamma italiana* could go to and back while having her pasta cooked *al dente*. I, on the other hand, a 25-year-old, walked down to the mailman's desk and thought I would never make it, for I was fighting against the windy weather, almost feeling like running the 26-mile New York City Marathon unprepared. The most tiring part of it is not so much the battle to walk, rather it is more the fight to keep myself away from believing that I will not recover, or at least, that I have lost that part of me that used to find happiness and laughter just around the corner. Once your body turns its back on yourself, it costs and hurts a lot to keep believing you will, one day, be that same (even though changed in a way) person again. I can put on a mask whenever I attend social events, but I know that once it has finished and the clock strikes midnight, I will be needing a couple of days (sometimes even up to a week!) to recover physically. The headaches have come back like a ghost at night, and my belly has never been angrier with me, almost showing off how big and swollen it can be. It is not a contest…hush now!

However, when I look back, I am proud to tell my therapist (yes, I dare call him that now; I feel confident and am not ashamed of telling myself I need his help, or at least, that I trust him more than I trust myself… We have already seen how deep I let myself drown) that there have been some important changes. We started our weekly/bimonthly sessions mid-December, and can now list the following steps I undertook to please my little person (how small and insignificant I might have considered myself, then and now).

One: I tried several times to go shopping for new clothes: all attempts were fruitless and resulted in a return home empty-handed – at least until now – for the jeans company has a grudge against my flat ass (sorry for the slang language, but there is really no other way to put it, humorously).

Two: Last Sunday, I went to the flea market with my father (he promised we would leave as soon as my legs were aching or failing to support my little body weight) and I had a smile on my face, a grin even, first when I discovered, somewhere forgotten on an bohemian booth with cuff-links on display, a beautiful pair of golden-and-burgundy colored earrings for my sister (that I bought right away, obviously!), and, next, when I came face to face with an old and abandoned copper pan for the very modest price of…five euros! The antique dealer – cigar in one hand and winking constantly with his eyes (was it the late morning rising sun?) – clearly had no idea what treasure he possessed. My father and I quickly glanced at one another, a smile in the corner of our sparkling eyes, and almost in chorus, chanted: SOLD! I am now the happy owner of not one but two amazing copper pans. I completed my set of copper pans with three others, of lesser quality, which I have received from my next-door neighbor, and even though those are very small saucepans, I am glad to keep them just to decorate my kitchen wall later, for I intend to hang them proudly just above the old country-style gas stove (not electric!) – a French Lacanche if I may dream, most specifically the Cluny 1000 model if I may say, and as to close the deal, preferably the armor or frangipane color, or shall I go for the burgundy red? My neighbor, a respected head chef in a hotel on the outskirts of Brussels, received those pans from his French mother and could not use them in his kitchen at home anymore (one would need to reduce portions drastically if he were to cook in them). Before throwing them away, he thoughtfully gave me his three-pan set, for he knew for sure I would treat them with great and precious care.

Three: I pierced my right ear! People have always known me with the same pair of earrings (still the first ones I had bought on returning from Salamanca when I wanted to embrace change for the first time). As I feel I have made some progress (first with my new haircut, a long bob, quite refreshing for my head that was killing me under the weight of the bun). I decided, last Saturday, to get my right ear pierced, but do not worry, for it is not a piercing; it is only a second earring: a silver star, right next to the first one, a boresome and common little ball. I chose a star because my sister always reminds me when going through fire and rain: "Always shoot for the moon, because even if you fail, you will land among the stars." I believe she got that on her Pinterest account.

Four: I went to see a massage therapist, not a traditional masseuse one might come across in beauty centers or spas – I utterly dislike these so-called 'healthy' public places. My mother dialed my doctor's phone number and asked him if he knew of someone we could trust and who would treat my body with the delicate care it needs after years of abandonment, for which I alone am guilty. The elder lady, in her 70s, made an exception after my mother called and told my story turned short yet summing up the years of exhaustion and (self) loss. I went to her townhouse last Friday by the strike of noon and did not quite believe what was happening. I felt comfortable enough to tell her the reason of my visiting, but it was, again, very tiring and hard to let out these suppressed feelings and be confronted with the reality of my being so frail and…may I dare say useless or desperate?

As I uttered previously, she is not a masseuse; she is in the medical field – although, truth be told, her essential oils may not be as fashionable as a pair of antibiotics and drugs to most Belgians. She treats lost bodies with reflexology and a hot, smoked oil that she carefully applies on your body in order for the warmth to travel up and down your body. Please, believe me when I tell you that I smelled like a burning chimney when leaving her house after an hour and a half. I was afraid my parents and sister would say that I had smoked pot or, worse even, that I had joined some secret cult.

This new experience was very intense, but she too did not hide her concern: she told me she could not yet 'feel' my body react, for it was too far on the edge of giving up. She told me I had not yet reached ground levels of tiny doses of energy, so, basically, what I understood that day was that, so far, I was still in a negative energy zone; whatever I would do, even resting, would not get me to the zero-percent battery charge of a brand-new Apple MacBook Pro. My body would need to reload the shutdown level, and only then would I be able to reach the first zero percent one sees on the screen, and only then would the battery start charging again for quite some time indeed.

However, reflexology comes with a downside: migraines, heaviness, and difficulties to breathe in. For three days in a row, I felt 'weird,' or weirder than the usual degree of exhaustion and frailty that overwhelms my body and soul. I am to go back on Monday, April 30th, and I expect the same bizarre incense (or Church-like) smell when passing through the door. I pray to God every night to listen to my heart and protect me from…myself. How could I, so peace-oriented, inflict such levels of destruction on myself, on my body? I believe I can be awarded a master's degree with highest honors in the art of body and mind destruction until the inner self is completely broken and lost, until even the soul decided to take a break and enter into hibernation or, worse, a (temporary) glaciation era. The only difference now being that I can come to peace with the previous statement, how bitter and severe it might be, and remind myself the following: "We lead our lives like water flowing down a hill, going more or less in one direction until we splash into something that forces us to find a new course." (In *Memoirs of a Geisha* by Arthur Golden, pp. 105-106.)

Right now, looking up from my writing pad, I feel like waiting for the skies to change colors and for spring to finally knock on my door. Renaissance is what I am fighting for with my heart and soul. Now, body, please, just please, will you hear my crying and just remember:

Even now, as broken as you may feel, you are still so strong. There's something to be said for how you hold yourself together and keep moving, even though you feel like shattering. Don't stop. This is your healing. It doesn't have to be pretty, or graceful. You just have to keep going. (M Dawuoh)

April 27th, 2018
The Avicii Wake-Up Call

AVICII cheered people up on the dance floor with his lyric '*life is a game for everyone and love is the price*,' but no matter how much we want to believe in love as a purpose of life, I have always felt like I was the odd one out, especially for the last couple of months. And even though I have no expectations as to whom and how to love, I just wish and hope I will first succeed in loving my little self and accepting my body and all its imperfections. It is crucial now for me to look for myself (and learning how to look *after* myself too) and just keep going, putting my hopes into the faith that God has a plan for me, that life has something more to offer, that light will appear. I know one ought not to be waiting for things to just *happen*, but I am still fighting against my body that keeps reminding me of how angry it is for all these years of abandonment, neglect, and suffering.

Last night, I cried once more. I do not hold count of the times I end up in tears, for I know I am a very emotional person and quickly panic-stricken. I had prepared one of my 'specials' for dinner, a quick-and-healthy vegetarian risotto with zucchini and green peas (frozen, I couldn't buy the fresh ones in time). For my parents and my sister, I added some *straccetti di vitello* or tiny-cut veal sticks seasoned with salt and pepper and sizzled in a drizzle of olive oil and butter, the latter being used only to better keep the crusty effect they so like. After dinner, we were discussing the sudden death of AVICII, the Swedish D.J. I won't say I am an enthusiastic fan of house or new music; quite the opposite actually, I am the kind of person who appreciates Mozart (all of his concertos), or the 'Spring Waltz' by Chopin, Telemann too, but also early '30s Jazz or Japanese Zen music, South-American flute videos, Latin-style Pablo Alborán recordings, because, let us be honest, he is GORGEOUSLY cute (girls, you know what I mean) and so very much handsome (again). Even so, I do, however, remember the few times I really did go out, back in 2012-2013, and these were the nights (late evenings to be more accurate) that I danced on AVICII, and, please, I loved that feeling when you forget about everything; you just dance along and go out, have fun with friends; we, the girls, always feeling protected by the 'guy squad' or our guy friends who would never let anyone touch us or do us harm and making sure one of them would not drink too much in order for somebody to accompany us back to our *kots*. We could thus be free of maniacs or machos and dance and move unpretentiously. We, the girl crew that would later that year embark on this military journey not-so-secretly named Salamanca, felt secure and united at the time.

Back then, I was still very naïve and innocent, and I guess I still am in a way, for I trust people too much, too soon; I believe everyone has a soft side, a kind and generous heart, a special quality. Perhaps that is the reason why I am so struck by the sudden passing away of AVICII. A part of me understands just what he was going through…at least in a way, a certain way. Right now, what I write may not yet seem relevant, and I have not the least idea where it will lead me, but I need to let it out and free myself and soul from the sadness and the guilt that have overwhelmed my body and, to a much greater extent, my mind.

Last night too, I read the press release from AVICII's family and discovered, to my utter astonishment, that he had actually killed himself, for his lifestyle had become unbearable to him. I know we are worlds apart, and we do not share the same way of living nor the same habits, the same experience, but still. I can relate to the demons that must have been invading his mind until they had reached the deepest hollows of his soul, one time too far too deep for him probably. I read that he was a heavy drinker, but that alcohol was his drug that kept him going, that kept him working, too much though. I was the opposite, a monk even, for I had not sipped an entire glass of alcohol and abhorred the taste (often too sweet or too bitter); but I was a binge worker and a body-and-mind freak, a master in the art of self-destruction. All this time, I have lived to prove myself to others, to perform, even to outperform. The truth is, AVICII and I both lost ourselves and our souls. We were – and I still am – an easy prey to the uncaring and selfish world we live in. One last time, I want to honor his memory by listening to his most successful songs while doing something I know I am good at and that I will enjoy doing: the baking of chocolate-chip cookies. So, here is to my new beginning, the starting blocks of which I am still trying to reach in order to finally find the road to recovery and make it across the finish line.

The real question though, is to find out how our world manages to drive us till the edge of the cliff. Some of us, willingly or accidentally, fall deep into the turquoise-water that seems – to them, at least – might be the answer to their prayers, an opening to freeing themselves from the burden they have been carrying for too long a time. Others, like me, are still struggling to backpedal from the appealing void. My body needs to recover and find the energy to pedal to a healthy lifestyle and start the engines to learn how to enjoy the little wonders that life has to offer; reaching for gold at the end of the race.

May 2nd

The Lotus Flower

My heart is racing, my throat is thickening, and my eyes get blurry. I suddenly do not have the faintest idea of what is happening to me, even though, deep down, I know. The world is spinning in my head, and the sounds and all the talking surrounding me are echoing in my head. It takes only a couple of seconds before I feel short of breath and my sister or my mother is already on her way to fetch a carton bag.

So breathe. I am breathing, but I cannot help but feel that most people around me will inevitably think that I am overdoing it; that, to them, this is some sort of exaggeration or some kind of overreacting. When the drama is over, I feel like wandering in my head like a stranger walks into foggy woods and fights to find his way back into the dark but marked-out paths of nature. Dizziness, as some call it, or, as I like to refer to, the mere and very common *après* of a hyperventilation/panic attack.

These episodes used to happen on a weekly basis, and I was bereft of any means or signs to anticipate the *when* and *where* my body would trigger the attack, taking me by surprise at the most inconvenient time probably. For instance, I remember that one time while riding the subway; another one in the car after dining out at a little Italian café; next, laying on the floor in my bedroom for no obvious reason; so many times at our dinner table while eating, or right after a family meal and because of an out-of-the-hand discussion about burnout and perfectionism; there was also a time I felt an upsurge of stress mixed with embarrassment when drinking the sweet-night tea and sitting on the couch. I have had my share of hyperventilation episodes. They have not vanished yet, but for the last three months, I can count on one hand the number of times that my brain froze and triggered the above-mentioned bodily reaction.

Still, I recall the last of these episodes. It was not so long ago, on a Friday, April 27th was it, when my father came home late at night and told me – while on the couch – that the minister had once again called him at work to solve yet another administrative detail the accountant of the embassy could not sort out for himself. Did he, or did he not, have to tell my substitute at work that her interim contract was to be continued through May? My sister, who has always been overprotective, especially when it comes to matters of Belgian work law, immediately informed us that the employer, when having questions about the medical condition of one of his employees, is supposed to call either the family doctor whose number appears on the medical certificate, either the health insurance doctor for any piece of information that he wishes to obtain, but most certainly not is he to call and disturb the employee herself or any of her relatives.

Ever since the beginning, ever since I crashed on my way home in the subway, we have been too honest with my employer. Nevertheless, I needed them to know, particularly the ambassador whom I had come to admire, that only time would heal my wounds and that patience was perhaps the hardest battle in the recovery process. After my father had told him that I would probably need another month of rest at home to try to get back on my feet and be ready (at least fit enough) to start working again, the minister, probably annoyed, hung up the phone. Just like that. He did not say goodbye or any other polite or complimentary close whatsoever. Startled as I was after hearing this, I think I just stared for a while, with wide-open eyes, so dumbfounded that somebody of his rank would lower himself to an indescribable level of selfishness and rudeness (ahem, *bad manners*, ahem). I was utterly shocked, and that is when the racing began, the palpitations, the loudly yet difficult breathing like a walrus, and all the common symptoms you are now familiar with.

*

On Monday, I went to see the massage-therapist for the second time in ten days, and it was, again, refreshing. I always feel more serene as I tell her about my fears and lifestyle (shall I call it the 'self-destruction style'?). She is in her 70s already, and I would so much like to call her 'Mamie Rose' or *Marraine la Fée*, for she reminds me of this very special character in the *Oscar et la Dame Rose* book by author Eric-Emmanuel Schmidt. It's a beautiful yet sad novel of this young boy in his final weeks of incurable cancer. While at the hospital, spending the last days before Christmas, he meets Mamie Rose, the oldest nurse of the block, who never grows tired of telling him stories about past times when she used to be a professional wrestler (or so she makes him believe). Although it is quite unlikely that the massage therapist used to fight into the ring, her sweetness and honesty are similar to Mamie Rose's: she is not afraid of telling me that she cannot *feel* my body, or that it seems to be disconnected from my mind, and that the level of exhaustion I have reached is severe, burning high even. I knew that already, but it took me weeks (almost months) to accept it, if one is really ever to accept the failures or frailty of one's body.

Oh, but, dear Reader, do not expect me to get a beauty treatment in some wellness center or spa! Far from the commercial hype for which the internet has millions of offers and discounts to get 'pay one, get one for free massage,' the meetings with Mamie Rose are a far cry from these oily rubdowns. I do not just lie there in my underwear on some towel-covered wooden table and wait until Mister Cute or Mister Six-Pack comes and gives me a massage that most females do not even enjoy, since their minds are busy figuring out whether he has a girlfriend or cooks shirtless in his home. Actually, I hope not, for if the steak is spitting in the buttered pan – sorry, he would probably be cooking with coconut oil – there will be nasty marks scarring his perfect tan.

None of this happens whenever I go see Mamie Rose. Quite the opposite, for I end up telling her about what had happened to me since the last time we had seen each other, telling her about my burn-out diagnose and how difficult it has been and still is (in a way) to cope with. I also list my daily habits and the classic routine I ended up losing myself into, while she sits behind her basic desk, the one you buy at Ikea but make sure you have picked the most simple design which has no trick and no additional screw when time comes to assemble your purchase. Sometimes, she will adjust the volume of her hearing device to better listen as I confide in her. She is wonderful at giving me advice and opening my eyes. At the end of the story, I wait for her to say something, but, for a brief moment, she can only feel compassionate about me and ask herself aloud how 'a young girl like me' can be harmed and destroyed by her own torturous mind.

It was my family doctor who advised me to go and see her in the first place, for I did not trust a Mister Six-Pack, especially not considering my condition, my zero self-esteem, my missing confidence, and my body shame. The first time I drove into her street, I was surprised to see a mustard yellow or orange-esque, old car whose plate was no other than F-L-Y followed by three numbers which I have by now forgotten. The curtains were of a plain old white, not matching the windows and hung up in an almost chaotic way. Yet, as she opened the front door, I was immediately carried away by the essential oils perfuming the hallway. On the wall straight to me, I could see a genuinely beautiful and extremely well-conserved Ancient Egypt papyrus, the sort of art I would personally tuck under bulletproof glass with an additional alarm system beeping whenever one is getting near. Perhaps this would be, only partially, over-exaggerating it. Anyways, the pale-colored paint on the walls and the glass entry-table standing in the hallway give away a sense of reassuring homey comfort which one would not find in a massage center let alone at a regular therapist's very clinical and smelling-of-disinfectant headquarters.

Her therapy could fall under the reflexology Chinese-medicine practice, and even though I must admit I was skeptical at first, this fairy godmother has proven over the months that her hands can move mountains, that her talking reaches my soul. At last, I have a feeling that she can really be the one who could heal my body and make it whole again, or at least cover up the wounds. The searching for equilibrium and the reconnection of the inner ways to fuel up the soul, to bring harmony to the mind and the matter, always leave their mark, their pains. So much so that for two days after such a healing session, I feel a dizziness taking hold of me; my belly feels like Pearl Harbor during World War II, caught by surprise by a sudden and terrible attack devastating the gut microflora which cannot think of any other way to react than by triggering stomach cramps and spasmodic acute pains in the lower intestines; and to make matters even worse, my head spins like a sick and nauseous ballerina performing on the deck of a boat during a storm. Nevertheless, when these side effects slowly move away, I feel like a tranquil flow is finally returning to my body before it reaches my soul, the latter asking itself whether *this time* will be a turning point in the destructive pattern I have drawn upon my body and myself. Honestly, I have no greater wish for me than finding back some peace and quiet; to return to a safe haven – well, safe enough at least – and blossom. I have been waiting for so long a time. Waiting to blossom. Waiting to feel the warmth that life brings to any of us who is willing to embrace it and treat it with great care. My time will come. It has to.

The flower that blooms in adversity is the most rare and beautiful of all.
(Mulan, Walt Disney Studios)

How odd that I should be writing about the blossoming of oneself only days ago, for I was blessed with a dream last night, or, better said, early before dawn. Usually, I open my eyes at 5 or 5:30 a.m., unable to go back to sleep and fighting against some fretfulness or not-so-trivial (at least to me) thoughts pondering in my head. That night, I had dreamed of a lotus flower.

The lotus flower, or kamala, stands for the purity of the mind and the soul. Its beauty lays in its capacity to emerge from the dirt of a pond, untouched by the mud, and still blossom. It is therefore said to represent pure spirit, rebirth, beauty, and resurrection in both Buddhism and Hinduism. Life does not come without its range of hurdles, but one needs to find the inner energy to rise above all obstacles and find peace of mind and spiritual growth. Only then can one be beautiful from the inside and reach out to others, this only when one has found quiescence and peace of mind.

I think of it more like the freshness of spring after the harsh winter months. My winter was not the happiest to remember, but even though it is true that past experiences shape the person you become, one is not to forget that those are only memories never again to be awakened yet never ever to be forgotten about. One grows wiser from the hurdles of the past, but there is a reason why they belong to the past. Never let past experiences dictate your future and steal your present; you may have stumbled, but I believe that you come out stronger once you have gotten up.

I guess I am still trying to emerge from the mud, from these winter months, and once I shall have risen from the dark, I will need to find sufficient inner strength in order to bloom out and shine into the world. Everyone deserves to live a happy life; I just need some more time. That is the reason why I like to remember what the Disney character, Mulan's father, had told her while sitting under what looked to me like a Japanese cherry tree: "*My, my. What beautiful blossoms we have this year. But look! This one's late. But I bet that when it blooms, it will be the most beautiful of all.*"

I am still trying to find a right balance in life, and God knows how destructive I have been toward my body and how torturing and uncompassionate I have proven toward my very soul. I thought I had lost myself, but, in fact, it has simply been wandering about for a while into darker corridors that had remained untraveled to before, and I need now to find the strength to emerge from the mud and rise into the light. The lotus, therefore, is seen as yet another wake-up call. It stands for patience, purity, spiritual growth, enlightenment, love and compassion (infinite for others, yet to be learned toward my body and self), self-awareness, faithfulness, and, most importantly, rising out of one's suffering. The petals of the lotus flower look so clean and pure, as if they have mastered darkness in order to bloom out of it and rise into the sun, until, finally, they blossom and are the most beautiful of all. At night, the lotus flower sinks back into the muddy waters until morning when it blooms again. It has been associated with rebirth, and, in a way, I believe my mind was whispering to me tonight, telling me that I need to find peace with the past and allow to rekindle the inner flame from the burning ashes.

October 2018, Ten Months

The Thirteenth Amendment to the Constitution of the United States of America abolished slavery and involuntary servitude in the middle of the 19th century. How come then that I am under the impression that something as strong and as serious a matter as slavery cannot – in practice and intrinsically linked to the human nature – be done away with? Eminent people have had the power over the years and all around the world to sign bills and pass laws and regulations in order to prevent their people(s) from being in the grip of madness or frenzy; from being ill-treated, discriminated against, or even exploited to the advantage of a conqueror, tyrant, dictator, and many others. But what if, instead of politicians and head of states or the great international organizations, it is us, each as a single person, whom have to abolish slavery in our minds?

Drawing on my personal experience, as little and unmeaningful this may be, I have come to the realization that the struggle between the mind and the soul is my new form of slavery; one which a person ought to be liberated and released from. For the last ten months now, I have been struggling more than ever in terms of exhaustion, guilt, low to zero self-esteem and confidence, hurting lightning attacks in my head (so far, I have not been able to find another way of describing the headaches that feel like spasms or powerful black flashes that seem to crush my skull or get it on the verge of blowing up), panic attacks, ridiculous and laughable levels of physical activity (for I could not even go further as the local bakery and back, and I would not even buy a pastry or treat for myself; I would just go to buy special ancient-grain loaves of bread), etc. The list goes on, but I now wish to understand how I ended up like *this*.

I look into the mirror and see the shadow of whom I used to be. Even though change is unavoidable and inevitable in every chapter of human life, it may sometimes be greeted with fright, silence, and pain. So, please meet me, the 26-year-old who, until now, has spent her life trying to please others and has shut her ears from life from the inside. I have always put great pressure on everything I did or undertook, said or thought, in order to never upset or offend someone's work, feelings, or emotions. I have always struggled to be the perfect *kinda* girl; the one everybody was proud of.

Nonetheless, all these years, I have failed to listen to my inner voice, to life from within, and I am now left with character traits such as indecisiveness, perfectionism, loss of self, and a need to control everything so that others would not be hurt or experience difficult or confusing emotions. The spark was fading away; the candlelight was slowly dying out, until that dreadful December day, ten months ago, when my body shut down completely as a way to protect life, what little of it might be left. I had, by then, become a working machine, whether it be for work or at home, at the supermarket or elsewhere. I needed to keep myself busy and could never rest, hence the impossibility of finding peace or tranquility. My body and soul were a 24-hour slave of the destructive lifestyle or habits that my tyrannical mind would order. I was the 2.0 version of slavery. Worse, I was both the serf and the ruler in Middle Ages terms. Serfdom was and is, until this day, the today's society in-fashion form of slavery that I am fighting against.

Until I have conquered my fears, destroyed inner slavery, and vanquished the mind – the ruler – I would ask you to let me be; please just let me be, let me see that I exist, for I feel a void inside my soul, as if I were a ghost wandering in the woods. I need more time to heal, and, quite honestly, can I really blame my body after it has been forgotten about for all these years for taking *some more* time; and can I really blame my soul for not knowing the warmth, love, and respect one ought to express toward oneself; or can I even blame myself for letting *this* happen to *me*? As I said, I need time, for all these questions deserve to be answered by…whom better than I?

These interrogations might seem easy-coming for some, or might not come as a surprise for another great majority of people. I believe it is incredible when one is able to follow his or her own route, escaping or overcoming the obstacles along his/her way. Of course it helps when that person is goal-oriented, determined, motivated, confident, and…certainly not going through this century's pain, the burnout.

November 3ʳᵈ, 2018

Naked. Just when I thought it could not get any worse, life has decided to take yet another road further down, further into the void. I feel totally deprived from the energy I would need to crawl back up, up to the edge, up to where I could feel the hope that I have come to lose or that I have already lost without really noticing or admitting it to myself. Naked is how I feel; impoverished in the soul, devoid of power over my own body, prey to the thousands and one flashes that flicker in my mind, dispossessed of any kind of emotion or feeling. Fear, I know all too well, for I wonder if there really is an *à l'eau de rose* future planned for me, or if *this* is what the next months – perhaps worse if counted in terms of years – will be like for me. "Hang in there, you still have a chance," whispers a little voice inside, to which the soul replies: "I have already lost too many battles; I need to find peace, for I cannot heal."

The harm has been done, and it will never completely fade away. I wonder how we are supposed to live with the scars that will stay open and burn forever; how we find light in the middle of the darkened skies; how we nurture hope in the silence of the mind; how we reach inner peace in the havoc of the war. How?

It has taken 25 years (+one) to be exposed as such: naked, emotional, even over-sensitive, too much of it some say. Only this type of hypersensitiveness or hyperresponsiveness brings a grave and unique *trait de caractère* to one's soul: exaggeration. One day, I am too much of a crier, the next, I am as bland as steamed, frozen fish sticks (which I certainly do not recommend). How many times have I not heard that I have everything a person can wish for to be happy: first, the good grades, next, the degrees, and next to next, a roof and a family to come home to, wonderful parents, and my person, my younger sister. Rest assured, I say my prayers every night; I thank God and my fairies my guarding angel even, for I feel most grateful and blessed to be alive even though it has taken a rather scientific (should I say medical?) meaning these past few months. While I *am* here, physically present until this day on the surface of the Earth, the life running through my veins, however, has lost its purpose, its sense, its light. It is not looking so bright on the horizon, rather dead quiet and dull if you allow me to say so. What then *is* your secret, Ô Life? How am I to heal my body and my soul if I can no longer rekindle the flame of hope and find the spark to continue the fight even with no weapons whatsoever?

Unfortunately, I am afraid I am bereft of the needed ammunition to fire the weapon and take up the battle, even just to keep up with the war, whether struggling or crawling. Who am I to think that after years of physical destruction, abandonment even, and H24 zero-tolerance, mental, must-have strength anyplace and anywhere, I would heal in just a blink of an eye. If only. On this day – a Saturday – I was reminded of the frailty of the shadow self that I and only I have created. The following lines will provide a glimpse of how I feel *inside*, even after a ten-month home siege.

That morning, we were at a crossroad. Actually, I was. Torn between going to the weekly fresh-produce market in Halle (a ten-ish-kilometer drive from our home) to get fresh-caught fish and Scottish salmon from the fishmonger and red grapefruit and veggies from the grocer, *or* going to the five-story department store in Brussels, for we have been missing new cooking pans for too long a time now, and Ô how I hate to fry fish and meat (for the rest of the family) in these absolutely obsolete and threadbare ones we got in our kitchen closet. I am always afraid the aluminum coating will come off and impregnate in whatever we are frying. Simply *not done* if we were to describe this to a chef.

As I have won my place as the family cook over the years, my mom trusts me when it comes to buying our set of cooking utensils. She kindly suggested to go on her own to the market (leaving me with the guilt of letting her go alone and carrying all the bags by herself – ten grapefruits and potatoes and all the vegetables to start the week do weigh a lot) while I would be in charge of finding a minimum of three frying pans in a jungle of cookware with no advice whatsoever worth taking from the ignorant sales assistants wandering through the aisles, making sure never to get eye contact with customers out of fear they might ask for help. To be honest, I will forever recall the 'it's a good pan to…argh…well, *cook things*.' Wow, thanks, that is some great piece of advice! How did I not think of it? This is groundbreaking and brain-activity-saving help. I thus walked through every aisle, comparing frying pans and cooking pots, evaluating the possibility to buy ceramic, inox, aluminum, or a combination of other materials, but needless to say, this was too much for me to handle. Decision-making has never been amongst my greatest skills; certainly not *now*, considering what I am going through. I then decided to go for – what I thought was the best price-quality offer – a three-set Lagostina Italian frying pans, just to replace the household-all-time-classic Tefal ones we have, instead of picking the chef-quality (with picture on the box!) utensils which come out much more expensive anyway. Easy shopping for many of you reading this.

To me, however, this Saturday shopping experience felt like climbing a mountain peak without oxygen or winter clothes to keep me safe and warm. I was an easy prey that morning, and my body did not fail to remind me of how unrealistically optimistic this outing was, given the discharged levels of the battery that has come to represent who I truly am. So when we got back home, and after my all-time favorite oven-roasted salmon *tartines*, I left the table and escaped to the couch. I am used now to eating just to feed myself properly, but I cannot really remember what it feels like when one does enjoy the food brought to the watering mouth and screaming belly, out of delight to get the yummy dish. This being said, I just laid myself down, and, suddenly, the body kept its promise and nearly knocked me unconscious. I had no fever, but my head was burning, the muscles in my neck all tense; I was aware of my mother and my sister talking somewhere around and about me, but I could not open my eyes nor was I able to understand what was being said. I needed to go to the bathroom after the chamomile tea I had sipped earlier, but I could not move – like, at all – I wanted to reassure my mother when she suggested to call a doctor on duty (even though we only trust our family doctor, especially given that he has saved me two times already from my inner demons caused by anxiety), but I did not manage to speak; I could only stammer, and even this speech defect was too much for my brain to handle. I had always thought, until now, that I had reached whatever lowest level there might exist in cases of burnout; but it was without counting the too-exhausting morning pan-shopping experience of the day. Lying down on the couch and being reminded of my frailty and temporary uselessness (I know I should not coin it like that, but I cannot help it, for this is how I really feel), my heart started to cry.

Zo vrij als een vogel, soms wil je kunnen vliegen
Zo vrij zijn als een vogel, met krachtige slagen slaat hij zichzelf voort's
Winters op naar de warme zon en met niemand rekening hoeven te houden
Doen wat je wilt; dat wens ik jou…
Was je maar zo vrij als een vogel.

Dear Mou seems to have found the words to interpret the inner cry-out of my heart. Weeks and months pass, but I am haunted by the same thoughts every night; the very same disillusion, guilt, incomprehension, sorrow, or, shall I say 'grief,' for I am mourning my old shadow and hollow self. My heart cried itself out of any energy I had left that Saturday; it emptied me of my ability to speak correctly; it deprived my brain from its power to find words and assemble understandable and comprehensible sentences (at least to others); it frightened me – worse, it frightened both my mother and my sister – for breathing proved challenging and painful, and last but not least, it reduced me back to the most original form of life, the vulnerability and emotional nudity of a newborn. The key, then, to open the gates to finding my wandering self and discovering its *traits* will lie in a nurtured hope and a strong faith. I am not quite there…yet.

*

As for now, I am an ostrich. I like to bury my head in cooking and baking. I can feel myself living while being in the kitchen, a confined yet secured and safe place for me. I would certainly not boast or pretend that I am a 'top chef' – far from it! – But there is this *petit plus* that I find in the warmth of authentic and very basic *cucina povera* dishes. Italian, of course, who would have dared to guess otherwise?

Growing up, we used to spend our family holidays in a little house on the Adriatic Coast, *vicino a Ravenna*, or a 100-kilometer drive south from Venice. This little place felt like a second home to me, to us, the four of us, really. The traditional no-brick and poorly yellow-painted villa is divided into four apartments, one of which, on the *piano terra* or the ground floor, belongs to my father's Oncle Ezio, a *pugliese*-born Italian who, when he finished his studies in Rome, followed the Belgian girl he had met on a school trip (of hers), already knowing he had found the soon-to-be love of his life. Oncle Ezio and Tante Anne are, until this day, a role model when it comes to living happily (ever after) and spreading around the love and the joy that one expects from a cheesy Hollywood romantic comedy.

My father has always had a very strong bond with his Italian uncle, for they shared a passion for *la dolce vita*. Hence, it will come as no surprise that my very first holiday – I was nine months old at the time – were to be in the *piano terra* in Scacchi. I would later grow up, knowing that, every year, we would go back to the little haven; to its quietness amongst the everyday *dolce far' niente*. I enjoyed the authenticity of the apartment; the fact that it was cram-full, every year with an additional piece of furniture, out-of-date (women and lifestyle) magazines, another set of cookware, another pair of slippers or soap or food to make sure one could bunker himself down and survive for as long as he wished. I have always pictured this house and our stays with the needed *lâcher prise*. I believe this word coins exactly the state of mind (and body) one ought to reach while on holidays: to be disconnected from any source of stress

59

or pressure, to loosen one's grip and start to let go. Staying in Scacchi was about forgetting how my room looked like, how much left to do there was back home, how another year would scar my body and grill my soul, how…whatever. Scacchi is our second home, and it does not matter whether you have the latest in-fashion bikini or item of clothing, the Italian *nonne* cross the street in a flower-power swimsuit while their husbands proudly walk through the streets up to the beach in speedo only, not bothering what others might think. Why waste time over judging and criticizing while you can just 'lazy down' on your *lettino* and gossip with your neighbor on the beach about your children and grandchildren or exchange recipes and making sure, however, never to reveal the secret ingredient you use and will not share, not even under threat.

I guess I felt safe there. I was comfortable with the pigeons' cooing in the morning and my mother trying to destroy their nest during the siesta hour by throwing a tennis ball right at the poor couple in love (be sure that was the only use for it, for there was not any tennis court in the neighborhood, and, like I said, many objects were packed in cabinets and closet drawers, never to fill their first and rational use). I liked how we pumped up our red boat, not to use it against the waves in the sea, rather like our very own swimming pool under the pine tree, right in the middle of the yard. I enjoyed the morning, ten-minute, bicycle ride to the Spar Market where my father and I would buy freshly made out-of-the-oven bread, *al olio* (Italian bread is traditionally made with olive oil and comes in all shapes and sizes: *pane mantovano, il arabo, la treccia, la ciambella, la tartaruga*, and many others typical from that area). We would finish off with a *bombolone* or a croissant *alla marmelata* depending on the day's mood and the recipient of the treat. At the beach, our first stop was *per comprare il giornale* to buy a newspaper and, again, here, my father would, one day, go for La Repubblica, the next for the Corriere della Sera (the latter being his favorite and we, the children, only very much interested in the fashion supplements and, later, the cooking ones, at least for me). These are only a few of the anecdotes and habits our family has come to gather over the years that we have spent at Scacchi's *piano terra*. We have built bridges of trust during our stays and are always greeted by our friends and acquaintances, whether it'd be the tenants of the fashion boutique, Centro Moda, or the local Santa Lucia pizzeria owner, the father first, the daughter next. Traveling to Scacchi is like opening a window to the past; a past which, to me, seemed undisturbed and freed from any worry or…let's face it, burnout and grief.

The yearly escape to Scacchi and later to Tuscany, where we would find the same second-home feeling in a little village near Arezzo, always renting the same apartment in Borgo Gaggioleto, with the rustic country-house style from early 20th century, was a welcomed break after the ten-month homework/sleep/repeat lifestyle I had imposed myself, at least until it no longer seemed relevant to me to have some rest, for I started to work too *while* on holidays. The same year that I came back from Salamanca, I had earned a summer scholarship from my home university to help a professor with a research topic, the use of metaphors in scientific written language and popular works. The summer job was not to begin until August, but I wanted to make sure I came fully prepared to our first meeting on campus and hence read books and all kinds of relevant documents to our research project during the month of July while sojourning in Castiglion Fiorentino. Oh, and, by 'reading,' I mean sitting down inside the house, at the wooden dining table, analyzing every word on every page, taking notes, highlighting in different colors, summarizing and making draft comparisons while my parents and sister were at the swimming pool, outside, with a charming 30 to 35 degrees. Quite often, they must have thought me mad for not joining them making *tufo*(s) in the pool, cannonball dives if you like, or enjoying the breathtaking view of sunflower and agricultural fields from the top of the hills while *in* the Jacuzzi and arguing whom would have to go out of it to turn the bubbles on again. The fall had begun, and how was I to know that I was into another kind of 'dive'?

Spill the Beans

Dear Mou,

It has been quite a long time since I have last addressed a letter to you. Perhaps there is no need in doing so, for you know the rest of the story the further falling down off the cliff: two years of the master's degree; the additional I.C.H.E.C. diploma in management; the stress of it all (obviously); the long-awaited dream of a Ph.D. in American interventionism and isolationism, and how it has shaped the world according to whatever foreign-policy stance the government has held over the years, especially since engaging in the Second World War; the pressure of not (never) being good enough; the zero self-esteem; the lack of confidence; the lifelong battle that I have fought to please others and make sure they were not missing anything – although, realizing now that it was *I* whom went missing in the battlefield, that I was quickly and dangerously losing my own self, that my body lacked the energy and the time to recover and build itself strong and proud. I froze myself to a 24-hour standby state; my body – or my soul – decided to hold an inner lockdown as a way to protect the fragile life I had masterly come to almost (yet not completely) burn to ashes. Instead of burning to ashes, my light just burned out. Luckily, as I should say, it just burned out.

Even though I know you will find this reading incredibly difficult, I wish you to know, dearest Mou, that no words will ever capture the truth in my heart, for the love I feel for you and the gratitude I owe you, for it is beyond any describable beauty. How blessed a daughter am I with a mother like you?

For months now, you have been my shield, my crutches as I slowly crawl my way back into…an unsure yet seeming normal life. Today, you have not failed to surprise me with the now weekly Wednesday tradition poem or quote, only, this time, Toon Hermans (a Dutch *cabaretier*, artist, and poet – yes, I did my research, and I thank Wikipedia very much) seemed to have found a way to let the beauty travel toward our hearts.

Deep inside, life still flows and fights its way back to health – how arduous this be – but only I can truly know that my heart keeps beating warm thanks to your patience, love, and care. You are there. Always. Everywhere. Even though darkness has not left my journeying yet, I am only starting packing my 'personal affairs,' almost as if I knew that this *voyage* will be the most important ever undertaken, for along the road I will have to learn how to live. Everyone travels with his and her own baggage, but all discover sooner or later which items to put in or pull out in step with the surrounding environments they encounter along their way.

On Sleep... As a Start Before Drifting Away

Pero la india les explicó que lo más temible de la enfermedad del insomnio no era la imposibilidad de dormir, pues el cuerpo no sentía cansancio alguno, sino su inexorable evolución hacia una manifestación mas crítica: el olvido. Quería decir que cuando el enfermo se acostumbraba a su estado de vigilia, empezaban a borrarse de su memoria los recuerdos de la infancia, luego el nombre y la noción de las cosas, y por último la identidad de las personas y aun la conciencia del propio ser, hasta hundirse en una especie de idiotez sin pasado. (As in *Cien Años de Soledad* by Gabriel García Márquez.)

Sleeping. I believe I have difficulties remembering the last time I have slept for over eight hours straight. What a funny and trivial thing to say, right? Especially when one considers sleeping as one of the very bare necessities of life (I now hear the famous Disney song buzzing in my ears, quoting Baloo from the Jungle Book). There is a reason and a rational explanation of why babies have the energy to cry out so loudly that they almost manage to kill their lungs and have their so fragile heads explode of redness and tension; they are amongst that kind of the world population who, let's be honest, lay all day and night sleeping in their cradle. The only worry their mind needs to register is to awaken on regular times (and, please, making sure their clock and schedule do not match their parents') and cry for whatever craving they feel or merely out of boredom. I might have put a teensy bitsy too much emphasis on these little cuties we so often stare at in awe or wonder. They are the future; they are the very own representation of springs of life; but what happens when they grow up? How curious to think that each will have to find and follow his or her own light; some with a little or much help, others with the confidence and faith they have already found on their way to radiance and, thus, not relying on anybody to guide them, since they trust themselves sufficiently.

All things considered, if we were to know beforehand which hurdles we would have to hop in life, we too *would* gather as much sleep as we could during the first years of our life, and this just to make sure we are fully loaded to overcome the obstacles while running on the tracks – or shall I say, staying on track, the eyes set on gold?

As I have mentioned earlier, I cannot recall the last time I have felt that sleep had the power to heal my daily hustle and bustle and reload the batteries. On this day, November 11th, my sister woke up at ten in the morning, telling me she had literally 'slept like a baby' and woken up strong and starting-block ready, running like a Duracell Bunny. It is Sunday by the way. Remembrance Day. Actually, it does not really matter what day of the week it is in the life of a lawyer *en devenir*. I admire her and feel so proud of her. I guess, I have always felt very protective of her, even though she is just 18 or 20 months younger than me, for I could not bear the thought that she would have to overcome the same obstacles as I have. It got to that certain point that I wanted to shield her from negative experiences or emotions. I wanted to be the cushion to absorb and soften shocks. And not only hers, but for all the people I care about, then all the people that crossed my path. And I do care about all people. Guilt and empathy invade my body and boost my mind and soul whenever anyone around feels angry, sad, or left out, treated unfairly, or is simply lonely. I want to heal their inner and outer pains; I want to do as much as I can to save their day and state of mind, forgetting – of course – how to run on my own track and find the balance I have never had.

I may perhaps never find the right balance. I have, indeed, always felt *different*, *uncommon* even, but not in the proud, pompous, or haughty kind of way; 'uncommon' in the very basic interpretation of it: out of the ordinary. Just like that. I feel that I do not belong; I do not follow the codes set and expected by society, the same social rules that are followed blindly and unquestionably by too many men and women of my generation. Unfortunately, *this* docile (and trained) attitude is particularly sought after by the coterie of world leaders and employers for their exclusive clans spread all over the countries – different in size, management, and (a)moral values, but all too similar in their expectations and goals. No matter in which hierarchy you find yourself in – and whether or not aware of the fact that you belong to one – each individual is free to take a pause for thought and reflection, even though the outside world encourages us more often than not to behave like lemmings.

As I scroll down my Facebook wall – and I am not talking about the waterfalls of cooking and recipe posts that literally and physically flood in massively every time I update the newsfeed, sorry, I am losing my train of thought – I was saying, whenever I open up the app on my cellphone (because we, Millennials, sleep with our cellphones, while we are slowly but surely detoxing from computer screens, how ironic), I come across pictures or 'likes' of in-my-network friends getting married or moving in together, sometimes even commenting on their first-time grocery shopping with their *beau*, or on the live coverage of a student's car that is being towed on my former university's parking lot, binged-watched by the whole community of students, including the ones from other faculties… In a nutshell, social media is the 2.0 version of the operetta: everyone is invited and encouraged to hop in while live streaming on stage.

Whether the *grand finale* be the happy-ever-after story hoped for, or quite the opposite, the totally and sudden fall off the curtain, the internet environment opens a window to peering in an unashamed and unannounced manner into the lives of others. I insist on the use of the plural version in 'lives,' since I believe no one really has a single life; all the to-be-seen adventures or tragedies are shared on social media accounts while best-kept secrets, hopes, or dreams are lived in the very heart and lavishly nourished by the soul. Hence, the greatest play is in fact a succession of shorter playlets in which the main actor is both the interpreter and director of his own lives.

However persevering and serious an actor might be, sometimes he too must call an entr'acte, for frenzy has erupted onstage and taken possession of his body, the necessary costume of the soul to illuminate the play and give voice to his shy inner spark. Quite honestly, I believe my soul needs a little more time to heal and keep up with the sequels unknown but yet to come…

On Unexpectedness…

Coucou Bella, je suis triste d'apprendre tout ça. Ça me fait de la peine. Je me souviens que déjà au Collège tu étais comme ça. Tu avais besoin de bien faire, d'aider les autres au détriment de toi et de ton bien-être. Tu n'as déçu personne, au contraire tes exploits ont créé l'admiration de tes amis, de tes proches. Peut-être que c'est ça qui t'a fait sentir cette pression de bien faire. L'important aujourd'hui c'est de prendre soin de toi, de consacrer du temps et de l'énergie pour toi. Tu ne dois pas avoir peur; cela va t'empêcher de te reconstruire. C'est facile à dire et compliqué à faire. (…) Le temps permet d'aimer à nouveau, de ne plus culpabiliser, de penser à soi, à son bien-être. Le plus important pour toi maintenant c'est de te reconstruire; donne-toi le temps nécessaire. Ne te force pas, ou plus. L'état dans lequel tu te trouves aujourd'hui n'est pas un signe de faiblesse. Ceux qui te jugent, te réprimandent, te poussent à guérir dans un temps record n'ont pas vu la vraie Alessandra. La jeune vie exceptionnelle que tu es, pleine de joie de vivre.

Warmth and comfort find unexpected ways to shove in the darkest woods and reveal the little fire that illuminates the path. I was the lucky recipient of the sparkle in the above message which is yet another proof of real friendship without borders, neither of time, nor of frequent and regular meetings.

The sender and I have known each other for years now, yet I know I will always be pleasantly surprised at what he says or does. We were freshman and senior-year buddies in high school, but our academic careers split our paths; each traveling our own journey and surfing or being swallowed down by our own waves. We ended up losing track of time, track of meeting up, save that one Saturday-night outing to an Irish pub in Brussels when we were in our first year of getting our bachelor's degrees, law for him, translation studies for me. I remember that we were joined by three or four other high-school classmates, girls only. That night, we felt like we were playing with the big boys: the high-school chapter was done reading with, and we were now enjoying the supposedly new freedom that invades almost all of university students as, for the first time, parents are not allowed to take us out (but very much appreciated when in need of a safe ride). All but me, for it will come as no surprise that the *kot* experience was yet another ream to the ship that would sink into workaholism and capsizing among the burnout waves.

This one-night-hanging-out episode would never be repeated again, but it did not prevent the two of us from sending the annual traditional and on-time birthday messages as well as the holiday and seasonal greetings. We stayed little in touch, but we never totally forgot the importance of these long-expected and most-welcome, cherished wishes from each other. The others, however, I have lost touch with.

It has been seven or eight years now since the pub night out, but only this past September, our birthday wishes opened up a window to a new and totally unexpected heart-to-heart. This time, we were both honest and true to each other in our replies to the famously disinterested answer one usually hears when writing 'I hope life treats you well' or 'hope you're doing fine.' Argh…actually, no or not so good if you want to know. Our *no* answers to the trivial 'How R U' were the start of couple of messages in which we came to the realization that we had been suffering – both of us – from our personal battles. The cry for help might be different and the fights unalike, but the pain and the suffering were as destructive to our bodies and as incomprehensible to our minds. I wish he did not have had to fight his own war, but he came out a hero and defeated his inner demons. He is a prime example of success: bearing the scars, indeed, but remembering he has managed to fight his way toward victory. Truce has been reached, the *ravage* was slowly taken care of, but the dust will forever have to be brushed aside, every day, by self-care and self-love in order never to pile up and ignite the demon inside. I wish him to find strength and faith, always; to rediscover marvel and wonder on his ways. Me? I am just not there…yet. But how dear is my wish for this 'broken girl to blossom into a warrior'!

On Benevolence…

On peut être bienveillant envers les autres tout en maltraitant son propre corps. (My therapist's saying, a wise woman, indeed.)

Monday, November 12th. The weather could not be more typically Belgian than a cats-and-dogs shower above our heads with the sufficient humidity levels so as to fuzz up the unfortunate, untamed haircuts.

After a bumpy and silent ride to the therapist's, we leave the car in a parking space downhill and decide to continue on foot the last climb until the beautiful cottage-style house. My parents and I are seven minutes late to our first group meeting. They want to know. They have been questioning themselves for too long a time now: why did we let our daughter do this to herself; why did we not take action earlier; why does it take so much time to recover; why can't she change her rigid habits and gain control over herself?

The whys and so many other questions had been popping up in their minds for quite a time now, and it feels right and just for my parents to have an open conversation with the wonderful therapist that has been treating and helping me since April. She is a psychotherapist, a psychoanalyst, but mostly a woman with a tremendous and remarkable experience in helping both children and adults in their quest to finding their true selves, their place and purpose in our ever-changing world and environment. I would often joke that she must have been a sorcerer in another life, for, in ancient times, they were famously known for being the village healers or medicine counselors. She laughs when I say she has 'healing hands,' even though, deep inside, she must know – somehow – that her putting her hands on my head soothes the pain; it triggers an immediate reaction as if my body and soul knew it means only but goodness to them.

Indeed, quite often, the tension I feel in my head makes me fear the worst. I *know* it is almost impossible, but I *feel* that my skull is about to explode under the pressure held in the hyperactivity of brooding over of my brain. Even so, whenever the therapist puts her hands on my head, calm and tranquility rapidly flood into me – the whole me – and soft pastel colors circle around in my brain, taking me back to happier memories I have left open in some dusty drawers, mostly childhood memories, when I thought of myself *not yet* as broken as I am now. Exhaling deeply. Breathing in…and out. I am trying to focus on my writing while fighting against a nasty stomachache which gives me a hard time even though I have adopted a yoga position which should give room to my belly to heal on its own and digest the food I had for lunch like a *normal* functioning organ of my system.

The healing takes time indeed, but only time can heal the deepest battle wounds, although never forgetting about the weapons deployed and the crippling bitter blows fired from afar. One may have won the war, but to maintain the title, the hero must, above all, conquer the black and white parts of his whole. Only when his inner fears are tamed and scrupulously monitored can each human being move forward, well-balanced and undisturbed. I believe this is key in the creation and further evolution of one's path leading to a successful personal journey.

Lieve prinses,
Zolang ik kan,
zal ik ervoor zorgen
dat jouw lichtje blijft branden…
tot het opnieuw
volop schijnt

(Mou, leaving a note on the breakfast table. Nov. 15th)

Wonder is the key that will open up the lock on the suitcase. Curiosity is a password. Gratitude, honesty, and love are the wheels to push it forward. Along the way, the suitcase will roll on different tracks of values; some more emphasized than others, some more difficult to understand and to live by than others, but in the end, all are to be discovered in accord with one's journey through life, and living is then a mere act of picking the values, right and ripe, to pack and grow your suitcase heavier.

November 22nd
Thanksgiving Day

On this almost-freezing-cold November day in Belgium, I think of the millions of American families and friends that will gather together and celebrate being blessed and thankful. One may wonder why giving thanks and making peace is not yet *fêted* all over the world; for I cannot think of any frontier that would stand in the way of spreading harmony and love, tolerance and respect. Giving thanks is not and should not be culture-rooted – the turkey potato salad and cornbread might be – but the fundamental values one learns, acquires, and passes on to their *entourage* can, indeed, be observed elsewhere, in the very hearts and souls of humanity. There is, thus, no geographical limitation, nor are there human boundaries to the art of living one's life in accord with one's principles and be consistent, always and forever, with respecting the freedom(s) of one's peers.

Deep inside each single heart, life flows and sails on the rhythm of the waves that epitomize the individual journey one embarks on – how beautiful or arduous at times this might be. This year more than ever, I wish to thank, from the bottom of my heart, my family, for they are my everything and my hold-on-to. I can truly tell from the last stormy couple of months that my heart keeps beating warm and has not capsized yet thanks to their patience, their love, and their care. They were there. Always. Everywhere.

To all, I wish to say that this *voyage*, with the eyes kept far away on the golden-sun horizon where happiness meets love and benevolence, is the most important ever undertaken for everyone, for one learns how to live while crisscrossing his own world. Everyone travels with his and her own baggage, but all discover sooner or later which values to put in or pull out of the suitcase, in step with the surrounding environments and humanity they encounter along the way. Happy Thanksgiving Day to you. May you always be blessed by the winds while sailing or conquering your true self. Love, always.

Ask My Favorite Artist, She Knows

Hiking the mountain high, one might be fortunate enough to find the person to share the climbing rope with, that special someone you are knotted together with and with whom you follow each other's footsteps, wherever they might lead, but both of you traveling together. Encouraging one another to continue, always heading forward, or, at times, forcing a halt when realizing your someone is dangerously hanging over the cliff.

I had already fallen from the edge, off the cliff, and deep down in a *crevasse* out of which I could not escape. This time, I was on my own. Helpless and cold was I laying in the darkest crack of the thick ice of the glacier. How long would it take to be rescued? I was fully aware of the necessity of gathering my own forces and leaving the cave behind. Although there was this one question that kept crossing my mind: how can one marshal its resources and get them battlefield-ready when deprived of the artillery and defense shield? Truth be told, my body had been emptied out because of my destructive self always seeking perfection and benevolence toward all but me.

It is Monday today. December has been inaugurated with the 29th wedding anniversary of my parents on the first day of the month. I was granted the honor to cook for them a not-so-ordinary *cannelloni* recipe of my making that I had never tested. Those close to me and familiar with my cooking already know that when they read *cannelloni*, they expect everything BUT the two-roll-pasta tubes stuffed with a meaty and gooey texture, covered with, then cooked in a gargantuan *béchamel* sauce, or worse, a cheesy 'cheap and cheat' version of it. Wrong. Go back to basic. Go back to simple and authentic tastes. Do not mix up too many ingredients. Do not ruin the *je ne sais quoi* touch that each ingredient brings on its own to flavor the dish just perfect. The beauty in cooking is that a chef, how little or much experienced he or she be, can create and prepare a recipe according to the palates' preferences of his or her audience. Mission accepted.

I was thus the *chef de brigade* for the night, assuming both the chef and sous-chef roles. Locked in my kitchen, behind the stoves, I feel the adrenaline. I always do. Time flies. I am not laying down in that *crevasse* anymore; I am out of the cave, and I can feel my body move again. I breathe in and out, powered by the only thought of how happy and – dare I say proud or impressed even? – my parents will be when tasting the new version of rolled pasta, my version: sautéed shrimps and *branzino* fillets (fancy sea bass, I will admit) with a *soffrito* made of finely chopped onion, crushed garlic, *peperoncino* (obviously) and a carrot, deglazed with a homemade lobster *fumet* (safely kept under lock and key in the freezer in our cellar and prepared following a recipe of my own inspiration when I had cooked lobster pasta and did not have the heart to get rid of the carcasses without extracting 200% of the flavor and taste, or what respected, old-school master chefs would quote #MakeYourOwnStock). Cooked for a couple of minutes and, most importantly, when not mixed, but sieved, this *jus* is the best stock you will ever have tasted. For my pasta stuffing, I had chopped the fish-and-vegetable combination in tiny bite-size pieces and had spent the next 45 minutes stuffing the tubes and had scarred the craters in my already-rusty hands with the *piquant* of the dripping sauce. Next is the assemblage of the rolls delicately on a *letto di porri* or bed of leeks, previously cooked in olive oil and simmered half covered for ten more minutes. These breaking-up-with-the-tradition *cannelloni* must further cook for 30 to 40 minutes, depending on the crunchiness you want for your pasta, in a pre-heated 180°C oven. Did I just share my recipe? I wonder now how many will try it…

Impossible. One never apes a recipe true to the original version. The same cook will not succeed at making one dish exactly the same twice. However, when writing down this new take on oven pasta, I wish from the bottom of my heart to share the attention to detail, the adrenaline and the love, the precision and the care which keep me up, standing on my legs even though I fear they will tumble down at any moment. I hope that anyone curious enough to try out the recipe will add his or her *petit plus* to embellish even more the dish and personalize it to his or her audience's tastes. It is then only a matter of… *Facciamo un brindisi e dopo andiamo tutti a tavola.* There is no such thing as sitting with our loved ones, all sharing dinner and anecdotes, past, present, or future tensed.

The evening after the pasta episode, we – at last, after a three-week break – had a decent traditional family meal. The four of us. It was still rainy, but that morning, I went with Mou to preorder and set aside our 2.50-meter-tall Christmas tree because if we don't, all the green giants are sold out, and we are left with the mocha yule log, the least favorite of the Christmas table, because, obviously, everyone prefers the chocolate ice cake. Mocha is merely too light a color to kin to chocolate and too strong a flavor to draw near the tiramisu one where the combination of coffee and vanilla with amaretto is the result of the perfect equation of a calculus genius in the culinary world.

So, instead of heading back directly to our house and lighting a fire (no, that we would not, at least not since the chimney-fire episode and the honeycombed, ashy-black, glue-ish, and shiny substance that leaked out from the ceiling, leaving my mother panic-stricken and a lifelong stern opponent of the fireplace *ambiance*), we decided to drive all the way up to my sister's house-sharing address and get her safe and warm in the car and bring her home. She would, thus, not have to ride the subway, take the train, and subsequently get on a bus to get home. Not that Sunday, and definitely not, given the horrendous weather circumstances. The four of us were finally going to spend a cozy, comfy, homey day and, dear Reader, be honest, what do you need more for a successful December Sunday?

She was home. My sister, my person. The one I protect against the shadows that have pushed me always further down in that mountain *crevasse* over the years. I will not let anything bad happen to her. Or to anyone as a matter of statement. I am too sensitive a being, some say (the therapist seems to think so, and my father was and is inevitably faced with my being so, always reminding me of it). Even so, when it comes to my sister, I would fight until I breathe out my last resources. Oddly enough, there are no two more different people as she and I. Since sharing the same room and fighting over who would ask our parents to let us have a cookie or treat or whom is going first on the staircase (you never know whom you would find upstairs when going to bed at night), we have been like black and white, yin and yang, zero to infinity, water and fire, actor to go-between. We could not love each other more if it were not for the opposite *traits de caractère* that define us, me and my sister, whom I also call Ze Bug (as in the exaggerated 'Ze Tooth' in the Chuck series, the name stayed from the time we binge-watched the episodes when our family arrived from the States and two of our cousins stayed over, a now-frightful ten years ago!). I admire her and feel like it is my duty to remind her to look for that sparkle in her life. I cannot tell how proud a big sister I am. She is feisty even, and, truth be told, if I were you, I would not ask her anything if (1) she is hungry or (2) she hasn't had her night's rest. Also, if you do not have the energy to fight back, do not contradict her argumentation, for she won't let go of you until you hear her side loud and clear. She thinks she is *petite* in height, but she is so *grand* a thinker (without the organizational skills, do not blame me for this, Bug, it is no big secret, and people will find out sooner or later). Over and out, for she has probably rendered you speechless and argument-bereft.

Her art skills, however, are too extraordinary, too sublime, for she draws a true portrait of who I am: a lost somebody, fighting an unjust war. She does not use words, instead, she turns to another kind of language: heart to art, water on paper, and charcoal sketches. And there she sits, legs crossed on an obsolete and lost, turquoise-blue yoga mat that has never been used accordingly. She is wrapped in an old business shirt of my father's that has become too tight for him but one that gives her the cliché look of a painter in children books, with a palette of only four colors, whereas my sister swears by her secret wooden case and only the back of a cereal box to mix her colors.

As I am writing this down, 30 minutes are left before I call everyone from the kitchen stoves to get ready for dinner and 'please be seated.' My sister is hiding back in the garage, sketching, but I cannot know. She won't tell me, nor am I allowed to watch. Suddenly, just before the piercing alarm of the oven goes off, she comes near me, a grin on her pretty, angel face. "This is you," she says. What? For me, really? "No," she says, "it is not 'yours,'" and she corrects me: "It IS you. I have drawn you." Obviously, "It is FOR you too, but, most importantly, I have drawn what I think you feel." For once in my life, I believe I am at a loss for words. She knows I am her greatest fan, but how does she do it? How can her 'heart to art' make my pencil go nuts, unable to find the words and fill the page? The artist has rendered the writer speechless, as if words have been stolen to put color on a standard white carton paper. She sees in me; she feels the suffering of the soul.

Les Mille et Une Nuits

Early this morning, I opened my eyes and listened to a light and gentle wind, followed by the knocking of an ugly but innocent drizzle onto the window pane of my bedroom. It was 5:17 a.m., and even though I had already woken up several times for the last six hours, I was calm and composed, not angry anymore about the injustice of scarce sleep nor fighting the attempts to doze off, for it will inevitably lead into a futile and failed endeavor. I made peace with this – hopefully – temporary condition, and for some time now, as I lie in my Scheherazade canopy bed, I gather my thoughts and listen to the first idea or word that pops up in my head. Warmth.

Whether a twist of fate or mere coincidence, Scheherazade has inspired me for the almost 365 nights that I have been snuggling up under the sheets and fighting my burning out. Never have I had so many dreams and nightmares; nor have I been thinking this much while trying to fall asleep. The *baldaquin* was my little girl's dream come true; a grand one-person bed, broad enough to make a 'snow angel' on the mattress, yet too small to big-spoon/little-spoon with a potential fiancé. The white linen lookalike, although cotton veils and the dreamcatcher hanging above my head make this Christmas present even more special to me, for the bed was given last year by my parents in a desperate attempt to sweeten my nights, already aware of but not entirely at peace with the shadow left by years of self-destruction, termed only the week before by the doctors as physical and psychological exhaustion. Or what society defines under the same roof: the burnout, the new-century affliction.

In the weeks that led up to Christmas one year ago, my world fell apart. I fell into pieces; I was physically and emotionally burned out. The lights went off. As in 'poof,' gone. Although it is still too soon for me to find out the answers that I need in order to live, feel, and smile with my soul, I have since come to the realization that warmth is the quintessence of the universe; that it holds everything together, that it connects everyone and everything. Warmth is found even in the darkest cracks of the soul. Warmth bursts from my shadow self and out of my void body, my temporary physical bunker. The brush strokes that my sister had painted could not be more truthful or precise, for they depict the warmth that keeps me alive. The body might be weak, but my soul has not just yet given up on me; both are protecting me from my mind by forming a protective shield and rejecting even the good sergeant troops ordered by the medical team to reinforce the original yet powerless injured and burned armed forces.

Perhaps the invisible strength of Scheherazade soothes me, perhaps it brings comfort to the torments breaking out unannounced and, while doing so, turns the inner voice unheard by my mind into words written down by my soul as if to make sure this story gets to be told. Deep inside, I have always known that the amusement I enjoy most is when I get to be playing with the words. Although never had I imagined that these would be lifesaving.

A Glimpse of Closure

Warmth again when opening my laptop computer and finding a note from Mou. She always makes sure to leave a little something behind, a piece of poetry she finds when I am already climbing the stairs to have a *rendezvous raté* with the Sandman. I hear her downstairs, ticking on her iPad, searching for something, anything. Surfing the web at 9:30 p.m. with the sole objective to unearth a however-brief couple of verses and write them down on a little piece of white carton paper, the same ones we have had for years and left forgotten about in my father's wooden, writing-desk drawers.

> *Nooit de moed opgeven,*
> *Kun je niet vliegen, loop*
> *Kun je niet lopen, ga*
> *Kun je niet gaan, kruip*
> *Maar blijf nooit stilstaan,*
> *Nooit dalen, steeds opgaan*
> *Kun je niet lachen, glimlach*
> *Kun je niet glimlachen, wees blij*
> *Maar nooit de moed opgeven.* (Author unknown)

Mou reminds me that even if she left for work at a little past six, braving the early morning dark and misty roads, she is still here. Always. The effort she has made to find and write down this composition and secretly slip it in my computer fills my heart and fragile soul with an indescribable sense of comfort and warmth, which reminds me that I am very much alive.

This recently found equanimity is, after all the battles fought and those yet to come, taking over control of my writer's quill. I believe I have hurt myself, my body, and my soul enough. Time has come to close the Salamanca nightmare; I need to write it down once and for all and make peace. I cannot forgive, not yet. Nor will I ever forget. I only wish to write the following words, although never addressing them to their legitimate recipient but hoping they will heal the wounds, partially at least.

Dear (at-the-time) best friend,

We did not interact that much with each other during our first year at university. We both had different groups of friends but shared the polite nod when entering the classrooms or auditoriums, and after a little while, even the daily 'ça va,' a typical French twist of conversation, for when asked how one feels, the speaker does not really wait for the never-honest reply. Oui, oui... we used to tell each other before walking along.

A couple of weeks passed, and when the distance became nearer between our shyness and differences, we found out that our homes were literally almost next door or just a village away. You had your car and drove the 50 kilometers up to our university campus every day (and back), whereas I had the kot, only a ten-minute walk to the main entrance hall of our faculty. The geographical proximity of our hometowns immediately inspired our first real chats and conversations. It was almost a throwback to kindergarten time; we had found out we were friends and would tell each other everything from that moment on. Our friendship was sealed, not with a cookie, but when I sat in the passenger seat and off we drove on one of the last days of June to our proclamation ceremony at the end of freshman year.

I remember that day as if it were yesterday. It was also the first time you told me about the coming to Belgium of your best friend from your tennis club, his trip all the way from Spain, where he lived with his girlfriend. Actually, you would not ever stop talking about him for the two coming years, leaving me as the sole listener and recipient of your anecdotes and adventures. I was left nodding from time to time and did not dare interfere in the unhealthy and tricky love triangle you fell into with him. I kept quiet about the injustice brought on against the naïve and too kind girlfriend of his; I did not tell anyone, for I was your chosen confidante, your trustworthy friend; I did not yell at him when I saw how poorly he treated you, playing both with your feelings and his girlfriend's; I did not ask you to end this intricate and doomed love affair. I just wanted to be there for you, to listen to you, to reassure you when he did not text back the second after you had sent him a note on Messenger, to bring comfort to you when I clearly saw you were struggling with some health and psychological issues because of your mal-être, because of him. Even with the benefit of hindsight, I seriously doubt I would change my being there for you, even if I had known then how little human care and friendship you were willing to give me as your best friend. I would still have been there for you.

Not once did you make me feel that I was worthy enough of your friendship; you were the eldest, one year older than me, and, most importantly, an additional year worth of experience abroad, for you spent time with a Mormon family in Oregon during a 'second senior year' in the United States, a very much in-fashion trend back among the 2000s' generation of high-school students, also called the deuxième rhéto over here. I believe I have always looked up to you, and never did I dare challenge your opinion on someone or something. I was the perfect prey to be tamed. It has only occurred to me now that you were a narcissist being, using me as your punchbag to let off steam or ease your own tainted or tarnished conscience.

Mondays during our second year at university had swiftly turned into the pasta-lunch days: I bought for each of us a takeaway white pasta box that we would eat between classes with extra cheese for you. The overcooked penne or butterfly pasta (depending on the mood of the shop tenant) that came with an everything but Italian tomato-basil sauce and gruyere cheese became some sort of weekly tradition during which you would base the whole conversation on 'that guy' again, who had promised you heaven on earth once he would have gotten rid of his Spanish girlfriend who, by the way, was his sponsor, since she provided him with food and lodging in Southern Spain. Somehow, he had marched off to Málaga and had left Belgium behind, yet he needed her and relied on her finances and naïveté during his selfish Spanish adventure. For more than a year, he lived at the expense of her family. And, during the short trips he made back to Belgium to meet up with his family and friends, he knew he was more than welcome to stay over at your kot, for you had managed to negotiate with your parents a little studio a block away from campus for your second year at university, obviously keeping your mother's company car too. How convenient. Truth be told, he might have had the best of both worlds…only, this sinful and immoral love (and betrayal) triangle had to cease sooner or later, and I was very much afraid of the consequences it might have on my best friend, you. Yes, I was afraid you might not recover from an unbearable suffering.

Perhaps that is the reason why I decided early on not to tell anything too personal or too happy about me. Because, yes, dear Friend, I too had a beau that year. An Italian boyfriend I was head over heels in love with, for I could not believe that a guy like him would be interested in – well – a girl like me. Typical, is it not? I had had a few insignificant boyfriends, but all had taken advantage of my goodness, or, shall I say, innocence, ingenuity? This time, this guy was really something, but my own experience told me to be careful, and I did not, not once, feel at ease with our relationship. I guess there was always this little voice inside my head telling me this could not be; this could not happen to me. As if from the start, I had known that it was not meant to be, but in spite of that, I had decided to let the butterflies intact because they felt like the grand finale at the opera. It leaves you trembling on your chair with sparkles in your eyes and tickles in your stomach. Unfortunately, I could not share my own little stories with the one person I felt close to: my best friend. I too wanted to boast about my beau.

The Italian passerby had gone as quickly as he had come, but for most of that second year in our bachelor degree, he had made me float. And, he was the first and only boyfriend to ever cook for me the yummiest farfalle al tonno using his mother's recipe and making the sauce simmer for almost three hours of heavenly flavors spreading across the apartment. Needless to write down how honored and blessed I did feel. Oh wait, I just did.

At the time, I did not yet realize that you were letting me down in the most selfless way possible. You were blinded by the impossible love affair and even forgot about the importance of moral values and principles. The secret is out, although everyone has always known about it: you slept with the guy who — tiny detail — already had a girlfriend and broke them up, not once but twice. Because yes, indeed, you felt the need to meet up with him again, challenging your parents' decision not to see him again. It happened when we were on a so-called girls' city trip to Madrid and Salamanca, to check out the place where we would spend our Erasmus. Every time, your mood depended on he sending a text or not, and I was starting to feel like the fifth wheel here, trying to get interested in some museum or other while you were off in the park with him. Thank you.

Nothing seemed to could have stopped you from seeing him. Unfortunately, your distress got a hold on your behavior and mood. And I was the punchbag. What had to be a great best friends' Erasmus experience — five months away from our homes to study in one of the oldest universities of Europe and, bonus, the best one to polish our knowledge of Spanish — quickly became a black hole from which I still need to recover, for you have reduced the little self-confidence I had down to nothing. You crushed me. If I had always felt inferior until then, you managed to break me. And I do not blame you, for it was not the real you. You were yourself the puppet of this guy that fooled you. And trust me, I am genuinely happy for you that you have found true love now, that the new beau with whom you have been with for the last couple of years, ever since coming back from Salamanca, is honest and true to you. You seem to have found a way to close that chapter of your life, but this also meant the end of our friendship, for I had had enough of it and told you so on the first day back at university when starting our master's degree. I was not a puppet to be played with. Not anymore. I too needed a confidante, a best friend, but I had never found a listener for the stories I wanted to narrate. Where were you when I, too, needed a real friend?

Bringing this letter to a close, I wish from the bottom of my heart that you do not know the pain you have caused me. I hope you are not aware of what has happened to me, for I do not wish anyone to go through the same battles, at least not as unprepared and unarmed as I am. I wish you well and hope you will take care of you, cherish what you have, and dream of what is yet to come. Farewell, best friend.

Undisturbed Rolls Royce Life

One out of the many things you learn when your inner light goes out is to observe even more than you have ever before. Look around, the people are playing a game of coming and going; they run east and west, back and forth, and see the minutes and hours slip away so quickly, they do not take the time to breathe, nor do they realize that the quality of their lifestyles and of the oxygen that is breathed in and out is deteriorating. Look to the left, look to the right; you will find the people standing up against the not-so-rosy future of today's society, upholding the same values they grew up with, promoting basic principles of life, and defending the rights of every human being while perfectly conscious that this admirable agenda is, in fact, a chimera, an utopian vision of the world. Left and right, and there they stand, the people who *would* like to shake the world by introducing new ideals, new policies, promoting their own revolution, but while their bravery must be applauded and saluted, they know they cannot challenge the ruling political class or at least not without any risk involved for themselves. Hence the status quo. Hence their continuing to having breakfast in porcelain bowls, buying the 12 o'clock (sharp!) sandwich or salad from the neighborhood's or the closest store without paying attention to the barmaid or service clerk, and most certainly making sure they never look into his or her eyes. Would it hurt so much to say hello? The daily routine will be left undisturbed and their minds appeased by their convincing themselves that they do their best and enough with this already. On paper, they are willing to hoist the sails, but once aboard, they get nauseous and are afraid of the depths of change. How inconvenient for a sailor.

I am by no means the new troublemaker, nor am I the Marianne from the French Revolution, far from it. I do not wish to meddle in politics or any kind of decision-making upper class. I am a mere observer of the world and the people around me. Alas, as I look closer, I am hurt, for I see beauty that is being neglected by the world population, by the people, by us all. And there seems to be no remedy to treat these ills.

In the weeks leading up to the winter holiday season, superficial beauty and generosity are prey to meeting the marketing targets of big companies obsessed with profit and, thus, not hesitating to pull the evil chord in their run to crush fierce market competition. In order to win over the naïveté of their consumers, the leaders are willing to close their eyes to some questionable, tarnished, ethical values, preferring to ensure a grosser and greedier cash flow for their company at the end of the year instead of investing some of the assets in people skills or enhancing the transparence of the production line and, in doing so, also improving the product's quality controls and the working conditions of the people at the start levels of the production chain so that the latter can enjoy a happy holiday season too.

Similar indifference can easily be found in the empty-word speeches of both great and lesser-known public figures, both from the political and the tabloid landscapes. Although I do not doubt that some are genuinely concerned about current world issues that are tormenting most minds of the citizens of the world (I hope so at least), I also know that these people will still sit and rely on a golden cushion and that they won't be disturbed too much in their everyday routine.

However, I wonder what would happen to humanity if we all started to listen carefully to the Christmas carols, the very songs about peace and forgiveness, about love and hope to us all. Let us, for once, try to feel united. Let there be peace. It starts within ourselves; it further spreads to family and friends, to colleagues and passers-by, to foreign people and cultures, to your next-door neighbor, whether he be from a different country of origin or supporting that other soccer team. Instead, why not light a candle when reading this piece and listening to the sound of silence for a while, meeting with your inner self before reaching out to others. And if not one candle, then many, as many as may bring warmth and comfort to your heart and nourish the joy in your soul until you feel like its light is spreading toward your neighbor.

There is something unique in lighting up candles. Three of them are illuminating my parents' living room table as I am typing out this draft piece, but, oddly enough, all three of them are shining in a different way; they bring light indeed, yet each does it their own way. One flame is quicker than the other in its up-and-down undulation as if it were a spring. Next thing I know, the light is only tilting the other way around, only to the right, then only to the left. But all three candle lights brighten up the room in marvelous – and awe-inspiringly harmony; they need each other because, on their own, they are missing that little something.

So, would it hurt so much to steal just a couple of minutes of our precious yet hectic time or schedule and look, undisturbed, for that light and warmth, tranquility and comfort that those red little candles stand for? Obviously, you may choose the color yourself. It is most definitely worth the detour, for the absence of words and this sense of peace and quietness will color (further or back) your inner light, your little voice left unheard, your true self. Think of it. It is worth a shot.

Free to Think
Yet Not Allowed to Ignore

I wonder now what would happen if humanity, all of us, would think a little more and let go of their known comfort. As I was surfing the web this morning in order to encounter the difference between a trout, a rainbow trout, and a salmon, I came across an interesting principle, but I will let experts discuss on the scientific roots or nature of it: the Bullshit Asymmetry Principle, coined and defined by Alberto Brandolini as follows: "The amount of energy needed to refute bullshit is an order of magnitude bigger than to produce it." Oh, I hear you. Dear Reader is probably frowning by now, trying to find a logical or rational explanation as to why a trout and the Italian computer engineer are connected. Well, rest assured, for they are not. It is yet another trick of fate that switched my attention from a trout recipe to the *legge di Brandolini* appearing on the right side of my computer screen.

An early adopter of the easy pose, in other words sitting crossed-legged, with each knee slipping onto the other as in the yoga pose (the Sukhasana they say – but do not worry, I have only just found out as I am typing this paragraph), I was surfing the web in search of a good definition of what *truite saumonée* is, aka rainbow trout. If I plead guilty for being a heavy consumer and number-one fan of Scottish salmon (skin on, please!), I had never tasted rainbow trout. And, quite frankly, I had no idea that it was a species on its own… I had thought it were a crossing between a trout and a salmon, explaining the rosy tint of this particular trout and its less-expensive price with regard to salmon. As it turns out, it is not the result of a scientific trial; *Orcorhynchus mykiss* is, in fact, a species of salmonid on its own, also called rainbow trout or steelhead trout in Canada. If any fisheries specialist is reading here, you are welcome to enlighten us on names and characteristics, for I may not be right and apologize if that is the case.

As I was scrolling down the blog of a French amateur chef and reading along the proposed distinction between all three species of fish, the Brandolini principle appeared somewhere in the explanation so as to highlight even more the ridicule of my thinking that a *truite saumonée* is, in fact, the scientific experiment of interbreeding trouts and salmons. How ignorant could I be? The cook seemed to take great pride in insisting that the argumentation it takes to convince people of this erroneous statement on rainbow trouts is much longer and much more intense than the time it takes people to adhere to their own theory on the matter (which is, more often than not, inaccurate and flawed). Actually, it all comes down to this: it takes longer to correct the idiocies one believes in than to blurt them out.

Impulsiveness might be as old as intuition; one can never really hold them in nor tone them down. We try hard to pretend we are all rational human beings, sometimes even overthinking situations or decisions, balancing them, doubting them, then mistrusting one's own capacity of thinking; but who would not be curious to find out about the daily habits we do not think about?

Later the same day, as I was watching a popular cooking show that airs daily on a leading Flemish channel, I wondered why none of the producers or the chef himself had not yet thought about giving the food to a different charity each week. That way, the cook would teach and show the audience how to prepare the dish, five times a week, in front of an at-home and comfortably seated set of viewers, while the food prepared and cooked in the studio would go directly to a weekly chosen food bank or a public welfare center or a café owner willing to serve an honest homeless man or woman and wanting the little extra touch to the already possible *café suspendu* option that we have in Belgium. Indeed, when one orders a coffee, some cafés and bars also offer the possibility to buy an additional coffee that they will serve hot in a near future to a homeless person: one buys an extra coffee, leaves the money in a jar, and when someone in need enters the bar, the owner will pour coffee in the previously paid cup. Here is to the welcoming of coffee with no exact 'pouring time.' *En accord* with this solidarity thinking, I wish the cooking show would feed a crowd in need instead of offering only a taste to the filming team (no offense), unable to finish the plate.

Of course, these good deeds will never make up for the injustice in the world, but small actions from everyone can bring us, I believe, closer together. So next time you stand in line to get your morning dose of caffeine, think about the warmth it could bring to the person who cannot afford to queue up.

The empathy and generosity inspired by the above-mentioned anecdote is deeply rooted in our own humanity, in each and every one of us, for we all have the power and the choice to reach out to others, starting with our own family. We have all, more than once, blurted idiocies or words we did not mean yet said on impulse, but as Christmas is getting near (only 18 sleeps away!), it is time to think again and speak, not with our mind, but with our heart.

I am by no means a judge before whom one is to organize their defense and justify their actions. We all write our own story and, unfortunately, no author can prevent some ink to be spilled occasionally and print a bad or sob experience on paper. Nevertheless, we have the power within ourselves to light up a candle, take up our pen, and fill in the rest of the page with the spread ink, creating color from black and white. The holiday season is not about forgetting the harms we have suffered from or are going through; rather, it is about our inner voice finding the strength to forgive our own self and others and consequently write the rest of the tale, or one out of the many other tales still unknown, but yet to come.

For the next coming weeks, our home will be the concert of traditional and classical chants and carols, starting, as always and forever, with the *Christmas Around the World* album that my parents got for free when they had bought a double pack of ground coffee at the local supermarket in the early '90s. Now that I think about it, one does not receive this kind of presents anymore. The super brands will more likely give away a little box to put your cookies into for the children at school and, to be honest, we all know that those little cases disappear sooner than they have come into the forgotten kitchen-pantry cabinet. Do not feel shame, for we all have one back home: a holdall or a hodgepodge of plastic and glass containers, aluminum foil, rolled-up baking sheets, lost lids and tops (probably belonging to a container that you have thrown away along with the garbage some time ago now), a wooden chopping block, perhaps even a so-said easy-to-use label maker (without any tape left, that goes without saying).

This completely disorganized jumble of things inevitably spreads to other parts of the house; a closet drawer, an unidentified carton box on top of a bookcase… To tell the truth, one may get rid of its content, whatever the container or furniture item it be locked in, without even noticing its loss or its missing. The human tendency to collect heaps of pointless objects over the years, doubled when getting married and later multiplied by the number of grandchildren coming to visit for the Sunday roast, never ceases to amaze me. Some of us convince ourselves that each and every single accessory has an emotional value, even though they had absolutely forgotten about its existence until that very fateful moment when faced with the decision of getting rid of it or not, or merely when being reminded of it more often than not by their children when narrating an anecdote during a family dinner. How thoughtful of them! Now what will you do? Dispose of it or stock it elsewhere for later (though never) use?

Real Christmas Tree

A two-point-five-meter-high, flamboyant, dark-green, Nordmann fir Christmas tree has been delivered by our landscape gardener, late afternoon on December fifth. Its beautiful shape and density, and its thick, shiny, green needles perfume the rooms downstairs and bring in the spirits of the Christmas past and yet to come, for it is indeed 'that time of the year again.'

The decorating-the-tree part has always been a between-sisters-only affair and one of the utmost importance. Bluntly uttered (and, here, I wish to say 'no kidding'), we do not joke about the right spots that are neatly and wisely chosen to hang the collection of ornaments, garlands, and tree bulbs gathered together over the years, although without ever disposing of the original 1990s items. Vintage is back on! First and foremost, there is the quick but necessary check of the string lights (we would not want to find out when it would be desperately too late that one particular light bulb is loose while having been busy hanging all the decorations for the previous couple of hours!). We then carefully spread all of our Christmas decoration panoply on the industrial-style coffee table, making sure none of the specks of glitter dust falls down on the antique Persian carpet rug which has been rolled up to its side for the occasion. Finally, when my sister and I have an actual *vue d'ensemble* of the whole trinkets and charms that are to give light and beauty to the little-less-than-a-month-to-last evergreen plant, we search for the first and oldest tree bulb of all: a military-brownish globe, the first and most valuable – emotionally speaking – item of our display. It had been bought by my parents when they had just met each other and has been decorating the tree every year ever since.

Second in line for most important is the bronze Angel Gabriel which does not have to take a backseat as to the beauty and worth of the *mappa mundi*. As from that moment when both items are on display and in full view, we cut the ribbon and inaugurate the Holiday Season. All other bulbs and ornaments are to find their true spot in the tree and are, let us be honest, the result of an almost-mathematical and geometrical thinking and discussion.

As I am writing down the last words of this paragraph, my sight takes a 45-degree turn on the right and admires the resplendent, sparkling, most appreciated plant of our *salon*. During dinners and breaks, we will hear the bells sing, listen closely to the refrains of peace, and, in chorus, we will be thankful for the love we have received and are to give and spread around us. I cannot wait to wish you all, a merry and most lovely Christmas time. May you forever cherish the memories of Christmas pasts and let the warmth of Christmas present permeate your future days and endeavors.

A Peep into Tradition

Several days have passed since the tree has embellished our home interior, but no presents have been put underneath our Nordmann, *yet*. Meanwhile, as I am lost in a daydream, I remember how we used to spend the winter holiday season back when I was little until I left for college. As soon as the exam session was over, on the very first Friday night my sister and I did not have to study, we would put up the tree and stay up late, binge watch a series (from Disney to Chuck, depending on how old we were) or listen to the traditional crooners and enjoy a treat or two (mostly ice cream) while snuggling up under the woolen blanket, carefree and tummy-happy. We would not receive our end results for another week, but we knew we had done our best at school, and past experience has shown that working hard pays in the end. That first week we were off school, we binged watched Christmas movies for the whole afternoon, sometimes getting out of our pajamas only before noon and barely leaving the couch, save to stock up on cookies and candies! To sum it up, it was a worry-free week. We had studied enough for a whole semester, and, now, we deserved a two-week holiday rest to celebrate Christmas and the New Year that was knocking on the door.

The official school break started as soon as we left the parent-teacher meeting to get our final results. Passed. Both of us. Always. Hot flushes, cold sweats, relief at last. Let the holidays start. In the couple of days that would follow, the party preparations were underway. On the night before Christmas, we would invite half of my father's side of the family over – the other half being more than welcome to join, but since they live across the Atlantic, they would not make it, not even for the chocolate and coffee yule logs (remember the mocha desert I was referring to earlier?). The next day, on the 25th, we would celebrate the birth of Jesus Christ *en petit comité*, just the four of us, my parents, my sister, and me. In past years though, my grandmother, Mamiche, would stay over and grab a piece of *panettone* at the breakfast table and spend the day with us, but for the last years, we have cut this habit down… and, honestly, I am not sure I know as to why.

Back then in Christmas past, I would run downstairs first, for I have always been a wake-up-at-dawn girl, only to wait a little longer until my mother would come down too and prepare hot Belgian chocolate and coffee to be served with breakfast. Knock knock, there is Mamy! My grandmother, also an early bird, would never cross the living-room door without knocking. It would not be long before everybody be up and sitting at the beautifully decorated Christmas table, red napkin still covered with the glitters of the previous feast.

For breakfast, my sister would sprinkle powdered sugar on her slice of *pandoro* (literally 'golden bread,' a star-shaped traditional Italian cake from Verona), whereas my father would slice up his *panettone*, the rival of the Christmas cakes, this one being typically served in Milanese families over the holiday period and especially appreciated for its candied fruits, zests of orange, and almond crust. I, on the other hand, would eat the *pandoro* covered with dark chocolate spread while stealing my father's leftover candied fruits falling on his plate. Guilty: there is no logic; even I do not find a rational explanation of the content of my breakfast plate. Back then at least. Anyway, the one thing I remember most vividly is the peace and quiet I felt inside my own body when I was that little girl sitting at the table, my feet almost touching the cold tiles of the ground, but not yet able to feel the shiver, and regretting to have come downstairs on my socks instead of putting some slippers on.

On past Christmas days, we would go for a walk in our village after late-morning breakfast; taking a left turn at the end of our street, first passing by the *Ferme Rose* to enter next a little further down the farm-smelling road, the mysterious woods, called *Bois des Pochets* where we would climb up a mount in its center and recite the Our Father Prayer. When in luck, when winters were snowy, we would bring the wooden sleigh with us and slide down the frozen and white-rug-colored wheat fields on our way to the medieval watermill that would mark the near end of our *promenade*, although not before stopping by the richly decorated window display of the local bakery. If temperatures were low enough, the smell of fresh oven-baked bread, croissants, chocolate pastry, *petit fours*, and *crème patissière* would seep deep into us and liven up our souls. A last effort was required before we reached our home, though, at the time, the last meters did not count, since our batteries were fully charged at the thought of devouring our just-bought pastry treats. Now that is a surprise (or is it?). Finally crossing the front porch, we would take out our mittens and put on our slip-resistant Christmas socks again: red ones for me, navy-blue for my sister. As a secret, I might as well tell that, for some time, we had the Bob the Builder red fleece slipper shoes, but please consider this unsaid.

I believe the Winter Holiday Season has always brought peace and tranquility into our home. At the start of the holidays, we knew we were 'done for the semester.' No working, no studying anymore; just playing and getting 'hug spoiled' by our parents when they came back from work. I remember those times. The first part of the celebrations were not over yet, but I was already thinking about New Year's Eve, for on the 31st precisely, my mother would traditionally prepare a chicken and seafood rich saffron-y *paella valenciana*! Olé – how cliché, even from me.

The last day of the year was, thus, absolutely worth the wait. After a quick round trip to the fishmonger in Brussels in order to get the freshest shrimps, scallops, mussels, and clams – making sure not to forget to buy the paella spices, the special Spanish *arroz bomba*, and a good bottle of white wine – my mother would get her apron on, and we all knew the show was about to start. Oysters with only pepper and a drizzle of lemon juice and *champagne brut* for my parents, chips and *amuses* for us, little girls. I would soon follow my mother's steps into the kitchen and be the sous-chef for the evening: chopping onions, crushing garlic, slicing red and yellow bell peppers, bits of chicken breast… The meal prep was the longest to take, and the challenge was to please the watchful mother's eyes. The cooking of the rice and seafood, however, was the quickest part, though not as swift as everyone gathering around the table getting ready to savor the now-steaming-hot-coming-to-us paella pan. *Buen provecho*, I ought to say, even though I did not know a single word of Spanish at the time. And *bueno* it sure was, exquisite even: a perfect blend of rich and delicate flavors reminding us of the warmth and the love we share. I will have to admit that, while writing this down, I cannot help but think how curious it is for us to end the year with one of the most emblematic and sunny dishes there is; almost as if winter and summer, when blend nicely, look palate-pleasing and even eye-catching together and remind us that opposites do attract and make up for perfect and lasting harmony. We need winter to welcome summer, and we need the latter to appreciate even more the comfort brought by the former. The icing on the cake would be that the people of the world would understand that their differences, no matter how great or small, are key to unlock peace and understanding in order to walk hand in hand. Let us be one, one whole, out of all our many parts, for there is no sturdiest construction than one resting on pillars of the most loving hearts of us all.

Waiting until the moment has arrived to countdown to midnight, the four of us would watch, each year, the same play, first because it was broadcasted on the leading francophone channel, later because my father had bought the D.V.D. in order to make sure we would never have to miss it if it were to be removed from the New Year's Eve television programs. As low as that possibility even is, one must take precautions. The play itself, *Le mariage de mademoiselle Beulemans*, is a 1910 comedy, but we watch the version that was shot in the '70s. The cast of actors is brilliant, and the popular language style (dialect) and folklore are to laugh with. It is a good-natured play; probably one of the most successful for the end of the year celebration. Dessert would consist of Christmas leftovers yule log – you do remember the mocha (false chocolate look, wrong coffee flavor) I wrote about earlier? Well, that is what our father would have – whereas my sister and I would decide over how many scoops of vanilla ice cream we would need to hold all the chocolate sprinkles we intended to add on top of it.

A little past nine, we would receive the first text messages with the New Year's wishes from the 'someones' who are afraid that by sending all the messages at midnight at once, from all the people around the world, the networks would break and be down forever under the overload. Actually, when one comes to think of it, that might have been true in the year 2000, but, nowadays, as I am writing, even Facebook is becoming out of fashion. Truth be told, I think I got lost in the whole Snapchat, WhatsApp, Tumblr, Twitter, or Instagram (and I am probably a rookie in using them properly). Some say mailmen lose their jobs; every year, a little more of them are forced into finding new employment. So, what has happened to sending out Christmas cards and holiday greetings to each other? Honestly, what has become of wishing truly and sincerely that the New Year would bring love, happiness, good health, and joy? Instead, we seem to prefer the posting of artificial pictures of wealth and abundant materialism, attracting only the greedy eyes of society and flattering the pride of the selfish. I still have mixed feelings over the deep-blue-sky pictures I see of friends taking a year-off vacation to travel the parts of the world where people have lesser means than they do while the West shows off its superiority complex and profusion of (empty) material riches. Humility might save some souls. It is not too late.

Christmas Wishes and the Sweater Present

Only a couple of days are left now before the night of present Christmas Day. As a *mise en bouche*, I first wish to address the following words to my sister.

There once was a little spot in the great wild, not too sure it would fit in and feel comfortable enough to keep warm and spread the light…

And so the story began. For this little spot fought her way up to the top. This year, more than ever, she has kept up with her resolute and determined pace and has proven her resistance and toughness more than once along her way. That is, until Christmas this year came around; for on this special day, time is infinite, kindness is authentic, and love is true. The richly and beautifully decorated homes hear the echoes of traditional carols played in the background, and smell of candle lights lit up for the night, the warmth of which announcing and welcoming the peace and tranquility into its walls.

On Christmas Day this year, I wish you to follow the tracks that have been laid out for you. Scale up, do not look into the void; the only way is up. Up you go, now. Careful, look to the left, look to the right, but, most importantly, I wish you to always keep your eyes set on the deep blue sky. In the distance, whether close or far, you will succeed in finding your balance with confidence and trust (wear high heels!), and even though I cannot promise you a perfectly smooth path, and although I know you too may encounter some potholes along the way, I can assure you that your inner voice will guide you to conquer them all with pride and shed light on your journey again and again.

I wish I could hand over a mirror to you tonight, in order for you to see your beautiful self and being as I do; that way, you would look at yourself each morning and see how bubbly and sparkling you are. However, it is too cold a present, and I do not believe it will get you comfy and warm, so I hope these loving cotton and scented spots will transform your mornings, noons, and nights, so that you can forever walk up head high. Merry Christmas to you, dear.

And, thus, I handed the sweater as a symbolic gift of the present Christmas spirit and everlasting love.

The Year 2018, I Have Not Seen
The Year 2019, I Hope to Live

And once the storm is over, you won't remember how you made it through, how you managed to survive. You won't even be sure, in fact, whether the storm is really over. But one thing is certain. When you come out of the storm, you won't be the same person who walked in. That's what this storm's all about. (Haruki Murakami)

December 16th. Exactly one year and 24 hours ago, I could not find any other escape route. I had been traveling for too long, disoriented and all at sea, for I had lost both my body and my soul. They had been hardening for some time into a thick ice mass, every day a little more frozen into oblivion, cruel and selfish *laissez-faire* until it went totally adrift. Whether it was destiny, fortune, or a sign of God, I will never know, but that day, one year back from writing these lines, I had only just escaped being submerged by the hard-hitting and killing tidal wave that had been chasing after me for a long time.

I have read somewhere that when the body or the mind is under high-voltage stress levels, fighting tooth and nails not to get electrocuted, the energy circuit reconfigures itself from within your body, saving the little power left in order to maintain light only for the most vital organs. Brain, heart, lungs, and guts will be so greedy that little or no energy will be left over to warm up the body from tips to toes which will soon color purple-gray or purple-black out of despair and abandonment. From that moment on, I have learned the importance of wearing layers, two pairs of socks (one of which woolen), and befriending the hot water bottle, although the latter plotting with the enemy and leaving tracks of semi-burned skin after it had been used. I believe that had it not been considered rude and impolite, I would have even dared to wear my knitted nightcap, for I have always had very sensitive ears, especially to the cold air of a bedroom at night.

For a long time – and I am talking months, if not years – I have known and experienced cold. From within, cold deep inside the bones. The worse it got, the tenser the muscles would be. Tips and toes, I did not feel them anymore, whereas the mind and soul were giving up every day a little more. My skin dried out, and no matter how many creams and balms or lotions I would try out, its cracking worsened, *ab und zu*, leaving hardened crusts of blood which would open up again each time I would wash my hands (often in my case, since I am always to be found behind stove pots). When I think of it now, I wonder why I did not get Band-Aid coupons for free, so heavy a consumer had I become. Fortunately, for me, Mou heard my crying and got me (no laughing) the kids' package, with happy drawings on it. Aces, Mom, aces.

Under Construction

Fighting off the rusty pain enveloping my bones, because of the inner cold, was not the only battle I would need to both fight and lead. As from the early stages in the wake of my tumbling, my body has shown signs of physical and emotional exhaustion. In order for the light not to get blown out completely and, thus, undermine or damage forever the most vital organs, my body has locked itself out from my tyrannical mind, which has proven too strong and too stubborn to ease off and slow down; quite the contrary actually, for whenever I got increasingly aware of the need to let my body rest, I decided to sail even further up the stream, although hoping never to go through the rapids and end up in a waterfall out of which I would most certainly not get out unharmed and unhurt. Because, yes, I never took my helmet with me, nor did I have a shield to hide behind. Actually, I was never really wearing any armor for the last couple of years.

I know now that I should have been more careful, but there is no point in dwelling on the past. The only person who suffers most from it is your fragile self. Be indulgent to yourself, as I have heard scores of people say. Take care of yourself. I wonder how many times people rush this out of their mouths just to bring a conversation or a quick and trivial meeting to an end, trying to avoid long and fearsome whining. Obviously, they do not grasp the original meaning behind this random and common phrase; they merely use it as a plain, common, and now-recognized form of speech to quickly end a talk. The American English 'take care' at the end of a natter is, thus, no better than the French opening line '*ça va*?' I cannot even think of the latter as a polite and decent thing to say to someone, for the speaker will, only on extremely rare occasions, wait for the honest reply of the person he or she is speaking to.

Nevertheless, how uncommunicative we, the humankind, might have become in the peak of a social media era (ironic, is it not?), we ought to take more precious care of ourselves. All of us, and if not out of love for ourselves, then out of respect for the ones who could not live without us and could not bear missing us. We, as in all of us, are the foundations of the world's most impressive masterpiece: the construction of a humankind; a whole out of its bits and pieces, how different might they be.

Considering the importance of a solid and strong foundation upon which will rest the construction works, it is essential to understand that every single life matters. You, me, anyone is worth fighting for. If early signs of giving up appear, let us remind ourselves and other selves that might be at loss, that their being, their doing, and their speaking are indispensable to the harmony and peace of this world. Let us spread the warmth to them all and make sure that their voices be heard and welcomed.

Landmines in the Battlefield

Over the years, my own heating system had dropped to the bottom of my body's priority list, since my brain was too demanding and too energy-consuming, leaving no other option for the inner light to go slowly out, disappearing into a forgotten corner of the landscape in order for the basic functions to keep warm and safe. Some might see a robot in this very basic description, a random shape only connected to an outlet and moving solely when switched on; but I would much rather compare myself to a phantom, for they wander throughout the day, not really feeling anything and looking only with the eyes set into the past, with the sole exception here that I am not dead. Life had not given up on me, no matter how hurt it might feel.

I had been erring for too long a time, until only very recently, I have started to feel again…ashes burning out and the charcoals still ember red, but out of which I would – hopefully soon – rise. It might have taken a year, but I believe I am ready just now to find a match and try to ignite the fire.

A different kind of fire did knock on my door though. It could not be more unexpected – trivial perhaps to some – but on Saturday, December 15th, I was hit by a flash of lightning in my head, and I realized one time too many how destroyed I was and how little left there was of me. It was a little after noon, and in the car, the four of us were: my parents, my sister, and me.

Actually, when I say car, I really mean the 'tiny car,' not the family 'all-terrain vehicle.' How odd though, to notice that, in every household, there is a bigger car for traveling with the family, *au complet*, and then the, *what I call*, 'little foot,' used by the one family member at the time for his or her daily commutes to work or for the 'quick-park-and-go' grocery shopping after work on the way home. The tiny car, as I said, is, however, only seldom used for family trips, but that day, we all headed straight to the white Fiat Punto, nine years of age (which would be swapped and sold by the time you read this piece). These are the memories I wish I could take pictures of, for I am sure we looked like the old French joke: *'Comment faire rentrer quatre éléphants dans une 2CV?'* I believe the proper English translation would need to use another car model than the French Citroën. An evergreen Mini Cooper perhaps? Anyway, sticks and stones may break my bones, as the saying goes.

There we were, all heading to the closest city mall, the one in Waterloo, low on gas because my father does not and will not sell the car full on petrol ("You do know the diesel fuel prices are skyrocketing, right?" he would say). Still digesting our lunch and, consequently, feeling both sleepy and quite bloated, my sister and I got ourselves out of the two-door and, mind you, not without difficulty – Cinderella would have more luck coming out of a real pumpkin. After a quick 'is my hair right' check, we entered the mall and immediately got pushed around by shoppers and passersby in desperate need of last-minute Christmas presents or something to decorate the festive table.

To be honest, I am quite allergic to this false and commercialized Christmas spirit, for, according to the last-minute shopper's opinion, any gift is good as long as they can put down a red-and-green ribbon package under the tree. They might get a bonus if the wrapping paper is reindeer-full. Only few people really think about the meaning behind the present and the emotional message they wish to deliver to the recipient, for the greatest gift of all acquires its dearest value if being person-purchased exclusively from a list of many more symbolic good deeds during the year. Do not buy your loved ones a gift for the material object itself, but for the time, devotion, and care it took you to choose it, pick it up, until you wrapped it up and handed it over with a satisfied and happy-relieved smile on your face. In the end, it does not matter whether bronze or gold, Christmas is about sharing love through acts of forgiveness, peace, and maturity of spirit and thought. And it takes great strength, I must admit, to know people deep down.

So, in the mall and once we had entered the *Passage Wellington* – the name of the shopping galleries, what else could it be in Waterloo, the very city where Emperor Napoleon Bonaparte was vanquished by a coalition under the command of the British Duke of Wellington, hence the name remained – we walked with decisive marching steps toward one of the few decent and classy shoe stores that one can encounter in a province-wide radius. And since the other two stores in cities further away from our home belong to the same manufacturer, one must not be a math genius or a market expert in order to find out that there is a real demand (and desperate shoppers) for footwear merchants; the real ones, not the sneakers and slippers you find at the local discount supermarket, with questionable 'real cow leather' tags. This being said, my mother sat down on the washed-out black leather couch, somewhat worn, and tried on a beautiful pair of burgundy loafers. What she did not know at the time was that I had ordered on the internet and only that same morning the Christmas present that my father would give her on the day of the 25th:

cream-colored woolen pants paired with a darker alpaca and wool-yarn jumper and a leopard-silk blouse (which I still need to convince her will suit her perfectly). Girls and women all over the world know that the burgundy shoes will be the icing on the cake and the perfect match to the outfit. As I am closing this paragraph, I am still waiting for the order to be delivered at our house, sometime between tomorrow and Friday. How curious of me though; I have this habit of feeling overexcited, hysterical even, when thinking how happy my mother will be when she will receive and open her gift; or how people in general, small and tall, close and random, feel when I do something for them, anything. I have always wanted to be as helpful as I could, but I still need to figure out how to be as good a guardian angel to them as to my own me whom has been abandoned since forever I can remember. I wish no one any harm, yet what have I done to myself?

I was suddenly struck by that thought, but I did not get too sad, because, before I knew it, I was face to face with a magnificent and elegant pair of stiletto heels, the ones my *former me* would have bought without even dividing the original price by two, for they were 50% off, but *who cares?* They are stunning, and I would have considered it a great wardrobe investment. Instead, the *now me* tries on the pair that is on display, zips it up, not seeming to be aware that the yellow-bee-spotted sock is an absolutely horrible fashion faux pas and a screaming blunder. The shoe has everything: class, elegance, *grand chic*, a leopard print at the back of the heel. Black pointy-toe booties. Comfortable even, however rare that might happen. Half off. And still. . .the sock that gets out of the boot reminds me how utterly ridiculous I look.

I did not need to count the sparkles in my eyes, for they had vanished the very second I had looked at my reflection in the mirror. A shadow. A fragile, sick, white, little thing, so exhausted she has bags under her eyes, wearing ragged-camouflage clothing only to make sure it is not too obvious for passersby to notice the lack of shapes, the lack of butt. It does matter, it does. Flat as I am, I cannot wear heels, no matter how gorgeous the booties are. Actually, to be honest, I do not believe anyone would buy anything when struggling with the feeling that they have dropped completely off the radar. It does not matter how loose the thick-cable woolen jumper is that I am wearing that morning in Waterloo; it does not matter how intense the effort I make in trying to disappear behind ragged clothes and a cap to cover my head; it does not matter how comfy my MOU boots are, there will always be someone or something reminiscent of the skinny piece of bones wandering the mall corridors, lost and terribly nostalgic of the time she would curse herself for having a muffin top, or so she thought.

Tick-Tock Bang

Destruction feels like a black hole now. The origin of it remains unclear, vague; the exit too far away to see. Light comes and goes, as a child expects to see the stars at night: sometimes he is in luck and counts them out of many more he cannot see; other times, however, he finds it rather hard to see their light illuminate the darker sky and counts none, whereas they are out there.

I disappeared into the void some time ago now and have just found the courage now to admit it. It strikes you as lightning, but it takes the storm to reach its peak to finally soften and demolish everything, leaving only debris and a phantom being, a shadow. If the soul had found shelter in time, it would need more than a hollow promise to emerge and spread warmth and light.

Ever since the shoe episode at the mall five days ago, I have experienced worse exhaustion levels than ever before; I have had ongoing nightmares when my eyes were closed during the night, for I am still not authorized a deep and sweet (fast and sound) sleep, or so it seems. At 9:15 or 9:30 p.m., my eyelids struggle to bear the weight of debilitation, tiredness and eventually collapse. I nevertheless manage to walk upstairs, old granny's pace, and fight with my toothpaste so that it won't leave white and dried-out marks on my lower cheeks because, obviously, I will be too tired to even notice and will eventually end up scratching in an attempt to take off the glue-esque and itchy feeling.

Aside from the toothpaste, I try my best not to think too much about when and where my electric toothbrush will hurt my teeth. Mostly in the back of the mouth, although, lately, I have noticed that I had lost some enamel on both the left and right canines. Depending on the intensity of the nightmares, their periodicity, and their lasting effect for days, weeks or even months now – I should rather keep track of the number of times when I am free of dreams and torments; I could count those times on one hand sadly, yet my teeth hurt and get increasingly more spear-shaped from all the grinding. Anxiety and stress levels influence my night(less) rest, and I have this horrible habit of clenching my teeth while my muscles get too tense for me to even relax. Nothing will do. Tension knots have been building up along my backbone from the neck until well into my lower back. Right side only. Careful, do not touch it or put any pressure on it, for I swear I will cry so much, it hurts. Worst case scenario is whenever I stand there, looking at myself into the bathroom mirror with a combination of aching teeth and a bloated tummy, along with flashing headaches and feeling like a ship that has been caught into a storm, not sure how to sail up straight without capsizing. I would then manage, at last, to drop the anchor in my own harbor, my bed, but having taken the needed precautions: orange-and-brown-striped woolen socks put on (they were horribly expensive at the time I bought them) and an extra three-layer cover sheets and blankets. Try to sleep tight, I whisper.

Unfortunately, no matter how warm and cozy I may feel under the covers, the falling-asleep part always frightens me. Will I doze off soon and end up dreaming after some time tossing and turning until finally ending up in the same predictable fetal position and leaving for dreamland? I usually firs curl my knees in toward my chest until I am warm enough or to feel safe, later stretching out my legs toward the end of my bed, although regretting it soon afterward, for it is still very cold back there at the end of the bed. Then I wait. When in luck, I unconsciously get to sleep, but around midnight and three in the morning, I am bound to wake up and fight against the same fear from earlier in the evening; or else, I am tormented by incomprehension, disbelief, solitude, helplessness. Those are the nights I cannot hold back my secret tears falling down my cheeks, nor can I prevent my soul from grieving. There is a life out there that my eyes and mind can see, but the carrier of the 'I' person lacks physical strength to live it up for real. For some years now, there has always been a double 'me.' The shadow one who wonders how to be and who feels she has faded away (and still does), hiding behind the power of the shaky and unsteady physical structure that does not seem to let go of the protective state of lockdown. The other one just bites her tongue and puts up with it, for she fears the look of passersby.

I wish, however, to reassure those who might look questioningly at me now that they have read the 'double-me' experience I have just mentioned. I do not *really* visualize a double image of myself, nor do I have any kind of hallucinatory images of another version of myself, almost as if mind and body were separated. I still feel no direct connection to the romantic poet and dramatist, Alfred de Musset, who suffered from a special (severe?) form of depersonalization, also referred to in neurophysiology as 'autoscopy.' How dreadful a weight his mind might have had to put up with, and I can only wish for my body to recover whatever meagre strength it may find to finally free my soul from its bodily prison. Let us fight back and demand the freedom of the soul, *i.e.* putting the first ruins together and start up the building of a new bodily structure, this one being resistant to whatever future torment or storm… Once the roots are dug tight and warm, I cannot see why I ought to fear the slightest breeze ever more.

It was only after I had put down the writing for the day, that I opened one of my Christmas presents, a book by one of my favorite authors (and probably the best one of his generation), the great Sebastian Faulks. I was eager to start his last fiction, *Paris Echo*, especially because it had been months since I had read one of his works of fiction. 20 pages it took me before I realized that I felt the exact same way as the character named Hannah, the American researcher on her return from a student's trip to Paris. I couldn't help but compare her experience to mine in Salamanca.

"When I finally returned home that July, I'd lost almost 20 pounds in weight, and my parents were shocked by the sight of me. (...) No sympathy from my mother or arm round the shoulder from my father could persuade me to confide in them (...). I was unable to describe the extent of my unhappiness. There was nothing in my own experience or in my knowledge of the lives of others with which to compare it; so I thought it best to lock it all away and try to think of other things. My mother told me I seemed 'cold,' and I found it impossible to convince her that when you've found yourself so far out of your depth, you cling to certainties, things you know you can deal with. And you keep clinging for as long as it takes."

I did not, however, lose all the weight on my return from the Erasmus experience. I had, on the contrary, gained a couple of kilograms, three at the most. That summer, I was already burying myself into work, for my professor had given me the books to read for the research on the metaphors used in English and French medical texts and documents that describe the role of bacteria. The subsequent assistantship at the start of that academic year was yet another reason to take a deep plunge into a workaholic attitude. Moreover, the loss of a narcissist best friend (I had to free myself from the chains; how hurt I might feel), the abandonment of myself, and the unheard (and snubbed) voice of my body screaming were the true red-carpet entrances into darker corridors of further self-effacement. The loss of a couple of kilograms at first did not seem so frightful after all and, surely, were nothing to worry about. It is only a matter of stress and anxiety. This episode will not last. Or at least, this was what I had been telling my inner voice to reassure it and to bring some comfort to my soul. With the benefit (not yet the wisdom of) hindsight, I realize that I had been ignoring these warnings by hiding behind the thought of a more-manageable life, one in which work prevails over the being, over life in general. I had, by then, become my own slave; the serf of a workaholic ruler slowly killing off her true, unknown, and yet undiscovered self.

Sending My Wishes on Christmas Eve

On Christmas Eve this year, many a man will listen closely to refrains of peace and cherish the love both spread and received. But what greater wish than reminding ourselves, the people of the world, to be one, one whole, out of all our many parts, for there is no sturdiest construction than one resting on pillars of the most loving hearts of us all. Merry Christmas to us all.

On the "night before Christmas" our party was in full swing and in between the *amuse-bouches* and the *pièce de résistance*, I had not noticed that my cellphone was storing a couple of text replies after I had sent my Christmas wishes earlier on this special day. I did not find the strength to read them when I climbed upstairs at 11:30 p.m. Oh I know, *that* early, some would say, but you will have to trust me when I tell you that for my skinny and still too frail body, my happy but exhausted soul, this it's-almost-midnight-calling-to-bed feels already like crossing a mountain-high border without really knowing what to expect *the morning after* and whether or not the "fast asleep" term will that day be a new word to add into my own dictionary of nightfall travels.

Nevertheless, I cannot describe the most pleasant and surprised feeling when the following morning at 5:17 a.m. – it was Christmas Day! – I unlocked my (charging) phone only to discover a 10-unread-message-scrolling-down on my screen. Ten! Even though I am grateful and feel blessed for the people who do take the time to reply and send their wishes back, one message in particular stood out from the rest. It was from my sister's godfather (my mother's eldest brother). He is yet another example of strength and bounce-back after he had lost his wife (and our aunt) a couple of years ago to a heart attack. It crushed us all. Not only does it take away the life of a beautiful person, it further causes an unprecedented rupture of our own still breathing hearts. Yet, when I see how stronger a person he is now, I can only admire him and wish him well. He has not closed a chapter of his life. on the contrary, he was able to listen to his inner voice and waited for the power within himself to follow his writing his life, heartbroken but a stronger warrior, and to prepare a sequel filled with new and bold memories. It took him bravery of heart to fall in love again, although without ever forgetting his wife. But then again, who says love cannot have multiple facets? Every love is different, every feeling is dependent on time and place. His reply to my Christmas wishes was the one that almost made me cry: *"The birds they sang at the break of day. Start again I heard them say. Don't dwell on what has passed away or what is yet to be. Ring the bells that still can ring. Forget your perfect offering. There's a crack in everything, that's how the light gets in.* Merry Xmas. C&G." Spot on. If my heart did not break, it had certainly melted.

I believe signs do come in disguise, and this Christmas morning – or better said, yesterday evening as my phone was ringing on the received messages while I was touring in our sitting room with appetizers and homemade sausage pastry rolls (Frankfurter, obviously, for the meat lovers) – when I opened the above-mentioned wishes, I felt the warmth fill my soul. No sooner had I discovered the inspiration behind Leonard Cohen's song, than I asked my inner voice to give me reason and hope to write my own sequel, the one I wish to share and tell, rather than dwell on the past, this past that had come to rule against me. I wish to inspire people with the person I know still exists and hides within my heart and soul. I need now to cautiously draft some color onto this shadow and cross off the faded charcoal pain. It is that time.

Time to realize indeed that the suffering has been too great already for my whole experience to bear whatever more. I have struggled from the very beginning of my life to be perfect in everything, always afraid to fail to please others and to suffer from their unconsciously judging eyes. Guilt has built up my existence. Until this morning, on Christmas Day. *Assez*! I have come at peace with the imperfection that rests in the true and authentic meaning behind the bricks of perfection. Similar to the unnoticeable, yet necessary airholes left in the brick walls to better sustain the house and let it last through heats and storms, human beings need their very own scars to better carry the wounds of their soul and remind their self that when the candle lights are lit, the lost wax stays fragile and warm for a while, only to soak hard into the soul and forever stain its past warmth and color the rosy sequel one deserves to hope for.

Wishes on New Year's Eve

Latin word *Salve* or 'be well' is still used by Italians to greet people and wish them good. I thus wave my hand and wish you to always listen beyond what can be heard and look future-further where your eyes will set. May your *passeggiata* welcome surprise and wonder, benevolence and care. But may love forever guide your pace and light up your soul. I wish you the most inspiring walk of all. Happy 2019 to you all.

And the Dutch version hereunder, just for my oma, because she does not speak English but admires an out-of-the-box message once in a while:

Lichtpuntjes, groot en klein, elke dag kan je ze vinden en zijn. Want lichtjes, waar ze ook zijn, toveren het bijzonderste uit elke dag en verrassen je, als het mag! Ik sta even stil en vraag stiekem aan de Engeltjes om elk moment voor jou zorgeloos fijn te kleuren, maar vooral dat er duizenden warme kaarsjes van liefde en geluk voor jou mogen branden en een fabelachtig Nieuw Jaar de weg naar jou mag vinden. Veel liefs.

Checking the couple of replies on my cellphone again, my eyes were caught once more by the beautiful message of hope behind my uncle's text. The same eldest brother of my mother. This time, he did not refer to a great singer; instead, he forwarded the old Irish blessing that follows. He did not have to add anything for my heart to melt one more time.

May you always be blessed with,
Walls for the wind.
A roof for the rain.
A warm cup of tea by the fire.
Laughter to cheer you.
Those you love near you.
And all that your heart might desire.

New Year

On the morning of December 31ˢᵗ, I had woken up from a terrible nightmare. I was on the Buzzsaw, a most daring thrill attraction of one of Belgium's most renowned amusement parks; at least, I thought I was. It looked more like the dark and foggy woods you would expect to imagine in a page-turner thriller, a forest you would rather not cross early in the morning after a rainy and stormy winter night, for even the air smells suspicious. The tall oak trees and the heaviness of the leafy greens only seem to allow the wind to give passersby goosebumps while intimidating sunrays and scaring off any warmth or light.

Fearing this eerie atmosphere, I could not help but rush and get a breath of fresh air. I was only given the time to bring my mittens to my nose in an attempt to keep it warm (safe from frostbite) and prevent it from breaking off from the cold, before I suddenly came face to face with a skyscraper scaffolding built in what seemed a rocky mountain. May I present to you: the Buzzsaw of the amusement park I normally never go to. The thrill-seeking and stunningly insane ride will take you – fasten your seatbelts and be ready – up and down at full speed and, while hanging in the air, will allow the joyful tourists to take a break from their enthusiasm and grasp for air. It further scares them off with a 45-degree-angle inclination which leaves them out of breath (obviously), and forces them to fight against gravity (because they will fear the skiddy seats), and to pray for their belts to be strong enough to keep them seated, even though not that restful anymore. It only takes a quarter of a second to be submerged by the intense-though-dreadful feeling of loosening your grip. You then feel your body slip away from the seats of the makeshift Buzzsaw scaffolding, only held back by the now slowly unfastening belt. Void. Earth, rocks, dust. Right below. Or, better said, right in front of you, since you are bent to form a right angle with *Terra firma*. Suddenly, this ride will confront you with one of the most primeval fears known, the falling down into a black hole of nothingness. The void. Again. I know this well.

Landing with both your feet on the ground, the dizziness will take a couple of minutes to clear up. In my nightmare, I found my body wandering cold and alone in the middle of these woods, escaping…death. That night indeed, I was nightmare-chased by the Salamanca *bestie* who desperately tried to kill me. A cold-blooded assassination.

I was running – typical, is it not? – forgetting how to breathe, chased by the narcissist ghost of the past, pursued by the same sense of powerlessness, helplessness, or by my too-long-a-time-lasting lack of self-confidence. She was there. Right behind me. Trying to pull the trigger and end me.

I woke up in cold sweats, trying to reach for some air. It was December 31ˢᵗ, the last day of the year 2018. The year I had not seen, the one I had not lived but had only witnessed from afar, from an alien body. Nevertheless, I could not spend the last day in pain, whether psychological or physical, be it the torturous mind or the aching bones. This day would be the first attempt to ignite the light, however little there is left of it. Light. Just feeling and sensing the warmth of inner light and the freedom of guilt-free and pure, authentic joy. Laughter even, perhaps. Why not?

The day started with a not-before-tested shower soap, just to make sure I could still appreciate an undiscovered perfume of (label-written) cotton-touch body wash. Surprise your abandoned self, I thought. It is indeed another step – small, I must confess – but no one will expect you to dive if you are afraid of the great depths of the sea; a first dipping your toes will do. After my out-of-the-ordinary shower, I headed downstairs to prepare my gargantuan breakfast ritual; it is not as if I was given a choice anyways so I might as well follow the orders, from the medical team, and, no, there is no argumentation possible whatsoever. This morning was also going to be different than any other I have had so far, for instead of concentrating on chewing and assimilating the different food constituents of my plate, I was thinking about what I should write for my New Year's Eve wishes. I knew I would send them later that day to the handful and dearest people I know.

I was not given much *food for thought*, however, because I rose very quickly from my seat to take my cellphone out of my bag in the living room. Beep, and then vibrating twice. This could only mean that I had just received a text message. 'Twas December 31ˢᵗ, and I had a feeling my sister would send some news. She always does when we are to meet her during the day. I had been proven wrong, since she had not sent any text message, preferring the Facebook Messenger bubble that pops up in the right corner of my screen. I was soon reminded of the last details of our conversation and the plans that we had been making for the four of us to meet up for lunch. My parents and I would drive to the Brussels city center, and she would take one subway, six stops, and one elevator to greet us on the last day of December 2018. We would sit down for lunch and take a little walk, meandering gently in and out the *chalets* of the Christmas village. Having escaped death earlier in my nightmare, I thought I deserved this posh touch of *je ne sais quoi* for lunch, a little something out of the ordinary. Again. Oh, you know, one has those days when they will binge on anything except for the usual or routine, in my case, the rye *tartines* with salmon and broccoli I usually have at one sharp in the afternoon, alone. Although I had been adding the extra veggies for the last couple of days, a week or two at the most. To hell with that. We are out, in Brussels, the four of us. Let us be fancy. I *wanted* something different, but not *too* different, because different means fear, different means anxiety. I certainly did not want to scare myself, nor did I wish to lose my balance. Some pains need time to heal; others need care and patience to accept they will stay forever. I sighed, for it is not easy a task to welcome change. Especially since change is everywhere.

I swiped the bubble downward, locked my phone, and on our way to Brussels we were! I felt the butterflies in my stomach for the first time since I do not know how long a time. To me, it felt close to going out on a date. I had made an effort not to look ghastly pale or yellow-sick and even applied some hypoallergenic foundation I had received over a year ago (still plastic packed), at a time when I was still a hopeless workaholic. The *biscuit*-color fond de teint was, thus, inaugurated for this lunch date.

Once the car was safely parked and locked underground – my father made sure all four handles were shut, checking them twice even, and if we had not been there, he would have checked them again – we headed to our meeting point. Yes, Papa, the car is bolted by now (sigh). My sister, on the other hand, would take the subway from the house she is sharing with friends, and it would be any minute now for her to arrive. A little past 1 p.m., I spotted her head and beige-spotted woolen scarf in the crowd, and we were soon mounting the stairs of our family topper hamburger restaurant of the Place Sainte-Catherine.

The Belgian *good* food chain, Ellis Gourmet Burger, has always caught my very special attention. It reminds me of better times. I had first gone there with my American godfather and his family on one of their trips to Belgium, and we all gathered there on the last day of my final exams when I was in my last year of my master's degree at university. I had just defended my thesis before the members of the jury that same morning, and I still had sparkles in my eyes. I seemed not to realize that I was done with university. Although, little did I know that I would enroll in an additional year in management only two months from then. Even so, Team U.S.A. and Team Belgium combined; we all went to Brussels that very hot summer day at the end of June 2015, and we sat down at a table on the first floor. We all ordered the classic gourmet burger, except for my grandmother and me, both of us preferring the 'sexy salmon and baby spinach' version. It was one of the best trivial lunches I had ever had. I felt free. And, now, on this last day of 2018, we would be repeating the experience, almost as if to make sure that we end this somewhat bizarre year with *classe* and a touch of *finesse*. Cheers. Oops, I forgot I drink no beer. Waiter, water for me, please!

This time was hot too, but only inside the restaurant, for it was too crowded. 20 minutes. That is how long we had been waiting, mouthwatering for most of that time, I must confess, checking every plate with garnished *ciabatta* breads and buns that came upstairs, passing by the tall glass door next to our table with view on the floor's corridor. No, not our order it seems. Still not. Surely, the next one coming up the stairs would be ours. No, again not. I was already observing very closely how our neighbors were dissecting their *pistolet* breads (that is how we call the 'buns' over here) and analyzing every layer of its content, both of them unaware that I had been eyeing them with discretion ever since taking my seat – at least, I hope they did not notice, and if so, well, the tourists would have to excuse my intrusion. How do you say sorry in…? I could not guess whether they were Japanese or Vietnamese. I only remember laughing and struggling to regain a straight face when the lady neighbor could not get any ketchup out of the glass bottle – seriously though, how difficult can it be to think of turning the bottle upside down while closed, especially closed, and shaking it for a bit, just until you hear and see the content sliding forward; or if you are in a lazy mood but still wish to stay classy and prevent any damage of unfortunate stain of color (because, let us be honest, it is ketchup we are talking about, and she was wearing a white silk blouse *obviously*), why not ask your neighbor's bottle…since our order *still* had not arrived, and that we had two anyway and would have been more than happy to help them out. Guilty me, I will admit, I had fun watching them. In the end, there were no fateful accidents. And they ended up enjoying their lunch with mustard solo. There was no crumb left, unfortunately for us. None for our hungry tummies.

Until finally, with view both on the glazed hallway, on our right, the *Place Sainte-Catherine* in Brussels, on our left through the window, the *Place* being invaded by little *chalets* with waffles and oysters and seafood popup bars, the waiter brought four burgers that we knew were destined only for our table. Four burgers, except for one, the sexy salmon filet. At last. Eat, people, eat.

Actually, mind the trap, for we suddenly felt all gossiping eyes around us, staring directly at us while we were fighting against our watering mouths and tortured mind. We were indeed at a crossroad (although, on second thought, my father probably not), teared between the sudden craving and urge to devour our long-awaited-for festive burger and the realization that in order to be socially accepted, we ought better look distinguished, polite, and classy, hence the delicate and posh slow-motion eating, with knife and fork, please. The three of us (and here, I am not counting my father in) decided to use the cutlery and to separate our burgers into two, then four pieces. How classy can one be? But for a burger, really? Nevertheless, we thought better of it and did not want anything edible to jump into our neighbor's plates; they had had their fair share; hence the carefully calibrated decision based on objective *art de table* factors: we're digging in, *people*. We sure are, and *to hell with* the extra sauce dripping on our hands, making them itchy and gluey. When you go for a burger, you do it in style. Although licking your fingers is perhaps a little too farfetched no matter how hungry one is.

Our appetite had been satiated, and all streets departing from the *Place* were inundated by flocks of locals and tourists – Spaniards mostly, at least during our walk that day, and the bright-colored apparel of Chinese groups you would find anywhere touring Europe, though not mixing or interfering with 'faraway' civilizations. All gathered here at the Christmas popup village, curious about the authenticity of the displayed honey, *confitures*, Canadian maple syrup, or just fancying an afternoon stroll following step by step the rich flavors of *tartiflettes*, *crêpes*, *raclettes*, Greek chicken *souvlaki*, beautiful pink cotton candy, caramelized almonds loaded with sugar and probably devoid of much of their original benefits, and other warm or cold snacks that one traditionally finds next-in-line after the churros, waffles, and French fries – sorry, that would be *frites* in our case.

Interestingly enough, as an aside, one can never stroll about any Christmas village without giving in to the materialistic impulse aroused by the joyful and appetizing atmosphere of the wooden huts. In our defense, we came to our senses quite rapidly, since we were still mouthwatering the pleasant and lingering aftertaste of our burgers. We were, thus, not much tempted by the rich and sometimes too-greasy full-fat or sugar-market street food that we could come across as we were wandering through the *cabanons*. Perhaps, there was a price to pay for our too reasonable and too sensible state of affairs at the beginning of the walk. By the end of the tour, we admitted defeat, surrendered, and succumbed to the urge (and sweet tooth) to buy a box of real *cuberdons* (please, how can one expect to resist the purple cone-shaped nose candy so famous in Ghent and Bruges, two rival cities fighting for its authenticity?), four better-than-the-originals-found-in-Lisbon *pastéis de nata*. These little Portuguese cream flans are a two-bite treat for my father, whereas my mother would save hers to eat on the following morning of our trip with a soft-boiled egg and whole wheat *tartines*, providing a contrasting view of how to savor best the pastry and do justice to the care of its making in the baking atelier. It goes without saying that we kept one as an extra for my father, one he would rather have as a treat after lunch the next day, served with his espresso, letting the flan, again here, disappear in just two crusty mouthfuls. At the very end of our slow walking through the Christmas village, I remember my sister insisting with two (were they Russian?) woodcarvers selling figurines that she did not need any white and clearly oversized plastic bag to wrap up her final acquisition of the Christmas stroll: a real wooden red-and-blue nutcracker. She had spotted it on sale for under 25 euros, and there were only three of them left, one of which was sticking out. It was the ultimate treasure of the day and, quite honestly, had it come upon a music box, she would have been bouncing off the walls. That is how thrilled she was. Had she heard Tchaikovsky playing, she might have fainted even.

Anyway, we were now leaving the *cabanons* of the Place Sainte-Catherine and finding our way back to the car, walking through the recently opened yet still under construction *pietonnier* – a pedestrian and, thus, car-free area in the middle of the city center that continues to cause much ink to flow, for it is sentencing to death the neighboring shops and trade in general, encouraging delinquents, troubled youngsters, or mere sheep to take over the streets emptied by the evening and letting monkey business and mischief thrive. However, that is a different kettle of fish.

Seatbelts fastened, my father started the engine and decided we would make a little detour and drop my sister off, the inevitable plastic shopping bag included, at her house share in a residential city just on the outskirts of Brussels. She would spend New Year's Eve with her housemates; I, on the other hand, would crawl into bed early, not waiting to see the fireworks on the stroke of midnight. This has become my traditional hop 'from one year to the next' for the last years. Skipping champagne and tumult, I believe traditions can be broken, at least for one's own wellbeing. Mine depends on an early under the covers. Before I close my eyes one last time in 2018, I will think about a wish for when I open my eyes again next year. Only time will tell, but hear me, please, just hear my desperate sigh, for I too dream of walking strong on the path of life, knowing where I am headed and how to heal the scars.

It was not on the first morning of the New Year, but very quickly, I believe somebody must have heard my prayers, otherwise how can one explain the quote that almost suddenly and quite unexpectedly popped on my Facebook wall, the latter usually being on the verge of a one-time too many cooking posts breakdown? Whether it were a trick of fate or a mere temporary Facebook disruption of my personalized newsfeed, Simone de Beauvoir made the *Madame Figaro* timeline cover that happened to break out on my screen just this morning during my porridge breakfast. Perhaps not so trivial a time at all, for she was born on this day that I am writing, exactly 111 years ago, on

January ninth, 1908. At 9:29 a.m., I had only just finished sipping my double coffee (black, no sugar, but you know that already) and realized that the post had already received quite an applause from the online community, because in just an hour or so, it had already been 'liked,' so to say in Facebook slang by 157 people. I could not help but wonder if scratching the honey out of the jar with a teaspoon and licking it off while drinking my coffee on the side and almost always finding out (too late a time) that the beverage is still too very hot was different enough a behavior or an attitude in order to fit into de Beauvoir's saying, *"Le secret du bonheur et le comble de l'art, c'est de vivre comme tout le monde, en n'étant comme personne."* Hence the honey with coffee. Who does that, *really*? Could this be my wish? Being…different? Am I not already?

Square Peg, Round Hole

Salty it does taste when reaching my mouth. It even tickles my nose and makes me want to close my eyes. Warm at first it feels indeed, as it slowly caresses my cheeks, yet it rapidly dries out and leaves a cold and sticky mark as if it were a consolation for the transience of emotions and life.

Silent tears are the heart's cry for inner change. As candle wax melts down slowly, depriving a room from warmth and light, struggling though to keep as little fire as there might be alive from the burning ashes, silent tears are the hourglass of a shift in time. It is indeed the right moment to hear out what your inner voice has been trying to tell yourself for too long now while your mind decided to continue to turn a deaf ear on your suffering, ignoring the alarm bells' ringing.

No matter how much I have tried, I cannot and will never be just like 'anybody.' I do not wish to sound posh, haughty, nor do I wish anyone to perceive a single trait of egocentricity in this statement; I would rather be understood as…just me. This is me.

All my life, I have felt the eyes of others upon me. I wish I knew why I had (and still do have) a constant and, may I say, self-destroying urge to please everybody; the need to be the good girl, the responsible one, the hard-working one. I could never live with and bear the feeling that I had or have disappointed someone, anyone, at any time. But who is this? Who is behind the shadow burden; who are the eyes I felt (and have been feeling) watching my every move?

As a little girl, I had already been inhabited by a fear of doing things wrong, fearing the expectations of others. Ever since then, I have always been at war with this never-ending battle of doing everything right, striving for perfection and self-control, leading me further on the self-destructive path one takes to reach such impossible levels of excellence and utter selflessness. The damage soon reached its culminating stage, and I hope there will not be another peak as I am writing down these lines. I pray for the worst to be behind me. Has my time to blossom come? Am I to enjoy something resembling a carefree life?

Or maybe just give me a glimpse, at least for a day or two. One would be enough. One.

'I don't know,' is probably the most likely answer I can provide to whoever asks why I seem to care *that much* for everyone, but me. I would literally jump high in the sky to bring back a little bit of sunlight if anyone would ask for or need it; but when it comes to me, I would simply crawl back into my rabbit hole and hide from my overthinking and dissatisfaction. "Later," I hear myself saying. "Let us first have the diplomas, the certificates; let us first make sure everyone is happy and blessed." I was never finished checking all the bullet points of my to-do lists and could not figure out how to start my life anytime soon. Put off to a later date. Again, until 'later' became an ever-stretching, almost unreachable period of time.

Ever since the kindergarten memory of folding socks and sweaters and tidying up the classroom until well into my first year as an employee, I had always ignored the signs of what would lead to self-effacement. After the Erasmus experience, alarm bells started to ring but were left unheard. As the sound was becoming unbearable and too high-pitched, I got afraid, so afraid that it was more mind comforting to do as many things as possible in order to care for others or dig my head into studying and work, getting high grades. All options seemed better than what I ought to have done really to save myself in time from falling. I did not. I had known for some time that I needed to prepare for the upcoming battle that was bound to break out, but I withdrew, for I knew I lacked the proper ammunition in order to fight for my own sake.

Needless to say, one cannot expect the mind to hush down its inner voice forever, for we all have a right to exist; we all have the right to let our soul take some time to keep up with our being, or better said, to find a more decent and respectful way to reach harmony and enlightenment. Are those of us pausing for a minute guilty for slowing down and considering a new wave to sail through the (hopefully more promising) winds of change, instead of plunging the paddles into rapid waters and ignoring the silent tears running down, thus risking to get lost and disappear forever into the ruthless power of waterfalls? Are those of us choosing hope over inner bombardment resulting in considerable personality loss condemned to be square pegs, unfit for today's society in which human beings are encouraged to be sheep, preferably not too strong-opinionated and pleased with their being mere daily routine subordinates?

This does, however, raise a question. Who and what defines society, precisely? I have been searching for an answer for some time, but I can only see *us*, the people of the world, perhaps not as united as we wish ourselves to be; *us*, human beings, whether yellow, white, a dollop of cream, *caffè latte*, macchiato, or dark-colored (see percentage of raw cocoa), we all have the right to live and exist, to be heard, and to feel protected from whatever potholes we might encounter on our way. All of us have the capacity to think and reason, to argue and to make peace. We have the power to choose to either dig deeper down into our rabbit hole, either extend our hand and reach for others. But, most importantly, we are all free in our hearts, and in this freedom, we find a haven to harvest love.

This freedom also allows even the best-kept secrets to find a comfortable accommodation, sometimes a shelter in our heart, whereas our soul will take charge of giving reason and true meaning to our wildest, perhaps most uncommon or audacious desires and hopes. Until, finally, wonder and awe, despair or sorrow will be left to the mind to be taken care of, though they ought better not be neglected.

Therefore, the human mind could be seen as the Venetian gondola of our own existence, of our own raison d'être. One cannot imagine strolling along the canals of the Italian picturesque *Venezia* without capturing the moment of a passing gondola, led by a dark-and-white-striped-shirt sailor. And just as the passengers are never fully protected from the little boat tilting a bit too much on the left or on the right – getting splashed is a risk you would have to be willing to take – our mind never knows how deep or how treacherous the waters will be. It will almost always find the best-built bridge to cross over; its mission being to reduce and control the damage, and to ensure a smooth and as much as possible unpainful outcome. At times, the mind might find itself at the edge of the river bank, not sure how to cross or how to prevent getting sunken into clear-blue or rather-troubling waters. These are the times when it needs protection and additional care.

Nevertheless, it does not matter how torn we might be, our mind will find comfort as long as there is faith. As I am assembling these words in the hope that it will make for a sensible piece of writing, my mind is wondering about the near future that lies only minutes ahead of me. I feel quite clear and serene, yet I cannot cast away a sense of murkiness. Silent tears are nowhere near, not today, but I hear my heart sobbing secretly, wondering what has happened to me? Where have I gone?

"I still do not know," I want to shout. I have, indeed, been looking for an answer for a little over a year now, and I must acknowledge that I have made some progress, I have. I now realize how destructive a *life* – huh, that would have to be *work* – style I had pressed upon my ailing body and increasingly stupefied self. I feel and see that my body lacks the wooden scepter of gondoliers to go with the stream, set sail, and finally steer on its own. Even so, I have learned never to lose faith. Easier said than done, agreed, but when the void is too overwhelming – as it is today – I try to find light, and if the skies are gray and all of nature seems to have gone back into hibernation, I light up a candle, just for myself. You have read correctly. A candle. As silence is my sole companion this morning, light has befriended my soul, for a candle is burning warm and slow.

Its flame reminds me not to give up. The constant need to be strong enough, both physically and emotionally, and consequently the choice to ignore and neglect the apparent physical liabilities and aches, the unheard siren calls from outside and within, will eventually end up in a complete self-destructive pattern, in the blowing off of your inner light and the total mistreatment and abandonment of the self. I have, indeed, lost any good treatment to my body, mind and soul. I do everything I can and more to care for others while I have abandoned in a cowardly way my very own right to be and to exist as *me*, a person too. I am now unable to take up the routine and repetitive plot of everyday life. So, how do I live? Tell me.

Knock Knock

The time has come to knock shyly, almost imperceptibly, on my heart's door. I cannot think of any reason to play hide and seek anymore. I have been wondering for too long as to why I do not seem to dare unlock the door of the secret lamp in which the heart has taken shelter. What could possibly be so frightful that I am afraid to discover?

To tell the truth, I was not born with a swift-decision-making power, nor was I born a daredevil. Ever since my early childhood, I would be pondering anything over for a long while before turning to the people around me and asking them: "What would *you* do?" Hopeless, so I have been told. Actually, let me rephrase that: I am a real puzzle, and this is the truth with which I have to live with. The use of the adjective 'hopeless' does imply that I agree it is subject to the noun it qualifies – the 'noun' being me.

Am I really? I believe I have not spent the last 12 months as a recluse to reach such a paltry conclusion. I only just need for something to click and illuminate my inner light-bulb for change to happen to my body. I alone can pull this trigger of change for the better. I have already grown so much on the inside – although the scope under which 'much' is considered ought to be taken as a very cautious and still-premature description – but I beg you to show mercy for every little step that I take indeed. Even the smallest of them bears its own significance, for I find myself one foot further out of the safe yet oppressive rabbit hole. I am also one step closer to reaching the clearing in the darkened woods. In the end, how is one to enjoy a starlit sky if they do not make sure that the earth feels safe enough to dare rest their feet on the ground?

Unfortunately, I am still afraid of the darkness I encounter when wandering in the woods. For the last two weeks, unpleasant and totally unwelcome nightmares have perturbed my already-quite-disrupted sleep pattern. It started with my escape from being murdered by my best friend before the New Year (you remember the nightmare) and these have not stopped since. I feel quite relieved that there has been no repetition of the running-for-my-life dream, even though I seem unable to find comfort in the other scenarios assembled by my hyperactive brain. If they are not too scary, they certainly are too burdensome.

"So, take a sleeping pill," some would shout. I thank you for the tip, but, no, I would rather not. Quite honestly, I have never been much of an advocate of generic medicine or drugs. I put my trust into the homeopathic or herbal medicinal products, and I rely on home remedies or grandmother's recipes to treat the evil ills.

However, rest assured, I am by no means an eat-only plants sort of guru, far from it. I would rather believe that, in the long run, the body and the soul must meet in order for us to find our balance. How can we then expect our balance to last if half of it is drugged under and suffers from its addiction to the not-harmless drugs? Moreover, how can we function properly if the soul suffers from the effects of physical malaise, the drifting in an ephemeral illusion of wellbeing, all preventing the mind to think clearly and see the light? Mother Nature knows best, I guess.

All right, guilty I plead, and there is no shame in admitting that I once took a quarter of the least-harmful sleeping pill my family doctor could administer, given the frail state of my body. He assured me that this type of substance had less risk of dependency and fewer side effects. Considering the fact that I would start with a two-week trial, I did not see any harm in giving it a go. Who knows, perhaps this little sleeping aid would make a difference. I only wished to make sure there were not any risk as to damage the already child-looking body, because no, I still do not have my sister's *derrière de gazelle* (she would totally roll her eyes and fake laugh if she knew I wrote this).

Actually, as an aside, when one comes to think of it, what is the *juste milieu*? Is there middle ground to be found between, on the one hand, the flat Mikado chocolate stick biscuits walking down the runway shows and praised by the fashion industry for their best attempts at disappearance-of-the-self tricks, and on the other hand, the butt-implants ardent supporters of fitness-trained 'curves,' internationally applauded by the plastic-surgery community or the body-positive Instagram gurus? I believe all are glued to keep up with their social-media diary and perfectly fake bodies, whether thin or plum, whereas average Jane and Joe are pushed further into their disillusion and dissatisfaction of their given bodies. Social media has certainly contributed to some evil ills ranging from eating disorders such as anorexia, bulimia, or orthorexia, to personality disorders and personal issues.

Bearing the silent struggles in mind, why does it seem that accepting the body you were given has nowadays become a million-dollar trick question? If easy access to the world wide web has undeniably liberated many a people and encouraged freedom of speech and confidence around the world (and I do believe we will continue to make progress and gain ground in our attempts to reach something resembling premises of peace and solidarity); the internet, sadly, has also triggered new and never-seen-before ravage in terms of body insecurity and so-called healthy eating habits. While surfing the web, one was also (unbeknownst oneself) swimming in troubled waters of low (not to say underground) levels of self-esteem or worse, self-love. Drowned was he or she bound to be.

Hence my calling to being good to your body. Care for it, and it will be grateful. You might even be pleasantly surprised when you discover a peaceful secret garden in full blossom. I wish I had read this somewhere before…before putting my body through this kind of inner suffering and physical ache, all this violence and tension. I wish I took greater care of it before almost destroying it and sending it to waste. I should have known better, I keep telling myself. At the time, it seemed logical and sensible to maintain my body just alive, only to be able to study more and get the highest grades or the approval of the shadow pressure I had felt forever, lurking behind my back, making sure I would not disappoint anyone. What then when one suddenly realizes that the one person they have disappointed most is themselves? And as I write these words down, I am reminded of a quote that had appeared earlier in the day on my Facebook newsfeed, a wise piece of advice and a motto to live by, uttered by the inspiring artist, Morgan Harper Nichols: "How liberating it is to pursue wholeness instead of perfection." Wholeness. As if it were the angels comforting our souls.

So tired of my lack of sleep was I, that I yielded. I took one of my kitchen knives on a late August night to cut the pill into four pieces, almost invisible to the naked eye, so tiny they seemed. I swallowed it with a similarly ridiculous amount of water. A two-week trial, or so it ought to have been. Unfortunately, I only lasted one week, for the experience was but a success. Seven sleepless and even more troubled nights. That is how long I lasted. I was soon to experience all the undesirable side-effects; from gas attacks in my bowels, dreadful stomach cramps to my skin turning yellow; from my heart that started throbbing to my mind that ended up spinning. I felt nauseous and down with fatigue, emotionally lost in this torment at sea. Never again, I told myself. Never again will I put my body in dire straits. I would rather have a cup of herbal tea, valerian root if I may, and experience the occasional recurring episodes of nightmares. My normal night routine without the sleeping pill was not so bad after all, for I would, indeed, still be able to close my eyes shortly after laying under the covers, and I *could* live with the fact of waking up twice or thrice during the night. However, I could not bear any more crying my eyes out because of the lack of sleep and the impossibility of closing my eyes; nor could I stand the battles my body had to fight against medicinal enemy substances that were trying to destroy my body from within with whatever drug-ammunition soldiers they had enrolled. *Assez!*

Please, do not utter the words 'Goodnight, sleep tight,' for it is yet too soon to joke about it. 'Don't let the bedbugs bite!' Drop it, please, for my dearest wish is that nobody is ever to experience such rollercoaster nights. I would very much prefer to wish all of us to have…sweet dreams, because dreaming we all do, and we'd better hope our own scenarios be love-tender and cookie-yummy, for we all agree in chorus, in unison (and in pastry), that it is the chocolate chip that adds a savory and delicate caress to the mixed dough, and no matter which other flavor you will want to bring into the batter, nothing will ever replace *la délicieuse caresse chocolatée*. It is sweet to wish an unperturbed night rest.

Monday, Somewhere in January

Monday morning, and a light drizzle gives rhythm to the wind beating against the window pane in the living room. There is no candle lit on the wooden table at which I am sitting. At least, not today. I did not have the heart to seek warmth and light from afar, for my only wish at 11:11 a.m. is that my body and my soul would, for once, feel safe and taken care of. I have failed. I am starting to get used to this state of being, this shadow life I have led myself into, the void which has settled down like an unwanted but unstoppable guest in my body, although the real host – my soul – would rather it were treated as a parasite and castaway. I have heard so many a people tell me that 'nothing lasts forever,' but how can they be so certain that I will walk into something better, perhaps being only just a couple of steps further ahead, but then again, where is it, and will it be something worth the pain I have suffered and the sorrow I have felt for so long a time?

There are tougher times when I wonder whether I will not eventually disappear into oblivion; the forgotten state of what living for real and feeling real are like. I went to sleep last night, and I was unable to feel any silent tear caressing my cheeks. I felt the sorrow deep down though, a deep and helpless sadness invading my soul, for I knew something had changed in me. Yet, I could not care less about my being, nor could I care about my inability to cry, even if just to prove myself I was still living. When it comes to others, I turn out to be an *extremely* hypersensitive person, and I would do anything to help out and act as a flawless Cinderella – the difference being that I take heart to carrying out these little tasks and, thus, ease the burden on everyone while bringing too many tasks upon my own shoulders.

However, when it comes to *me*, I play guilty at holding the record-breaking and lowest level of empathy and self-benevolence, for my mind is as cold as ice, a master in the art of body and soul abuse, perhaps torture. It was only a matter of time for near-destruction to hit rocky hard and save the life within me.

How curious though, for exactly when doubt invades my mind and soul as I write these lines, an enormous sunray illuminates the living room. It has stopped raining now, and the cloudy skies are still hesitating whether to keep moving with hints of anthracite gray or rather turn into a sweeter and more comforting heaven white with traits of orange-red sunlight in the background. Is this some trick of fate to tell me not to give up? At least, not yet?

I do feel blessed, for it was only yesterday when I heard on the evening news bulletin that my father was watching that the first two weeks of January had been very dark – weather wise – with only two hours and 17 minutes of sunlight. Although I am very well-aware that Belgium is no sun-friendly champion host, I cannot help but feel grateful for the little exception made today, perhaps even on purpose to boost the morale of the still unwilling-to-give-up troops that are fighting for my freedom in the hope life will return. Am I too desperate to see a sign there? Am I *that* freakish to believe I have been chosen to be the worthy (and needed) recipient of a sun's caress? Oh wait, here, it hits the window pane again! Double strike, I should say. I am blessed, am I not? Welcome back; please, do shine bright. Am I too pushy to ask the sun to guide me too? Any chance I *am* the chosen warrior?

Hear my prayers, Sun, show me the way to blossoming. I still wish to be the lotus-flower self I dreamed about back in…April, was it? Guide me to break free. I still aspire to flourish and encounter inner peace, for the latter will prove key to open the door to harmony of the body and soul. Give me strength to dare and let go. Somewhere I know I must endeavor and embrace the change. I still hope I will one day find the courage to ask my body, myself, my heart, and my soul for forgiveness and treat them all with benevolence and good care. However, am I to stay here in the bubble I have created, or shall I burst it and travel to a path yet unknown?

Before embarking on a different and utmost challenging journey, I first need to come at peace. After years of abandonment, mistreatment, and oblivion, I need to apologize to my body and ask for forgiveness to my soul, for not only have I opened the door to let it wander on its own, unprotected and too easy a prey, but I have also pushed it further out of my body and left it forgotten about in the dark, up on its own, desolate and wrecked.

Truth be told, I still need to take my first steps into the healing process. When hitting the ground as hard as I possibly could and reaching similar malevolence toward my being, both the material envelope and the inner living spirit, I realize that I will need more than a good night's rest to wake up, one day, scarred but not too badly fixed.

Well…well, are signs flying in today as joyous chipping robins? You know what I am talking about, the little birds on the first days of spring when it is still too fresh and humid early in the morning to put on your peep-toe flats you have been wanting for so long to take out of the closet, yet getting sunny and warm as the day goes by and regretting you are wearing the extra layer and carrying your trench coat on one arm, leaving room in your empty hand for the needed umbrella, at least when wandering around and about in the Belgian clement weather zone. Ahem. Bless you. And the signs.

The weather being poor or mild, the fact is that on this somewhat blue Monday, I have been offered a surprise appearance of the warmth and light of the sun, peeping unannounced yet more than welcome into our living room. I was, thus, not expecting any other present on this day, and still, as I heard my phone beeping twice around 2 p.m., I knew it was too late for the *Le Monde* newsletter and too early for the *Cucina italiana* and *Figaro Madame* recipes of the day. The only explanation I could think of was that I had received an email, a real one, not the spam or newsletters that inundate your mailbox yet that you are too lazy or too tired to erase and sweep into the dustbin. An actual email. To me.

I had, indeed, received an email, and so intrigued was I that I almost deleted it when sweeping my finger on the screen. Reading the first lines, I discovered I was the winner of a two-person Japanese cooking class; the contest of which I had even forgotten I had participated in. I only need to send a reply back, and I am free to attend the Brussels-held event, learning how to make sushi, yakitori, and miso soup. But here's the thing: I have never eaten Japanese food, and even though I am a fish kind of person, I am not a *raw fish* eater. Even so, I just feel girlish happy, for I have won something, and I wish I could have enough strength, physically speaking, to attend the evening session, but I will not claim victory just yet, for I know I cannot possibly stay up until 10:30 p.m., adding an extra hour to drive back home and feel completely void and floppy.

Tomorrow, after breakfast, I will reply to this email, and I will try to give away this unique and fun experience to my sister who, by the way, is no queen of cooks. She will be a master in the art of bringing chaos into the kitchen area, but she will pass the exam with honors, of that, I am sure. And, bonus: she will be allowed to bring a friend to share the laughter with, because, quite honestly, there will not be much of learning involved; it is more like cooking with kids, keep their hands busy but away from the flour, for no cake will get baked, only the floor will be covered a beautiful snow white. My time will come, of that I am sure. By then, I will have bought a worthy apron.

Tuesday, Still January

Although I must admit that for the great majority of passing days I feel like I am a complete misfit, on this chill January Tuesday morning, the remnants of a tranquil red sunrise are slowly fading into a bright yet partially cloudy blue sky, similar to the tracks left by planes flying by left and right, but all following a straight journey line.

I could not have picked any better day to be the one-time-happening 'happy' outcast of society, however inadequate and ironic the adjective might be, considering the other 364 days left of this year. Happiness might, indeed, not be a fitting account of my emotional-state description after only a double espresso. I might need something stronger, but, then again, I do not drink nor do I smoke, so what left is there for me save…let's say, irony? All rum or brandy little pick-me-ups aside, I will not shout out loud that I woke up all gleeful and ecstatic after the three wakeups and a too-early 4 a.m. inner clock preventing nightmares for one thing, but inhibiting back-to-sleep rest for another. So no, I do not feel particularly 'happy' about my recovery process; however, I do feel reassured, comforted even in the temporary and 24-hour-lasting definition of a misfit.

On this day indeed, January 15th, as I had only just opened my mailbox and social-account newsfeed for the latest recipes of the morning check, I found out, to my great surprise – and subsequent disappointment – that U.S. President Mr. Donald Trump had not found any better idea to tackle the government shutdown than buying all-American and only American fast-food for the National Championship-winning Clemson Tigers during their White House visit. There is not a single thing to boast about, dear Mr. Trump, but I will hail your efforts for not letting hunger strike the members of the football team when they are invited into the people's home – not your showoff and 'mocked by you as the *grand* person' cartoon mansion – and since your house-personnel workers could not prepare a feast worthy of winners lest a solution be found to the shutdown, you felt the urge to insist that you had paid from your own pocket money to order some of America's finest: McDonald's, Wendy's, and Burger King. How thoughtful of you to fatten the sportsmen and ruin their probably strict diets to the chagrin of their well-rewarded nutritionists. I cannot think of any more preposterous solution than sending your puppets to fetch drive-thru and present the cold menus on silver plates. The only question that pops into my mind is whether the president will punish the civil servants for locking the country down and incidentally putting him in a difficult situation when having guests over, by forcing them to do the washing up. Free of charge, obviously.

This is the time I am happy about being a misfit. I do not belong to a society in which one of the world's leading countries is ruled by a cartoon character who gets politics and reality television mixed up. I am still trying to come to my senses after hearing a Second World War anecdote from my beloved grandmother (mother's side), and I cannot understand how the people of the world can seem to forget so easily the pains suffered and the rights besmirched during the previous century, remembered in the collective memory for its deadly conflicts and dark times, and choose from amongst a panoply of talented and capable candidates (with their own backgrounds whether dark or bright) the least-fitted occupant for the White House. Such incomprehension and disorientation qualifies me as a social misfit. At least in this kind of society. And cheers to me for welcoming this definition for myself.

The society I wish to remember and which I would like to fight for and be part of is one made up of genuine people like my grandmother on the day she told me about that Second World War anecdote… Please be seated and listen up (or read).

Last Saturday was market day in Hal, and after collecting our fresh produce, fish fillets, and chicken breasts (for my parents, they like the eggplant *parmigiana* version I make for them), my mother and I stopped at my grandmother's apartment in the city center for the weekly cup of coffee, a lump of sugar for her, and *een wolkje melk*, a 'cloud of milk' as they literally say in Dutch.

As I was peeping into the books she had just received for the New Year, I could not help but notice the one I had on my own wish list by Heather Morris, *The Tattooist of Auschwitz*. I told my *omaatje* I meant to buy it in English soon, for the copy on her coffee table was, obviously, in Dutch. She had read it, she said, between two deep breaths, revealing just how poignant a page-turner it is. Being myself a passionate reader of war testimonies and especially fond of Sebastian Faulks's research and masterpieces, I suddenly realized that I had never asked my own *oma* about her and her family's wartime experience.

Late that morning, I saw a sparkle in her gray-blue eyes and a willingness to wander down memory lane. It started with discussing the weekly price tag of our one kilogram worth of potatoes that we had just bought an hour earlier and me commenting on the fact that back in 1942, when Paris was occupied by the Nazis, women from all social classes gathered food coupons, sometimes trying their luck at the black market in order to feed the hungry mouths of children or the elderly they were taking care of. With one coupon, they could buy only one kilo of potatoes, one kilo. How on earth were they supposed to last a week if these *carbs* were not tidily divided into bits and pieces? Back then, people did not have the choice to avoid carbs on their own accord like the Dukan diet gurus and so many others.

My grandmother remembers the rationing in Belgium too, in her childhood home of Ruisbroek, on the outskirts of Brussels. Born in 1933, little Jeanne was only ten at the height of war when Nazi Germany was still confident and strong. She grew up the youngest in a family of four, her parents providing for the very basic needs even though they were poor, financially speaking. Her mother collected the ration cards and saved them up by keeping them in a black leather purse that she would always bring with her in the bedroom upstairs, for the *coupons* were the golden treasure during the war. In the yard, the father arranged for a little potato field in which neighbors could also plant their own vegetables, for there was enough room for the salad and green beans to grow along with the potatoes and peas. Coupons were often traded for flour, the diamond dust that would feed their whole family and neighborhood during wartime. Omaatje's family was amongst the lucky ones, for they had an oven in their kitchen indeed. The ten or more kilo sack of flour was to be handled with great caution, and the children were better not caught spilling the precious dust on the ground when adding a spoonful to the blender bowl. In addition, my great-grandparents were careful not to turn the oven on too often, for the smell of homemade bread loaves would soon reach patrolling officers who shamelessly stole their intake if so inclined that day.

Belgian families did not suffer famine during wartime, but somewhere in between the occupation, my *oma*'s parents, Maria and Felix Ocula, were to face a difficult and brave decision when they could no longer, she told me, feed their children's hungry mouths. They were four of them; my granny having three elder brothers already in their teens. Back then, online shopping and discounts could not save their however humble way of living. How then to cut back on your spending when you already possess so little? It did not take long for the parents to decide to sell their house for a negotiated price of 7,000 Belgian Francs. Only seven-thousand francs. Next to nothing, but still a small amount. One would need to check the purchasing power at the time and real-estate prices in order to know the equivalent sum in euros or dollars these days, because it does seem quite out of context to believe they would sell their home for the bargain price of 173.53 Euro. *Du pain bénit*, as they conveniently say in French. It's a godsend. Still, as small an amount it was, the money would buy them freedom. For the next days or weeks at least.

Packed and ready to move out, the Ocula family traveled the five kilometers on foot with wheelbarrows and carts to carry varied household goods to a little farm in Sint-Pieters-Leeuw. The only rule prevailing being that when under attack or when hearing gunshots, one must seek shelter, lay down, and cover one's head until silence can only be broken by the whispering damp treading the ground.

In times of war, fighting troops and commanding officers have little if any consideration for architecture and do not hesitate over the destruction by bombers of ways of access between towns and cities or any other important monument standing in their way. Ruisbroek had already lost a bridge, preventing the people to cross the canal until the end of the war, but as my grandmother recalled, the town could have lost far worse: its mill. There were plans to blow it up, but it was without banking on the courage and determination of one female villager, a cunning one if I may add. The night before the blow, she headed straight to the mill with a wicker basket containing glasses and a little pick-me-up for the soldiers who were to carry out the order. She knew how to best accentuate her assets and ended up inviting herself over for the *aperitif* she had slyly prepared. There was a serious amount of alcohol involved, mixed with laughter and pleasure to ease the tension, so much so that the men were too ashamed of their behavior and ran away before dawn. In times of war, the failed destruction of the mill was not a top-list priority and would soon be forgotten about by the military and the town council.

These were only two anecdotes told one Saturday by my *oma* and, to be honest, I wish there were more to follow. Nevertheless, I am already grateful to her for sharing with me such moving memories, for I can imagine how hard this must be on her. And, therefore, *lieve oma, dank je.*

Barriers so High Yet Must Be Overcome

Something is falling into place. Three candle lights are spreading warmth and light and make for a bittersweet contrast with the heavy winds smashing against the higher plants in the backyard. I have come to admire the outdoor landscape of still life. Rough winter months welcome more rain into our already-so-fortunate and privileged country, weather wise. Belgians even have their own word for this weather: *il drache encore*! *Dracher*, French impersonal verb, apparently comes from the German transitive, *dreschen*, or to thresh with the flail, to hammer out, which the educated (polite) French turned into *une pluie battante* whereas the English prefer the 'cats and dogs' to be involved. But amongst all normal populace, *il drache* is on everyone's lips when opening an umbrella (when in luck of carrying one). All this to say that tears are falling down from heaven, and I am a silent spectator, my eyes frozen into oblivion.

The grasses in the backyard have become messy after the passage of winds; some straws lay abandoned hither and thither on the almost-frozen and definitely too-humid soil. I wonder whether I might just have found the perfect way to disappear from my worries: one foot in the drenched lawn and I might be swallowed down into the very heart of the earth. Could it be that simple?

Still considering this escape route sometimes, I am, however, constantly amazed by the beauty of nature and how it reminds us that there is hope even in the deepest, most silent cry of our heart. As I am looking through the sliding glass door, a timid sunray illuminates the apple tree, stripped of its fruit and foliage, as if it were standing in the spotlight, right in the middle of the stage. Light has appeared for the first time today as the clock strikes midday. After any winter break comes the sun, and I am starting to believe there is nonpareil experience to cherish what we are: an ever-going, still-evolving, and inner-growing form of life. But as in the cyclic turn of seasons for nature, time will slow down and eventually freeze before steadying itself back on track and moving forward. Take the time to heal, nature says, for against all odds, (weather-wise) the bare tree will recover its foliage and eventually allow the apples to be plucked when beautifully red and ripe. Compotes are back in season.

As the weather is clearing out and the hours are passing by, I cannot help but think of me as a bare tree. Only, mind you, it was not nature that had stripped me off of my foliage, but rather a despotic, self-destructive mind and lifestyle. Little left of me was there, bar a not-yet-frozen lifeblood running through my veins. My soul heard the echo of my inner voice crying out for help while my mind had already given up taking care of the body. I, on the other hand, had already gotten used to the inner suffering which, unfortunately, was also increasingly showing on the outside as if thrilled to frighten away caring and preoccupied people. I did not need any scarecrow; my mind did the work by controlling my every move and thinking. For too long a *winter*time, my body, my mind, and my soul have been accustomed to this ugly truth, still walking although struggling most of the months and incapable to stand on her own. Light had gradually shifted from that center-stage apple tree, but before it got time to rot, light was saved from switching off and the fruit from a terrible compote fate. The bare tree was given another chance, but this time – being the last straw it could manage – it would be a long way for its lifeblood to fuel up and blossom out.

Winter has been lasting for over a year now, but I have heard the first crackling sounds of ice that would, day after day, let the life that had been kept prison-frozen break free. I would climb over the steep slope and culminate at last, planting the white flag. Even though winter is far from over, I am already yearning for spring. The time has come for me to make peace with myself and ask my body for forgiveness. It has suffered enough. On the verge of being erased completely, I ought now to acknowledge the inner crying. Only then will I be ready to welcome spring. Only then will I truly embark on the journey of recovery until, finally, light will appear and summer will announce my comeback to living a full life. Changed, yes. Spoilt, no.

Burned

Can you forgive me, please? I will try my best and walk away from the shadow that has been gnawing me on the inside. I will try, indeed, I will; and from the ashes, I will rise. Hope. Do not leave my side.

It took me years of involuntary, self-imposed slavery to light the fuse, but once the fire had broken out, the subsequent blast was bound to happen. It was only a matter of time. I lasted one more year; the last 12 months of which I spent behind an office desk in an only a-couple-of-square-meter, dark attic room on the fourth second-to-last floor of an old yet prestigious townhouse, the private property of the embassy where I was employed.

After two months into my first job, my hard work had paid off, and I felt honored when one of the diplomats told me (in the elevator) that I was to move to the second and most important floor, though feared by many, the office and salon of His Excellency, the ambassador. I had come to admire him and would not let him down. Anything he asked, I checked and double checked. I was a rookie, but a fast learner and, most importantly, a resourceful one. I ended up doing much more secretarial work than I had first imagined. On the day of the interview, I had thought I would be hired essentially for translating and interpretational tasks, or so I made myself believe. From the very first day, I was shown to my office but had no training, no explanation as to what exactly I had to do to fill my day of work. I could not learn from a same-position yet older colleague, so I took on most of the managerial tasks and caused quite a wave of change in the blurry seas of insurance and accounting. I was horrified at the lack of care with which my predecessors had managed the contracts and the day-to-day missions. I had quickly made up my mind. I enjoyed the challenges and would put my heart and soul into everything I undertook in order to facilitate work for everyone involved. I felt extremely happy and complete, for I had gained their trust, and never was I going to disappoint them in any way. Or so I thought. Until December 14, 2017, I guess. I failed them. By my leave of absence. The worst part being that I did not know how long my body would need to heal itself, nor did I know if time would really bring me back to a more-balanced and healthier lifestyle.

The email was sent on December 26th, 2017. The news must have sent shockwaves through the work house. For some reason, I do not remember what I had written, nor if I had myself sent my sick leave's notice or if my father did. Truth be told, I had put on a mask for most of that year because I had seen the signs; I knew my body was letting me down more and more, struggling to hold on during the ten-minute walk to the subway, the 20-minute ride, the crossing of the always-so-chilly and long tunnel connecting the subway station and the main hallway of the train station, waiting for the too-often delayed train to take me home, resulting in 30 minutes more spent reading if my mind was not too exhausted, and, eventually, the driving home in my car, being careful not to miss the reverse gear otherwise the white Fiat Punto's engine would let out a bizarre noise for finding itself in fourth gear. Every single day, in every single thing I did or not, I was reminded of how frail I had become. Save face, I told myself. Stay strong.

I spent three hours daily (at least, not counting the delays) commuting from home to work and back. I woke up at 5:30 (5:20 if morning routine included washing my waist-long hair), prepared breakfast and ate it fully at home (I needed this me-time, fueling up), and gone was I at 7:15 to catch the 7:49 train to Brussels, platform one, in order to arrive before nine in the morning at work. By then, I was almost emptied out, rotten, but I kept it together, drank my coffee (brought from home), and would accomplish the great variety of daily tasks until late afternoon without much of a break. Not that I was not allowed one, I simply felt guilty about *taking* a break from work.

I tried to fuel up with omega three and six rich fatty fish, whole-wheat bread, nuts, or blueberries (only if need be), anything that would give a little extra energy to last longer, work harder…but my efforts had proven useless. No matter how much and how protein-rich my diet, I felt the void growing inside me. What I did not know at the time was that my body had long ago gone into shutdown. It had frozen from the inside to preserve whatever left there was, for frost is the best guardian of life. It sort of knew that it would take long to hear the first crackling that would break the ice and encourage the first signs of recovering *some* life; but wary and alert the body was, to make sure the mind would not outmaneuver the back-to-health construction plans and blow out the light as soon as it peeped out.

Nevertheless, the daily commute and the pressure I would put on my body and self in order to outperform my unconfident, unsatisfied, perfectionist, control-freak, and too-strict, too-severe shadow was not the triggering factor associated with the burnout. As I have mentioned earlier, it takes years for the fire to destroy one's secret garden; and years it takes too for the damage to be repaired and the scars to be healed, although never will they completely disappear. I shall have to live with them, bear them…proudly, eventually.

So, please, meet me: a girl who slowly faded away behind the idea of perfection, guilt, outperformance, distrust, and selflessness, until her own personality and character were frozen and inaccessible to her soul. She had forgotten whom she was, what she liked or disliked, and the more she realized that she was disappearing for real, the more she would find an escape in work. First when at school, at university, at work, yet also…at home.

Hello you, my name is Alessandra, but please, call me Alice. I was burnt inside and out, until the outer walls were *presque* tumbling down after a major fire broke out, which swept through the inner corridors, only to leave behind proof of the wreckage and disbelief of the soul. The heart had been crying for years, but the mind would not hear any of it: 'Hear-asable,' that is who she was when she stopped listening to her inner voice. It feels like being erased from what seems to be a normal way of life; yet, it takes courage and time to acknowledge your voice.

Scared to Remember December 14th, 2017

It has been a little over a year since that fateful December Thursday when I left work somewhere early in the evening after a hectic nine hours of secretarial tasks mixed with ennui and peaks of stress. The last one being about the stamping of an envelope which was to be posted the very next day. Since offices were closed at this hour in the evening, I did not see the point in putting the letter into the envelope and sealing it before the next morning. But if your boss tells you to seal the envelope, you hush and oblige.

The weather outside was in accord with my inner despair: damply cold and bitter; one could almost hear one's teeth gnashing, so much so that even breathing, as I ventured outside to catch a subway and train back home, was a burdensome and self-evaluating task. The moist of my breathlessness would soon be captured into the questionable, *real*, woolen scarf. The static electricity hitting my neck now and then made me believe the fiber used was not so much real lamb or alpaca wool as indicated on the label, but rather real sweaty acrylic and stretchy iron-free elastane. The snapping cold would tickle your *presque* runny nose after which you would be forced to take off your – again – not-so-woolen glove and feel how the icy wind would lash your already-cracked hands in your courageous attempt to take out a tissue paper used earlier that day on the subway ride. At least I had a tissue left in the pocket of my coat to save face, hence limiting the damage of being less-presentable because of the testy weather. Entrance of the *metro* and more ice, this time on the descending stairs (mind the slippery ones!). And then a smokehouse, so hot it is in the depths of the Earth as if all people were gathered in a sauna homeward.

Next thing I remember is seeing you, Mou, platform six in Central Station, meeting for our tearful commute back home. We both knew the night was young and unclear. As soon as we got home, I would indeed have to swallow up a microwaved leftover of overcooked white fish and broccoli (no potatoes; there were none, nor was there time left to steam some) before heading out to my first encounter with the therapist. An unknown somebody who looked more like a recent graduate than an accredited and experienced psychologist. How much older is he anyways? Silence between us, Mou. Not a word after the meeting. Only tears and disbelief. Finally, at 10:30 p.m., I dragged my feet straight to my room, not minding washing off the *biscuit* concealer I had applied earlier in the morning.

Neither my mother nor I had slept much that night, but however haggard we looked on the outside and distressed or shaken we were on the inside, we both still woke up at dawn and headed to work the next day without speaking a word to each other. It was Friday and clearly not a *fun* day to look forward to. We did not know how we would keep it together, yet we were very well-aware that the wound had been opened, and it was I that was bleeding out of life.

With hindsight, those are amongst the most dreadful 48 hours I have ever experienced, for no such pain and incomprehension, no such powerless and hopelessness have ever tortured me to such an extent than the mute morning commute to work. My inner light had been blown out. Of that, I was certain.

I still cannot fathom how I managed to uphold my trembling body that Friday, the day *after*. My swollen eyes reminded me of how desperate I had been for the last couple of years; preferring to ignore the telltale signs of deterioration and extreme damage in order to maintain at all costs what seemed to me as a manageable life without too much of self-care involved. There simply was no energy nor time for that. I paid the full price; at my own health's cost, at my own self's existence. I had lost the right to feel, the right to be.

The next hours and days were cadenced by blurriness, incredulity, shock, helplessness, and guilt. So much guilt. How could I have gotten great honors at university and have failed to such a shameful extent at my own growing? The following 'house arrest' ordered by the family doctor whom we visited first thing on Monday would give me a series of panic attacks and sloppy emotional meltdowns. The sentence would later be reinforced by reports of one psychiatrist, one therapist, and one massage therapist, all of whom making an unparalleled leading medical team to whom I owe my being kept alive so far with no need of hospitalization. They would continue to follow me twice a week (thank you, Mou, for driving most of the times with me), and in exchange for home treatment, I had to promise to do as they told. At least until I had found a way to truly and genuinely take care of my body and soul; to listen closely to the hopes and needs of my body.

Well, the rest of it was quick. The first month of sick leave would lead to another panic attack, more tears. Other sick certificates to be sent over the months, and the same hollowness torturing me and controlling my every move. Today is January 19th, 2018, and the roofs of the houses in our *cul-de-sac* still look half-melted and frosty white. It has been over a year since my burning out.

As from now, as part of my New Year wish, I endeavor nonetheless to better recognize the blatant signs of weakness, frailty, and suffering, although it will prove an arduous and challenging task for the otherwise so-accustomed and thoroughly selfless me. I took (and always do take) at heart the caring and comforting of others; in the hope of alleviating much of the workload of others, yet having failed to realize such behavior and thinking – however noble or brave – had slowly killed me from any humanity and good-heartedness toward…myself. I was soon to lose the remnants of self-care, and, instead, I struggled only to survive, frightened to disappear into oblivion.

Remembering the First Months: Despair?

Well into the first weeks after the storm, my body dropped the anchor in the middle of these turbulent waters, and I had lost what little control I once had over the rudder. Although the waking ups in the morning were no longer timetabled to the nearest minute, I still arranged my day over a detailed and to-the-clock schedule. I guess I did so in order to prevent my mind from getting into deeper and darker waters of thoughts, out of which it is much more arduous to swim back to a healthy shore. I needed to keep busy in order not to think about my pain and guilt. Over the first weeks and months (sometimes even until now), I have fought hard to make people around me aware of the difference between a *burnout* and a *depression*, the latter being a 'persistent feeling of sadness and loss of interest,' as explained on the Mayo Clinic website. Quite the opposite actually, at least in my case, since I was mentally too strong-willed, mulish even, and perhaps too proud of my ambition and my forever-strong desire to help others out. I have always scheduled my day around people's needs. I have always pressured my body to go too far beyond its own limitations, hence the ignoring of the alarm bells once I had gone too deep into trouble to sort things out on my own. I got scared because I did not see any issue. Why would I stop if the daily tasks I managed to fulfill were righteous, self-sacrificing, and honest? The more fear took a leading role in my life and being, the more I burdened myself with my constant need to make things easier *to others*. Long story short, the more I got scared from my body's going down, the more I did for others, only to make sure I erased myself from my mind's preoccupations. I knew I was not 'doing fine'; but at the time, I was not ready to admit that.

Truth be told, when one has reached such low levels of self-esteem, lack of confidence, body insecurity, and self-loss, one feels warmed up by an inexplicable, almost-puzzling feeling of comfort and satisfaction when one is able to act as a good-doer, a good Samaritan. Nevertheless, as from the moment I felt so encouraged by my 'heroism' in focusing whatever meagre strength I knew I had left into the coloring of a brighter life for everyone around me, save me (obvious by now), the burgeoning integrity and selflessness quickly provided me with a good and human argument to give up on my body and stop taking care of my soul. So stubborn was I to believe I could live a more-manageable life if I forgot all about myself and, instead, took charge of anything. I could render *la vita bella* for every character crossing my journey, except for me. I had all forgotten about my life.

Unfortunately, the sailor will have great difficulty in getting the curious tourists aboard if the ship itself resembles more of an unstable, vacillating, and neglected dugout canoe, rather than a full-star yacht sailing on turquoise waters. This forced body shutdown has helped me realize the importance of both the soundness and resilience of the hull in order to welcome people on its deck and promise them a lifetime experience resulting from my personal commitment to them: friendship, benevolence, and a caring heart. On my next travels, I sincerely hope I will have found a healthy equilibrium and more self-care – perhaps a bit of self-indulgence could not hurt either – or just a kinder heart toward both my body and myself. The healing process will end when I have learned to hit the brakes, and, from then on, I will start the journey to recovery; but until then, I need to listen closely to what my inner voice has been whispering for too long, something that I have deliberately ignored and buried deep.

As a result of the ill-equipped, shaky, and bandy-legged raft serving me as body, a compulsory stop was necessary and inevitable; if not, it, *i.e.* the body, would have sunk with no guarantee of lifejacket being thrown out there in the open sea. I would have been a DiCaprio on the night of the Titanic tragedy.

I would lie if I told you I was not scared. My soul was consumed by frightening thoughts, undeciphered mysteries, and deep puzzlement. No one in the surrounding waters would properly understand what difficult challenges were weighing upon my body, nor would they believe the poor descriptions I would narrate of my state of being and thinking. The danger, however, is lurking everywhere: this precise feeling of being socially excluded is always waiting for you as a cat would be for its prey. It is only a matter of timing for desolation and loneliness to push you further down into a downward spiral. The role of parents and close relatives is, therefore, paramount in order for all the struggling-to-survive sailors out there to feel supported and loved, only just enough to keep them on deck, untie the ropes, preparing to make sail until they are ready to cast off whenever the appropriate time has come to pursue their journey.

Twelve

For the past 12 months, I have been on this deck, in an ocean which waves were cadenced sometimes by existential questions and windy storms, debilitated by crocodile tears and confusion. I was, thus, to surf different waves and make sure I would not capsize and drown, although my every efforts were bound to result in the further emptying of my strength and willpower. I have learned since the meaning of the old saying, 'one step forward, two steps back.' Sometimes, one must simply accept to retrace his or her steps, for they were only just misleading him/her from the true journey he or she would embark on, the experience of a lifetime, the sole path worthy of his/her endeavor, struggle even. 'Fall down seven times, stand up eight,' or so goes the Japanese proverb. I would like to hold onto this saying.

I have no intention of recollecting all that has happened between Christmas 2017 and this year's, at least not just now. I am too much in awe of the darkening and nighty landscape that is unfolding before my eyes as I am writing these lines. There is a snowy background of winter wonderland, just enough to cover the tracks of a daredevilry explorer in the backyard, slowly disappearing under layers of wool and knits. But, then, perhaps not. You caught me; it was the neighbor's fat and lazy cat, answering to 'Leo,' busier than ever with its evening *toilette*. I see him walking off toward his home. I'm guessing bedtime is near for him, and so it is for me.

Next morning, no Leo, king of the jungle, hopping up and down behind the grasses on the horizon. Only a tranquil and empty backyard, save for a leaf or two. The tree helps me remember that nature too has its pause, rewind, and play buttons. So does my body. I paused or have been forced to. Yet, now, I feel like I am ready to rewind and tell.

I thus wish to start writing about the *now experience* which is the result of months of battles fought against all kinds of winds, all unfavorable to raising the sails back again and press 'play.' As I am standing alone on the flagging deck, too often confronted with the bitter truth of my possible faltering or tumbling down, I have come to realize that fear has also partnered with my shadow enemy. Although, on the one hand, there is a voice inside my head telling me that I cannot and ought not go back to my first job, on the other hand, that same voice has come to intimidate me, daunting me with a horrible feeling of an even lower self-esteem than ever before. I am, sadly, starting to consider myself unfit for normality. How does one lead one's life? How does a 'typical' day look like?

Still, what falls under 'the norm,' *really*? Incidentally, is it not society that is encouraging a game of hide and seek with and between its actors? They who contribute to its *grandeur* seem to be trapped. Society 'hides' those amongst its subjects, those who do not fit into the prevailing molds; it 'seeks' only the sheep that are most likely to blend in without ever questioning their being manipulated as puppets. Nowadays, it seems like the people that are pulling the strings are also masters in the art of make-believe: they – or most of them – promote their own interests trying hard to fake-echo the answers sought by the great majority of the populace while, in fact, securing their government seats and prioritizing their golden tickets to ever greater *hauteur*. Society is, therefore, anonymizing a still-greater proportion of its sheep; the black ones amongst them being further isolated and monitored closely. All the while making sure that they are the ones who feel as uncomfortable and lost as possible; that they somehow are…wrong, missing the point.

These informal yet widespread social understandings between a community of people living in a certain environment govern most of the actions, habits, and thoughts of these people as a whole. Norms, or so they are called. Yet, what happens to those who, like me, feel as if they are unfit to stick to an almost-unchangeable daily routine, this sheep-esque attitude?

Growing up, I would always picture myself as a young woman who would get up early in the morning, take a short but warm and decent shower, and, while finishing my morning toilette, think about the knit or sweater combination, a mini or a pencil skirt, perhaps a dress, the high boots or moccasins, or would I dare to wear stilettos that day? It all depends whether the pavement is not too slippery during the winter months and, of course, if the walking time is not too long before I reach the office or whatever destination I choose. Breakfast, I imagined, would be taken at home, but where was this 'home' supposed to be? I cannot remember.

Even as a child, I already knew I would not be the kind of person who would be satisfied with a coffee and pastry to go, the kind of breakfast that Italians would order before getting into the overcrowded subway line in Rome. *Un ristretto e presto!* Well, talking about a quick-and-go sort of breakfast, I do not believe that this would be praised by health gurus and nutritionists.

Later, back at university and the first three years of my bachelor's degree, I did not mind much what I would eat in the morning. Nor would I overthink my eating habits back then, although I already hated feeling bloated quite often, to my surprise. I did not read about nutrition or healthy meals, since I had never really been surrounded by fast food or garbage takeaway. My mother did her best to cook Italian pasta *con gli ingredienti giusti e sani* or bring fresh vegetables along with quality poultry, meats, and fish, seven days a week. If she was not behind the stove, then my grandmother would be, as she used to come every Wednesday (it was my mother's day off work and our only half a day at school). My grandmother would thus meal prep for one or two nights, and on Fridays or Saturdays (depending on the quantity of meal-prep leftovers), we would order *real* pizza, pasta, or a *scaloppina* for my sister from the Italian restaurant just around the corner, Arcadia. Mind you, by 'real pizza,' I mean freshly homemade dough, quality ingredients, fresh tomato-oregano sauce, and mozzarella directly imported from Italy's finest milk farms, not the industrial greasy and fat mozzarella sticks or shreds one can find at the discount store. The latter is not cheese, rather a bad-cholesterol substitute. All this to say that I was brought up with good-quality foods and drinks while enjoying the occasional Sunday breakfast with a chocolate-pastry indulgence, the *couque au chocolat* (what the French call *chocolatine*) or a *boule de Berlin* (to be honest, I was only interested in the rich vanilla-pastry cream and powdered sugar on top of this European fried doughnut, only missing the central hole for it to be American). The four of us would toast over a glass of freshly squeezed orange juice, mixed with a drop of lemon or two just to get that pleasant bitter-and-sharp aftertaste so as not to render the drink too orange-y sweet. *Tchin-tchin*, as we say.

If the orange crop had no effect in the awakening of our taste buds, my sister and I would wait (a huge grin on our angel faces) for our mother to suggest a little yet very luxurious treat, highly appreciated when in the cold December month. Mommy behind the stove again, this time for some *real* hot chocolate milk, with Belgian chocolate, extra dark or *noir de noir*. We had a preference for Côte d'Or over Jacques, but any quality chocolate would do actually. A teaspoon of vanilla sugar and our eyes would sparkle while our mouths were watering. Then came the dipping of our cut-in-four slices of bread with *speculoos* or chocolate sprinkles. Sometimes, we were even too lazy or hasty to even prepare any topping for our sandwiches, so we would end up with a loaf of plain white *pain de campagne*, plunging crust first into the chocolaty mug. Now you must admit that nothing compares to fresh-from-the-oven and *cuit sur pierre* traditional bread from the local bakery. The true worth of this *savoir-faire* can only be best appreciated by time and a full-house happy family breakfast.

I was not a picky eater back in my childhood days, nor was I in my teens. However, I quickly came to feel the pressure from 'the girl's squad' during my high-school years. I would not really mind swallowing the sandwich I had for lunch while hiding in the toilets, just to make sure I fed my stomach – gave it a little something before anyone could notice – and could, thus, stay focused for the entire afternoon classes. I only had to make sure that 'the girls' did not catch me. It was considered cheating on their so-called daily requirements. Two girls from my group of friends were always on some sort of diet, so if they could not eat, then nobody was allowed to. Ridiculous, I know, especially when considering that your body is undergoing some radical changes and battling against hormones and all sorts of emotions. Moreover, the five-day-a-week classes and homework, the frequent testing times and final examinations were also very consuming activities. Hence the necessity for nutrients, for food. Last but not least, how was I to survive the overcrowded and damp bus ride home if on an empty stomach? I could not fathom fainting before a crowd of mocking children and popular students (that we, in French, would surname *les people*, how convenient). No, I would not skip a meal, not any kind. That is how I ended up swallowing my lunch while taking a break from the girls' silly talk in our high-school restroom. My eating habits have, thus, too often been the result of overthinking. It must come to an end. It just must. Period.

Away on February 6th, 2019

Azzurro is the color of the light blue Dolce-and-Gabbana-esque sky presenting itself in front of my sliding window. It is late morning, and for the first time in ten days, I find myself sitting quite uncomfortably at the round-shaped breakfast table. Alone. Free of any sound bar the occasional humming of the refrigerator. I cannot help but notice that several crumbs have resisted the too-rapid and hasty movements coming with the cleaning of our plates, some of them still a bit sticky when I try to collect them. I pause and determine the need to further clean the table, for I know it be invaded again by the crumb special forces when my father will put his teeth in his *baguette* for lunch, almost fearless of the crispy crust that could damage his palate and…'crumbdus ' the place all over.

It has been ten days since we have left our home in Belgium for a needed (and well-deserved) break deep into the mountains, somewhere between Grenoble and Gap in the French Alps. We are currently staying in a tiny and perhaps *risible* village known as La Joue du Loup – literally, The Cheek of the Wolf.

A thousand kilometers I am from home; a thousand signs that are yet to be discovered, only to be multiplied by an infinite number of reasons to welcome and embrace change. At last. It is a two-week escape in one of the most sunniest ski valleys in the Provence-Alpes-Côte d'Azur French region, a little village not too well-known from the outside, although overcrowded buses with Dutch, German, and English tourists tend to arrive frequently every Saturday morning after a (wild or sleepless) night ride; the chauffeur dropping some off while waiting for others to come onboard for the return home, engine rolling. He will be given only a short rest before hitting the sinuous roads back to wherever his passengers came from.

Sitting at our table, I admire the *azzurro* landscape that is on display. To my left, if it were not for the humming and buzzing of the refrigerator, I can hear the snow melting from the *chalets'* roofs, unfrozen water dripping before touching the still-icy and skiddy soil. The view to my right is less enchanting; I spot a lonely, messy, wooden *armoire* with hearts carved into its little doors which, when opened, only reveal more hearts; these painted onto the bowls and plates. As for the mugs, they are free of any design – good heavens! – and make for the fair description of the French *jatte*: white, no sparkle, no fuss. The espresso set, however, is made from ceramic, is colorful, and – who would have guessed? – heart printed. Oh boy.

Aside from the omnipresence of hearts on the red tableware, there are a series of eating incongruities. One can indeed rent the most luxurious apartment or stay in the best possible hotel, there will always be a piece of furniture or a closet destined to be messy and in which one would hide the half-opened/half-empty bags of chips (*grissini* in our case, French-bought, although Italian-made, the real *torinesi* ones, but who cares), Mentos candies (the mint-flavored ones) only bought for the car trip, never opened save for one during the trip back home, the rest stored in the cellar until next year when, in the spring, we will be reminded of their stealing too much space amongst the cookies and candies box, inevitably leading to their throwing away in the garbage tin.

So, in the closet on my right, second plank above the cutlery drawers, lays a red tray – abundantly decorated with hearts, obviously – containing a mix of chips, salted peanuts, liquorice, and mint candies. This luxurious collection of foods do not, however, measure up to the French 'guillotine,' the official name of the salami-slicer machine. Dead serious here. But, again, who would mind if the French enjoy giving fancy names to the in-the-Alps daily, useful *accessoires de table*? May I present, the *guillotine à saucisson*, mountain (colloquial?) language for salami slicer? Fortunately, there are no hearts carved into the wooden, miniature, slicing machine this time.

Next in line in that same closet are two Opinel pocket knives; two, because one is never enough, I hear my father say, especially true if one, for instance, puts one of the knives in his backpack and, thus, saves the other for cutting a slice of Tomme de Savoie cheese for lunch. Two knives. Two. End of discussion. Nevertheless, the 'two' amount quickly mounted to three, for he bought an extra Opinel knife in the sole, local, miniature supermarket there is at the Place des Boutiques (central square), arguing they are twice cheaper than the ones you can purchase in Belgium (an assessment to which I seriously remain doubtful).

Finally, reaching the end of our closet tour, I spot two pairs of glasses, another one of unused shades, and the sporty ones that my father puts on when on adventure in the snow. They are facing the warrior of glasses named 'The Mask' that my mother wears on snowy days; a mirror ski-mask in which it is impossible to notice her eyes. The 'normal' fashion sunglasses are too far behind in the closet, ashamed of their uselessness in the mountains. They are merely and shamefully used for the car trip when the sun shines a bit too much on the road, hence rendering color-blind the appointed driver and giving way to the endless debate of who is going to hand over the unshaded glasses when entering a tunnel and back the sunglasses when exiting that couple-of-meter tunnel. A *fourre-tout*, as I like to call that kind of closet or living cabinet. Be honest, we all have one, a holdall I mean, no matter where or how far we travel to.

Left and right have, thus, nothing to boast of, but right in front of me, the view is breathtakingly beautiful. The clock almost strikes midday, and I am a front-row spectator of the *lacher-prise* and end of the tow rope of the beginners hill, known here as the *piste verte*. Early in the morning, the first sprouts, some not even four or five years old, follow like little lambs the red uniform of their ski instructor; their whole helmet and ski outerwear weighing more than the children themselves. I sometimes wonder how they manage to control their skis, let alone stay upright after being hit by the ski rope on their attempt to free themselves from the circular pancake that tows them uphill. Who would not melt before their woolen mittens swinging back and forth out of their ski jacket?

This is center stage today. I am the luckiest spectator there can be. Apart from the baby penguins learning to ski, I am also admiring both the courage and the tenacity of determined adults trying their best to find their balance on the snow; their skis still untamed and their heads red of perspiration. These are the ones who, tonight (tomorrow morning at the latest), will suffer from muscle pain and sweaty, stinky socks. We all wonder, indeed, how the instructors of the *Ecole de ski français* manage to look like models on the runway, whereas normal people look like astronauts landing on the moon when walking with their ski boots in the snow. Could it be that the people born in the French Alps or in ski resorts all over the world possess a special gene that immunize them against that sort of preposterous walking or the sweaty ski boots and the not-ever-happening runny nose symptoms? They always seem so classy and undisturbed by sudden changes in the climate outdoors, whether from the mountain-top freezing temperatures to the impossible heating and solarium conditions when the doors of the village shop open, they remain calm and, what looks like, well…photoshopped. Their hands will not get rusty, their lips will not suffer from cracks or from the occasional bleeding, their nose will not get rosy nor runny; *bref*, they are the hero mountain-men.

Mid-Winter Holiday

We had left on a Friday at the end of January, after a four-time security check of locks and keys, started on my father's initiative – unaware or unwilling to accept that he suffers from a compulsive checking disorder. He would climb the staircase up and down to make sure all the plugs are out and that the front door is under lock and key, sometimes nearly breaking the lock because of the strength with which he turns the key.

All ready and quadruple-checked, it was now 10:45 a.m. I was already feeling nauseous from the typical smell that invades the car while ready for departure and hence welcomed with relief the opening of the front doors for my parents to take their seats, Mommy behind the wheel. The fresh current of icy air felt like a caress on my cheeks. I could breathe again and was ready now to open my book and disappear into a couple of hours of quality and undisturbed reading time. Seatbelt fastened, my mother would drive the first couple of hundreds of kilometers, leaving the last quarter for my father until our arrival in Mâcon, the city of the French writer, Alphonse de Lamartine, and our *étape* for the night. The following day, we would hit the road after a rich and healthy breakfast until the Wolf destination be reached, *i.e.* La Joue du Loup. Woof!

One could wonder why such preposterous details (to some at least) bear a significant importance, if not a paramount one for me. I do not recognize myself as belonging to the category of the populace that tends to oversimplify events or people – most of the time being ignorant of the very subject or question they criticize. I, instead, belong to a group of other '*mes*' out there; the ones who struggle too; they who know and truly understand the pleasure in noticing details or in taking the time to seek out these little features, mostly because they too share a similar experience or a battle of their own. To them and to me, details are considered transcendental and ought to be duly noted, for they behold the power to soften the pressure felt in our mind. There are too many questions to be answered, to many ways to tackle a problem, and, mostly, a common sense of indecisiveness that leads to a frightful and feared anxiety based on the impossibility to choose. Details matter, period. However, there is a downside. If one may think of this balancing pros and cons as a quality (or blessing) in life, I can assure you that it can prove a burdensome personality trait at times, one that empties our bodies of the little energy we have managed (so far) to save in order to keep the most basic organs functioning. Detail can kill.

For the last ten days (our holiday stay being almost over), I have had to cope with *details*, but not in the transcendental nor in the killing way. I was, instead, forced to deal with the details brought about with *change*. Even though it might not seem as a groundbreaking advance to most 'normal people' (but again, who falls under this so-commonly referred to stereotype?), the answers I would need to find by myself during our mountain trip had been the scenario of many nightmares and sleepless nights on the days (even weeks) before our actual leaving.

With a 650-kilometer car trip that Friday until the first stop in France near Lyon, I had time to list some issues I have been struggling with: where would I find fresh fruit other than a banana or a kiwi in the little French Alps village? I obviously need to include fruit into my breakfast ritual. Moreover, will the shop tender sell any kind of exotic fruit such as grapefruit perhaps? No, probably not. Then what would I choose? What will the options be? An apple? Why, there must be apples at least. Perhaps I could chop one in bite-size pieces and mix them together with the morning porridge? Luckily, I am on the safe side, since I have packed my own oatmeal and goji berries and carob powder. I would not be *that* flexible in the morning or *that* prepared to embrace change…at least not to switch from a porridge breakfast that I actually enjoy to the French baguette with jam that I know would not satisfy nor nourish my body properly.

Next item on my list was my water intake. Truth is, we will be in France, and, conveniently enough, the water that I'm used to drink is French labeled and, bonus, a lot cheaper when purchased in France than the bottles we buy in Belgium (where there is a tax on plastic bottles that inevitably boosts the price up in our supermarkets). I will not need to worry about this, so I might as well get this quadrupled checked on my list. I will, thus, be safe with the water-supply chain during the holiday.

The central issue, however, had been daunting me for some time. What about fish, my needed protein intake? I knew beforehand that the lunch and dinner parts would be challenging for me, since I follow a (truth be told) strict high-protein/hypercaloric/high-fat diet with rye bread, a serving of greens, and fresh skin-on salmon fillet. I sometimes switch to sardines or Belgian *crevettes* if Scottish salmon is unavailable, but those are already considered a step back, for they do not nourish me enough, at least not as much as the salmon does.

The latter keeps me full and spares me of headaches attacks or sudden losses of balance in the afternoon. *Somme toute*, as they say in French, I try to eat at least three sorts of vegetables a day (broccoli being almost daily on my menu), white fish in the evening, salmon for lunch, an egg in my breakfast porridge, only to make sure that I reach high levels of protein to make up for my not-eating-any-meat diet. There is a sensible reason to this: I simply do not like the taste of meat, whether plain or processed. To make matters worse, I do not digest cheese or cow milk. I hear you, what on earth was I thinking to go and hide deep into the French Alps, the holy ground of cheese, raclette, casseroles, and first-quality meat? Well, there is always room to be surprised.

Actually, not so long ago, I would not have coped with such drastic changes; I would not have been able to address these questions, let alone experience such changes. I would have stayed in my rabbit hole where I was left undisturbed of the common twists and turns on the very track of life. However, the status quo would also have left me…unlived. I understand now that after years of self-erasing, I urgently need to learn how to live. Again, like 'normal people' do or try to. Hell to the shadow me! Get the engine rolling until we reach the Wolf and I be faced with change.

Upon our arrival that Saturday, we unloaded the car and quickly headed down into 'town' for some grocery shopping. I was happily surprised when I found frozen salmon fillets. Perhaps not first-choice, but I will not make a scene for coastal-Chili-farmed salmon. I also added to our cart some frozen Alaska hake fillets, 100 grams a piece or what seems a ridiculous amount for a fish to be cut into, but with ten fillets a bag, I could not argue there would not be enough. I did not, however, find any quality bread other than *baguette* and the industrial-white *pain de mie* for toasts, so I decided I would introduce change into my lunch plate and eat boiled potatoes instead. This would be my first inner *Révolution française*, for I am not a potato eater. How odd though that my mind was prepared for the worst while, in the end, it looks like a very rewarding sign, a blessing even. I will not be too disturbed into my eating habits *and bonus*; I will sketch a first-experience change pattern into my (compulsive) need of keeping every detail (of my diet) under control. I would lie, however, if I told you I am not looking forward to coming back home and savoring until the last crumb, a fresh plate of Brussels sprouts, spinach, broccoli, and, most importantly, market-fresh premier-quality Scottish salmon (skin on, mind you!), fish and shrimps. Delicious.

I was quite taken aback when I found out that I did not need to miss home at all. If not the salmon, then for the fresh fish. Surprise number two was on its way when one morning, while heading downhill for some water and beer shopping, I looked into the menu of a restaurant. The gods must have heard my craving for fish. Quite unexpectedly, during that morning walk to the *Place des Boutiques*, my mother and I came across a new restaurant, one that we had never been to in the ten years that we go to that ski resort. Our family has been holidaying for years in *La Joue du Loup*, yet we have never really eaten out; except for once, but the buns and burgers were not of such an exceptional quality for us to come back the following years. Instead, we have always cooked our own meals with a makeshift kitchenette. L'Envie des Mets, so it is called, has most certainly changed that habit, and I keep my fingers crossed for the local people and tourists to find their way to the tables of *the* best restaurant downhill. The chef and owner is proud to present his *menu du terroir* with fresh and first-quality ingredients, and to my *grande surprise*, a modest but satisfying choice of fresh and grilled white fish, and not the least may I add, a whole *daurade royale*. As soon as I spotted this on the menu, I melted where I was standing.

The next evening, we were waiting for the doors of the restaurant to open. It was 6:40 p.m., but the curtain would only go up at seven sharp. The 20-minute wait seemed endlessly long, especially since we had come downhill with heavy snow and sweaty feet, the three of us hiding under our umbrellas. I had been wearing the same in-fashion black mountain shoes for a walk earlier in the morning, again in the afternoon for a stretch-your-legs walk, and then, now, to walk down to the restaurant. Needless to say, my feet were sweaty, and my toes were frozen. 20 additional minutes of wandering about and, now, I wondered whether my toes would fall off from the cold, until, finally, the door did open, and we were showed to a table, window side, where a cold stream of icy air was caressing our backs, this feeling being totally unwelcomed. But, hey, fish was on the menu. Fish. The iciness would do. I knew the *daurade* would be worth the cold.

I had to wait another (what seemed to me endless) 30 minutes and could not help myself but hasten my mother and father to swallow their first course so that our mains would be ready sooner. Suddenly, the clock stopped at 7:34 p.m. when a beautiful, stuffed-with-fennel-seeds, grilled sea-bream lay presented among a *brunoise* of zucchini, carrots, and leeks. Wild rice on the side. Heaven. Beyond celestial frontiers, for there even was an in-triangle-shaped cut lemon presented alongside the fish. *Bon appétit*, indeed! Please excuse my selfish *tête-à-tête* with the fish; I will come back to you later in another paragraph.

Last Days Away

Looking back to the nearly two weeks of our mid-winter break, I am unfortunately unable to comment on any great or definite improvement of my being lockdown. The tranquil white landscapes have brought some new inner peace, for I have indeed come to accept the sleepless half nights that I get as night pattern. So, just after the clock strikes two or three mostly, I now lay on my back, under the covers, wondering. Some nights, I know all too soon that it will be difficult if not impossible to get back to a siesta sleep state. Instead of tossing and turning, I prefer to take up my reading where I have left it. Books are bringing me comfort, and I must admit that I quite like their company, for at least my mind enjoys a little rest while being concentrated on the story. It is easier to follow a course of action than overthinking the least important detail or gnawing on my sorrow and fate.

At 4 a.m. this morning, I did not read at all; I could not help but organize the schedule for the last day of our mountain break. It has already been two weeks since our departure, but I am a little prouder self today. I have been able to adjust quite rapidly, and I have grown accustomed to the surrounding area, the no-rye-bread lunches, the fear of not getting my daily intake of fruit and vegetables, etc. At first, I went for a walk twice a day, mornings and afternoons, and enjoyed the cooking dinner part too along with the little chores and treats, *i.e.* preparing my mother's tuna *baguette* for lunch one day or her mozzarella and ham salad the next. I have found a new environment where I could, again, spoil my parents and give voice to the Cinderella act I so enjoy to play. True story: I do like to take care of the people I love. To me, it does not sound that odd to clean, set the table, prepare lunch or dinner, and make sure everyone gets his treat.

Nonetheless, I know that I tend to overexaggerate, up to the point where I completely forget about the 'I' person within my body. I have been neglecting her for too long, since I do not remember when, and I have the greatest difficulty of finding her back and giving voice to her being and her existing. Honestly, it is not as if I were giving her any chance, for I do not know how or when to rest. Reality hits back, always rocky-bottom-hard, but just when my mind was echoing signs of despair while tossing and turning in the children's bunk bed of the holiday rent, my phone was buzzing in a WhatsApp message that I had only just received from my little doll sister (was she awake that early?).

"And in those moments, where the sun is setting and the house is quiet and you are weary of the day, may you know that there is grace for you in that space, and no amount of heaviness or loneliness can take that away. And because of that grace, you are free to slow down. You are free to breathe and rest, no matter the things not sorted out. There might be some mystery here, and there might be longing, wondering, and waiting, but there will also be boundless peace that goes beyond any understanding, running wild like a river through everything, no matter how heavy those moments feel. So rest easy when evening is approaching. Tomorrow is surely coming, but in the hours in between, you are free to rest till then." (Morgan Harper Nichols)

Am I, really? Am I free to rest? I cannot help but sense the burden that is upon me, the piercing and watching eye of *others*. Who are they? They are the *everyones* and *everywheres* that I feel hamper my way up. Perhaps I needed the last two weeks to throw my body and self into a new and unexplored environment where I could appreciate, quite obviously, the many, wooden, heart-engraved *accessoires* of the rent apartment or, to a more serious extent, the new changes and train of events that make up for the adventure, the term being too strong for, again, 'quote-quote' normal people. However, for me, staying in a different environment while fighting against my shadow and destructive self feels like departing for a backpack expedition to Antarctica.

Nevertheless, in hindsight, I see a new step forward. I welcomed positively this wave of changes; I even felt relief for the first time since long when, instead of pushing the button of the five-star coffee grinder machine we have at home, I was able to go back in time and pour full tablespoons of pre-ground packed coffee into the old-fashioned coffeemaker. I measured eight of them and filled the water compartment until reaching the eight-point-five dose for a pure, intense, and strong flavor of *Plaisir*, a golden (well, black) hot beverage to enjoy every morning, the smell of which invading the breakfast room while mixing harmoniously with the simmering of my carob and goji oatmeal. I only need to crack an egg, and here's to our last day away from home.

Two weeks, yet I have still not found out how to rest, nor have I given me the green light to rest. Improvements ought to be made as to that area of my treatment, but I need first to change my restless behavior, the one I dangerously aggravated during my studies and, later, during my first year as an employee. That self-destructive behavior was also the one that I would come to adopt at home, in my *yet-so-safe* surroundings.

I have come to realize that guilt has been gnawing on my soul for too long, because I am now staying at home – although forced to recover from a body shutdown and a threatening destruction of the matter and soul. I, thus, quickly ended up convincing myself that I ought to better make myself useful at home while my parents were out at work. It was, or so I thought, the least I could do. Be useful. And while we're at it, be the ostrich, I heard my soul saying. It suits you so. Until it has completely annihilated the vestiges of what you thought was your known self. Work hard and erase yourself even further off the road.

Spectator

On our way back from the mountain interlude, I dreaded the week that presented itself ahead. Three medical appointments, one of which on Monday, the day after our return, with the massage therapist. The next one would be that Tuesday, for the weekly meeting with my psychoanalyst/therapist, and last in line would fall on the Friday, same week, for a follow-up interview with the psychiatrist, this time in the clinical facility. It had been more than three weeks since I had last seen one of the experts treating me and following my case. The three-centimeter covered-in-snow roads had impeded our driving to the therapist and general doctor's appointments the week before we were to leave for La Joue du Loup in France, leaving me 'out of hands' for all this time. I was, thus, in desperate need for advice and counselling.

On Monday morning, after the heavy breakfast and one (no double this time) cup of pure Arabica Costa Rica coffee (sweet and balanced it says on the store-bought package), I drove off to whom I now call 'Marraine la Fée,' Cinderella's fairy godmother. She knows me well-enough and has been treating me for the last seven months I believe. Rough and feisty, despite her being in her 70s, I tell her everything. That Monday, yesterday actually, it was different though. I felt a connection, a click, a little *je ne sais quoi* in her eyes that gave her away: I had become her little *protégée*. She was caring and understanding; she was there to listen to my crying, to my incomprehension as to whom I am to find in my quest of myself, to my disillusion of and not-belonging to the world we live in, to the rupture between my body and my mind, the clear-cut division between matter and soul.

While I was sitting on a beige, vintage, suede *fauteuil*, searching for a handkerchief in my bag to dry up my tears, she had an answer ready and did shoot it out, her voice trembling and her eyes red and wet: "*Tu sais petite,*" she started, "your brain is consuming you. It empties your body of whatever little energy there is left, impeding the food you eat to reach the organs, for it all goes straight up to your hyperactive and too-demanding brain." Because of the rupture between body and brain, the latter absorbs everything out of my high-protein/high-fat diet and keeps the engine rolling H24, whereas the body is left with crumbs, leftovers if you like, and consequently does not end its shutdown out of protest or as an act of salvation. By keeping the barriers locked, the body protects the little activity there is left in that frail *matter*; it ensures the maintenance of the basic functioning of the organs and prevents any further damage of them. One cannot fool his/her own body: it feels only too well when a wave of further destruction is on its way. It thus anticipates the damage by locking its harbor down. No trespassing. None.

Marraine la Fée interrupted her speech at the sight of a raven devouring the fat tennis balls of bird food she hides in the bushes, originally meant for the little birds, like sparrows or robins. It does not bring her any comfort to see the winter food supplies swallowed up in a bite or two by the big black-and-white unalluring birds, the very ones that are strong enough, she believes, to chase their own daily share of food. Selfish creatures! It made me smile, and it had brought a sense of relief, of *lacher-prise* that I had not experienced for a long time. She is quite someone, *Marraine*.

From what she had told me, the most arduous battle I am to fight is against my own behavior, my own mind. I must break from the actual *plan de bataille*, for it only leads me further down the edge of the cliff. The guilt that has taken over my mind must be shot down. Done with the au pair routine, exit the governess. Enters a new 'me.' I must free myself from the role that I cannot help but take; from the *everyones* and *everythings* that I carry on my shoulders, too frail now to help out, even though I wish I could *be there* to ease and alleviate the *everythings* of the great *everyones*. How odd though, considering the growing selfishness in the society we live in, that I should be told to take care *less* of others and *more* of myself. I must lessen my emotional experience of the surrounding reality and, instead, learn how to sit as a spectator of a real-live comedy, at least for the time being or until I find back a decent state of health.

However, truth be told, I have absolutely no idea how to distinguish duty from joy. I had mastered in the self-effacement, with high honors in the wiping away of the self. Am I then to break free from the *whats* and *whos* I know here and be alone somewhere to meet my own self and give my body the time to recover quietly and in peace? If so, where to?

Am I to start over someplace new? All alone? Forget about it. It is too soon: "Do not run away, not just yet." Actually, this is my therapist's saying. The Tuesday psychologist that brings back some balance and reason into my life. I went to visit her private practice yesterday, on a cold, late-afternoon Tuesday. It is mid-February, and the wind snaps at me like ice cubes do when getting them out of the freezer with your bare hands, unprotected. As the days are starting to stretch, the little birds have chirped early in the morning for the last couple of days. I know that, for I hear them when I wake up at seven and appreciate their singing to each other as if to welcome spring earlier than weatherly possible. They remind me that, no, I am not ready yet to run away on my own. It would further destroy me.

During our one-hour Tuesday *tête-à-tête*, I spent the first half telling her about the mountain trip, the positive and the negative points, the fish (obviously, I could not skip that part), but I also mentioned the agitated half-nights, the unexpected discovery (and health benefits) of bee pollen, the unbelievably rich and savory acacia honey, although a bit on the dark color side. I continued the description with the sore muscles and the unceasing *au pair* behavior, the rupture between the body and the soul; all of it, I had to tell her.

Nor could I hide my fear of what the future holds for me, as if I were not meant to be part of this society. I do not fit in, and, quite honestly, I have not the least idea of how to live and work, be happy or to learn to enjoy, to feel the pleasure, to trust people, to trust…anyone, starting with myself. As I am sitting on the square and cushioned little wicker stool in her salon, tensed, the warm tears caressing my cheeks, I am unable to find any tissue, even though I was sure I had put a whole pack of them, ten, in my bag before leaving home. While I try to sniff discreetly although shamefully aware that it will not go unnoticed, the therapist remains calm as she listens to my fear and sorrow. In the end, I ask her if ever I will recover the energy *d'antan*, my former existence.

Why that, I will not; instead, so she said, I will encounter a new form of energy, a new stream or flux of life. She put the record straight: I suffer from a severe form of burnout, and I ought to consider myself lucky that I have gone off the radar at age 25, for I have a whole life to build. Some people crash in their 50s or 60s, and, truth be told, it is far worse a challenge for them, for they will question their whole existence on the surface of the Earth until now; they will face the dreadful and most-feared reality and ask themselves what phantom life they have been impersonating for so long.

Before I knew it, I was heading toward the table, ready to let her hold my head in her hands as if carrying me quietly and softly laying my head on a pile of books in order to lay ruler-flat on the table. My knees are up while she puts some order in my ugly and clinging toes (I guess it is safe to share a universal secret: nobody likes his or her toes, come on). I close my eyes and try not to surrender to the aggressive tears invading my soul. What have I done to myself? Where have I been? How am I supposed to function in this world? Actually, I need to learn from others, so…what is *your* routine? What do *you* eat for breakfast? How many slices of bread do you eat a day? Do you have snacks? How long before you go to work and tell yourself you are tired? How tired do you feel? Can you still stand upon your legs? Can you still go out and have dinner with friends, or do you isolate yourself from all the rush-hour agitation? And what happens when you come home? What do you do to treat yourself a nice, cozy, and comfortable 'me-time'? In short, how do *you* live? Please, tell me. Feel free to share your secrets.

I am deeply sorry to intrude as such in your personal everyday routine, but I am in desperate need of an example to follow, for I am lost. I do not know how to live, lest it be to work, to perform, to help out and forget – especially forget – about the struggles I keep avoiding by behaving like a governess, an au pair, an ever-performant workaholic and busy bee. Life to me has proven very self-destructive, yet, in almost drowning, I have been forced to gasp for air. Here I am.

Mill for Life

There once was a Belgian gastroenterologist, so my Tuesday therapist told me, a very renowned professor at university and author of scores of articles in medical literature, a married man was he and a father as well. Until one day, he too suffered from a burnout. He too had outperformed his own body, although without noticing in time that the matter could not quite follow as rapidly as his hectic mind which had been changing gears at more than full speed. He lost himself while his body broke down, yet not completely, for he managed, after months of therapy (and questioning), to find a new stream upon which to flow. He, thus, quit the *everyones* and *everythings* he knew and bravely gave himself the present of a new life; one in which he was the original author of, instead of the mere actor he had been so far, always trapped into secondary roles and always feeling the pressure from the outside world, for he were to be ever more performant, ever more strict toward himself, ever more *something*.

Until that day when his world had tumbled down. He changed gears and bought the last flourmill of Belgium, somewhere deep into the Ardennes, located in the south of the country. As a medical specialist, he knew what sorts of flours were best and kindest to the human digestive system. He seized the opportunity that presented itself to him, and sooner than he had imagined, he was to become the 2.0 version of ancient grain millers. Whether spelt or rye, Khorasan wheat or simply millet, he would welcome time into his milling and, a pinch of salt later, would add homemade leaven to let the bread rest before letting it rise in the oven and finally getting it golden rich in both texture and flavor to please the ever gourmand's palate.

Aside from the treasure of time, the miller had also taken up his writing, although not where he had left it. He would now let his pencil find its way through excerpts and articles in the service of his newfound interest, knowledge, and experience in ancient grains. The rediscovery and the use of ancient grains turned into flours by this former medical surgeon are amongst the best used (and purchased) by organic bakeries and *grands pâtissiers* in Belgium and Northern France. He healed himself from the destructive phantom that governed his body and mistreated his soul. He kneaded until he had rendered this demon flat, although making sure this life-changing experience would never rise again. This newfound peace was bound to last, rather than go stale.

Upstream

Many a people strongly back and unquestionably think of energy as a large bowl that can either be empty or full. However, only a few, among whom my therapist, prefer to give a rather modernist twist to that definition of the energy of a human body and soul. She and other partisans are the ones adopting perhaps a more metaphorical view of *our* energy, seen to them as a river which waters sometimes flow at torrential speed, sometimes snake in and out the narrow brooks. Depending on the surrounding environment, the water can be a magnificent crystal-blue or just the opposite, a morose, troubling darkness. Nevertheless, after having given voice so intensely to my inner sorrow and pain, I shall be obliged to consider that life has not yet disappeared completely from within me, even as insignificant and discreet a rivulet it can be.

Rivers, seas, and streams allow the daily functioning of the human body; they nourish the mind and take care of the soul, the latter finding its peace only when harmony is reached through an equilibrium between composure and strength, time and speed, relief and benevolence. Unfortunately, at some point, I must have paddled loosely, for I headed directly and uncontrollably into the rapids. These fast-moving troubling waters have engulfed me for the last four – almost five – years now, and I have had the hardest time struggling to keep my head above the water. At age 26, despite years of taking swimming lessons, I feel like I am drowning. Is there a shore nearby so that I can catch my breath and find some quietness?

There is no point in mourning my past and phantom being. For a while now, I have lived out of fear; the fear of disappointing, the fear of failing – first at school, then at university, at work, at home – the fear of misunderstanding the meaning of life, the fear of time. That last one was probably the engine driving all the other sources of fear into a sort of endless spin.

I have, indeed, always been afraid of not having the time to accomplish what I had pressed upon myself, whether this would mean arriving ridiculously early at appointments or isolating myself from everyone and everything, only to be able to work or study more (and better) and realizing afterward that I still had *too much time* left before handing in a paper or sitting the examination.

Whenever this were the case, I would not allow myself to sit comfortably in the little IKEA armchair I had back in my student's room, nor would I sit in the vintage leather faux Louis XVI sofa that we have in our living room at home. Quite the opposite happened actually: I would revise, not once, not twice, but up to as many times as possible the notes and summaries that I had made so as to prepare (even better) the exam. I would recite my lessons, but despite the door being closed, my mother and sister would hear the recital loud and clear as if they were in the audience next to me, or, worse, behind the scenes. Although being very assiduous in my summaries, I would, however, end up on a sour note because *so* exhausted was I that I never, not once in my six years at university, knew the last page by heart. Read it, I did, but to recite it by heart, that I was not capable of. My sister had come to tease me about this strange habit of mine, and we both had a good laugh, praying the teacher or professor would not go into too many details listed on that particular page. Luckily, there was never a question relative to last-page content during the many examinations I have sat…and passed.

All little anecdotes aside, there is no use, as I have mentioned earlier, in mourning the past 'me.' Yet, I cannot recall when the waters began to change color. It does not seem fair, but who is to give a totally objective definition of fairness? All of us move our oars in all sorts of directions; some find a propitious current, others need a little more practice before finding their rhythm and controlling the stream.

One Year and Two Months

Last Friday was February 15th, or one year and two months since going underground. I have had time since to realize that I could no longer blindly follow the way I thought was set for me; still walking on that road, although I need to halt. Indeed, once I am out of the tunnel – this black hole – I ought to figure out my own path by assembling not bits and pieces of concrete but beautiful marble *pièces détachées* that I have borrowed on my way through the tunnel and out. I will slowly create a road to recovery until blossoming out and blooming eventually; breathing in the air so fresh, so light, with touches of linen, aromas of spring, and scents of recently cut grasses. The bee pollen will sprinkle its dusty fluff *en arrière-plan* while the bees will be busy stealing (not so secretly and unashamed) from snowdrops, crocuses, lavenders, lilacs, hyacinths, hydrangeas, and poppies, for all colors will do for the honey to be syrupy golden and healthily sweet. I will, again, breathe in deeply and contemplate the almost-transparent white veil covering the first sunrays of yet-too-early a-spring kind of day while timidly attempting an appearance on our sunny-side terrace, scarf and woolen blankets by hand. While fighting off the many questions and thoughts wandering in my head, I try as best I can to close my eyes, suddenly finding myself smiling when hearing the neighbor talking to 'the girls,' aka the chickens, one of which named after our former queen, Paola. The other names are not worth mentioning when compared to Queen P.

It had been a no-coffee morning, for I was to meet with the psychiatrist for a follow-up. Hence no coffee, because I do not want to find myself in the very uncomfortable position of having to pee and not being able to. My father had taken the day off from work to drive me to the clinic. I did not mind arriving too early; at least we could wait outside, on a sunny-side bench, in front of the main entrance revolving door, a little to the left. The sunrays suggested a cloudless sky and the weird impression of being overdressed, wearing indeed too many layers for the abnormal 15-degree-celcius temperatures.

Tanning over with, I was to head to the clinic facility, detached from the main hospital. I tried to gasp for air when telling the specialist how I felt, clearly aware that the physical condition had not improved yet indeed. I come a long way, true; but although I have made great progress, psychologically speaking – accepting the theoretical foundations I have been taught by the medical team on cognitive behavior and nutrition – I still sense there is a sharp rupture between the body and the mind. The former does not give up so fast and holds onto its 'no-trespassing' guidelines. It will simply not lift the barrier up. It manages on its own, tries its best, and seems not to give up the survival mode it has gone into months earlier in order to preserve life. I suppose only time will heal this wound; only time will stitch the pain, even though leaving the scar open forever.

In the meantime, I ought to learn how to put into practice these theoretical guidelines dictated by the medical team. Although I *know* I need to let go, I find great difficulty in *really* letting things go. Hence my sometimes-boring questions to the people around me, for I try to gather all the useful information as to how *they* manage to *live* their life. I think I must annoy them at times, often even. So, when they least expect it, I just observe them. I like sensing and experiencing the surrounding reality. Talking is superfluous, since only the eyes are called for this investigative type of activity.

I wonder whether observation might enter the much-debatable domain of art (in general). While sitting at the living-room, vintage, wooden table with industrial accents, I enjoy the warm caress of a mid-February shining sun knocking smoothly on our window panes. I even dare say that I enjoy the first fly that is buzzing around from the kitchen to our salon, creating its own interludes in the midst of the otherwise-so-annoying greasing sounds that flies do. Yet, today, I cannot mind too much, for I am being transported away by the chirping of little birds. As I turn my head to the left, I catch myself smiling at the view of a bright-pink, plastic, soccer ball comfortably and almost majestically installed on top of the green-leaf bushes separating our yard from the neighbor's. It was probably left forgotten about after the kids' game yesterday afternoon, on returning home after school. I already picture the mother of three calling for her little rascals, among them twins (boy and girl), to come inside because dinner is ready. Quite honestly, if you were a child, would you think of the pink ball shot up in the air which had fallen on top of the bushes? Perhaps not, and who would be cross when knowing that the hungry football team were about to devour their spaghetti and meatballs with extra cheese on top? All we could mutter is, well, enjoy your meal.

To the question 'is observation art,' I would like to answer favorably, for the spectator can quickly and boundlessly turn into the author of his own imagination and hence contribute to illuminating his own experience of the surrounding reality. I believe anyone can master the art of observation and appreciate both the applause as well as the creativity behind it.

I have spent too many years neglecting not only my body and self, but, most importantly, I have been deserting my right to being the observer of the life around me and how it is experienced, if not by myself, then by others in general. My 'to be or not to be' personal challenge was for me to understand how *others* spend their time.

Although I do imagine that most people share the same troubles in finding a balance between work and self-care and their hobbies, I also believe that many *everyones* still find a way to smile genuinely and generously despite being (sometimes or oftentimes) quite overwhelmed at work or by life. I wonder how this feels. Perhaps that is the reason why I prefer to write about the balance to be found between work and *care*, rather than the traditional opposition made between work and *personal life*. In 'caring,' one goes further than in leading his or her personal life which can be anything from brilliant and enjoyable to broken and unsatisfying. Hence my suggestion to talk about *care*. Generally speaking, one cares for oneself (the human being is selfish), but I believe that many a people still kindheartedly care for others, *i.e.* for the *everyones* that are part of a person's *mise en scène*, whether Shakespearian or not.

One year and two months ago, my scenery collapsed. I was left with no décor, no colors, no disguise. The mask had fallen off; the curtains were up, leaving me naked and frail, humiliated to the bone. I had failed. I had disappointed the worst critic of this play: my own self. Exit self. Switch off lights.

All these months since December 2017, I have fought hard against my body. Up to this day, even though dark has not been vanquished yet, I continue to resupply the weaponry while my mind keeps the headquarters busy reflecting upon the revolution that is inevitably bound to happen, if it is not already underway. I wonder what victory will bring.

Nevertheless, no matter how poignant or puzzling these written words may seem to some and others, I consider myself blessed and lucky, for the naked creature standing upright in the spotlight – humiliated to the bone – has been given another chance to rediscover beauty and sound, emotion and humanity. All are not mastered overnight, obviously; they are taught to us while walking forward on our path, step by step.

So far, I have enjoyed being the observer of life around me, but I have been even more fascinated by the stories behind the players. Any kind will do, any anecdote or story; any smell reminiscent of the past, any sound that immediately transports me back on memory lane. But as thankful as I am for remembering these past souvenirs, I am also deeply aware of the hidden danger it bears. One cannot *stay* in the past, as comfortable and securing a haven it might seem, simply out of fear of facing the uncertainty – good or bad – of the future. Therefore, one must welcome and embrace change when it comes across one's path. One ought to look forward to the rising sun and have faith. And as faith has healed the wounds of the past, faith too will heal the scars that have been left open and will prevent them from destroying us again. Never again.

While waiting for time to heal this particular wound, I try to empty my head, although I shall confess that I am no genius at it. The overthinking is too natural and too intrinsic an activity (shall I dare say *past-time*?) to me. Nonetheless, *if* the thinking will not capitulate even just for a while, I have decided to take advantage of these marching soldiers and let them busy themselves with a well-defined mission: the recollecting of the thoughts of the past, not mine per se, but *everyone's* or *anyone's*. Those who rub shoulders with me must know that I am a strong advocate of remembering and spreading our cultural heritage, our History especially – with capital *h* mind you – and more specifically the First and Second World Wars that have shaken humanity only decades ago. I cannot quite tell how I ended up being so interested and so curious about these events of the 20th century. Yet, I have realized mostly through readings that we must remember, always and forever, the atrocities that have divided and crushed our souls in order to identify evil when it knocks on the door.

Back in high school, I was deeply moved by the *Schindler's List* movie that was projected onto the wide and white cloth of our classroom. I was 14 at the time and already experiencing the drawbacks of belonging to a not-so-popular girl squad, the leader of which preventing us from eating in front of her (she would always be on some diet), thus forcing *me* to swallow my lunch between classes or hidden, unseen in the restrooms. The movie made a strong impression on me, and from then on, I was more interested in our history classes, the peak of that focus being in senior year, on the one hand because the recently graduate and dandy teacher was handsome and the only teacher ever wearing ironed shirts and matching ties (the pink and baby blue ones being the absolute favorites of the girls attending his classes), and on the other hand because the same teacher was the most singular and unique storyteller of past events, whether landmark or random. He knew how to draw attention, for he was a unique rhetorician. Finally, when I left high school for university, I knew something in me had changed. I was suddenly aware that one's knowledge of history was key to determine one's place in this world; that it was a springboard in one's attempts to live one's life rather than be the sole spectator of the others' doings.

Later, at university, I mostly held this interest hidden somewhere in a corner of my mind, for I was trying my best to prove myself with regard to what *others, i.e.* the *everyones*, would say about me being different. I was brought up in two languages at home, hence the 'liability' to translate as accurately and as smoothly as French-speaking boast-offs, *des m'as-tu-vu*, as I like to call them in French *justement*.

In addition, I was convinced that I had to prove myself to my father, since the translation studies in English and Spanish were perhaps not considered as bold a choice as the study of economics, law, or engineering (fortunately, I am not responsible for the calculus and equations behind the building of bridges and houses; I would not trust myself too much in these fields). I still felt I had to make my way into these specific fields and consequently focused every work or paper that was to be handed in – unsurprisingly – on economic or political themes such as the economy within the European Union, the 2008 economic crisis, the conflict tearing Israel and Palestine, the nuclear threat posed by Iran (research made when in Salamanca, during the Erasmus experience), the building of the Panama Canal (first year of master's degree, Spanish class), and this to name only a few projects that I had been investigating.

The two years of my master's degree, I had the chance to be taught by the crème de la crème of all English professors. One was to become a role model to me as well as the director of my thesis, while another one would quickly serve as my absolute mentor and the professor I most looked up to. The latter introduced me to English literature and to writing as a form of art. The American literary works, on the other hand, were being taught in another class by our faculty dean who I could listen to for hours, especially since we were following closely the U.S. Presidential Election and the swearing in of Mr. Barack Obama for a second term.

The summer before entering my master's degree, I had just come back from my Erasmus in Salamanca. I found out that I was slowly but surely isolating myself from everyone and everything that had, would or could hurt me, so as to take the necessary precautions. I did not trust anybody bar myself and my hard working. On campus, I was a teaching-assistant in English for our faculty's freshman students, and I had already set my mind on working ahead for my thesis during any spare time gaps I could find. How was I to know that I was about to fall into the void?

What I did not realize back then was that I had just tanked the car gas full to better drive me on the road to self-destruction, to abandoning myself on the pavement, and to ditching my body and the care of it behind. Although the personal and physical levels of devastation are probably not the best to remember, even today, the insight and the knowledge that I have gained throughout this whole experience are priceless. And, for that, I am thankful. We might not choose the enemies that cross our path, nor can we mourn forever the wounds and the scars that are tattooed deep into our souls; but we hold the power within ourselves to feel blessed with our capacity (and boldness) to tell our own story and to color it brightly instead of sketching it gloomy and darkly. How was I to know that four years from that (lack of) realization, *I* was about to become the very artist whose soul had been torn and whose paper had just gone blank?

Yet, here I am, sitting, this time, not on just some ordinary chair of the living-room dinner table; instead, I decided that this late afternoon, I would pick the one leather *fauteuil* face-crossing my usual spot. Just to change habits; have another view of our backyard (and perspective on life maybe). I am already proud of myself, for I have eaten my protein-and-honey nut bar, 40 grams of high fiber and protein content. 'Good healthy fats,' I hear somewhere in the background.

Seriously though (no laughing), I seemed to have lost this sacred ritual of 'snacking' over the years. I had lost the habit of it. I did not think it normal to have a little something to munch on at ten or 11 in the morning nor somewhere late in the afternoon. So 'thumbs up' shall I say, or that is until I swear the hell out of my body for the cramps I now feel in my lower guts. This must probably be a direct cause of too much fiber at once, resulting in the overload of activity pressed upon my frail-and-often-stubborn digestive system. "Get used to it, foe of mine!"

Moving on from those unwelcomed spasms, I am now trying to clear my mind from any personal thinking and switching it to a forgotten anecdote of our family, starring *mamy* more precisely. Mamiche is my father's mother, and I do take a lot from her. I have no idea how I came to think of this interlude, but I would like to share my thoughts. It often helps me to put things into perspective. Mamiche and I are both very determined and obstinate in our caring for others; we both hush our inner pains and suffering and smile to helping out others. I have always known that her family had fled from their home during the Second World War and that one of her little sisters was born in France. It would be the adventure of a couple of months before returning to their bourgeois hometown that they had previously abandoned in 1940. This is her story, the story of Mamiche's flight from the Germans, of her courage in the face of adversity.

It was 1940, and Mamiche's parents, *Parrain* and *la Grande-Mamy*, as my father refers to them, were still very sour from the last seen marching German soldiers, *les Boches*, that had been crossing their beloved and free countryside.

Under no circumstance would they bow once again to the German will and so, when the Belgian frontier had been trampled on in May, 1940, by Hitler's troops, they decided to organize a convoy with some neighbors and friends to depart to south-western France, near Bordeaux.

A great-uncle, a priest, even kept a diary in Dutch of their journey, which I am very eager to read if I am allowed to and if – mind the hypothetical statement – the diary still exists. I wonder why it had taken so much time for the story to come out again. I remember Mamiche being invited over for dinner recently, and it was in the midst of our paella dish that we found ourselves traveling back onto memory lane. How has such a brave and poignant adventure been locked for so long? Is it too hopeful from me to expect there might be pictures too? Only Mamiche will tell. Do tell me, Mamiche, do tell me. I wish to read this diary. I am all ears and ink-ready to write it down and print it in our history, the common book of human stories and travels. Do tell me. Please, do share.

Sameness in Portraits

Today is February 22nd, and the skies have printed out the interior of my soul: an undisturbed light-grayish tint hides the sun and keeps back the light. I wonder how 'they' know, not sure who or what is behind them. I manage to smile though, out of the corner of my eye, for I still spot the pink soccer ball majestically installed on top of the bushes in our neighbors' backyard. The children do not seem to miss it too much apparently; instead, they prefer to play with one of the other soccer balls they have for spare in their toy chest. The birds are still chirping happily, and I wish I could be the only guest invited to their concert, at least if it were not for the humming of the fridge or the occasional long-distant roaring of the passing planes, flying too high in the sky for me to wave back, probably at a little guy or business-class passenger looking through his window, wondering also, perhaps.

This morning though, the same skies seem as bored as the depths of my soul. The gray uniformity is *en accord* with the emptiness that I feel deep inside. After the regal breakfast, I had decided to spice the house up and fill the atmosphere with a warm and comforting smell of star anise, ginger, and cinnamon. I cannot help but think of my sister who would literally melt if she were to know that I have just taken the freshly baked gingerbread out of the oven.

The modern twist given to this gingerbread cake is yet to be tried for the first time. The cake in itself is far from a perfectly risen one, nor is it a perfectly round-shaped golden bread, but I honestly like the authenticity of it. It is my special recipe, my own, and I will not change it unless I got a bad grade from my family's taste approval. I was in luck, for it had already passed the granny test. It had, in fact, been enjoyed and delicately savored by both my grandmothers, *Oma* and *Mamiche*, when they had come over for dinner, and who would dare question their taste buds anyway? Grannies approve of it!

Both of them have inspired me throughout my childhood and still do until this day. I have been fortunate enough to learn from them ever since standing on that crutch next to the kitchen sink, waiting for anything to be licked off the used spatula or any sauce that had been left on the wooden spoon. And may I say that it is indeed a matter of utter importance to use *wooden* utensils when cooking pasta, give a turn in a sauce or preparing a risotto recipe; actually, the quality of one's utensils is as transcendental as salt going with pepper in every *cuisine*, period. Which also reminds me that I would insist on the use of pink Himalayan salt or Breton Fleur de sel, the white one from Guérande. But I guess that is just me sharing too many cooking details, perhaps uninteresting to many a man.

Is this really a bad thing? I shall have to admit that I find it fascinating to be able to nose around in other people's kitchens. Do not be mistaken; I will not fall into the trap of telling you that I wish I were a bird or a little mouse to fly or wander about in the cooks' ateliers, for I would only end up being chased after and hunted down, either by a wet and stained dish towel, either by a flour-dusted pastry roll. So, no, I will not fall for that. No bird nor mouse reincarnation, no thank you.

Instead, I will secretly share my wish to stand next to a *mamma italiana* to see and learn as much as I can of the art of giving. Italians sure know how to win everyone's heart with the simplest ingredients and their most generous savoir-faire. Furthermore, I also wish to peep through the windows of any kitchen, only to watch how any family, whether big or small, any couple, anyone really, takes great care of bringing the most honest and authentic food to their table, night after night. Yes, I want to witness how food brings us together, we, us, the peoples of the world. Cooking, therefore, opens the door to a greater mutual understanding, to the sharing of wisdom and savoir-faire, to the awareness that only by holding hands, we, the people, will reach (inner) peace and heal centuries of self-inflicted wounds, our owns and the world's.

After lunch, I still felt the same emptiness in my body, even though I had savored every bite of the fresh oven-baked garlicky *rosé* salmon (it literally melts in your mouth, so soft a texture it is, and this despite the fish being frozen Norwegian salmon, not the Scottish one I fancy so!). As a side, I had steamed once-in-a-while so intense and flavorful a broccoli, rye *tartines*, and last but not least, two little *peperoncini*. A feast that I had indulged myself into, especially when letting the spicy juices drizzle over my bread. Yum. This is my favorite 1 p.m. appointment of the day, and I am thankful, for I can have this little face to face as many times a week as I wish. The icing on the cake – or better said, the additional sunrays on my plate – is a teaspoon or two of acacia honey as dessert, and this, only seconds after licking up the greasy salmon knife. The honey adds just this sweetness and glueyness to which I cannot surrender.

Yet, it was now nearing two in the afternoon, and I had decided to try an outing. This was a first. I would be alone, obviously, and outside the house.

There would not be too many passersby at this time of the day; most people are at work or commuting already from the big cities to the local schools to surprise their children by fetching them early and baking some pancakes. The neighbors' children often get back home at around four-ish, and perhaps now would be a convenient time for them to dethrone the pink soccer ball from the bushes? Only time will tell. Tick tock.

I had only taken my cellphone and keys, and out was I. It did not last long, however, before my legs felt wobbling. I had only just climbed the first 50 meters further ahead than our street. This little digestive *passeggiata* would take me first up to the cemetery, then through the Rue Auguste Latour, a road alongside which I am often tempted to admire the tiny yet cute townhouses, one of which resembling a white cabin you would find near a beach. Whenever I walk beside that house, no matter what year or what month it is, the owner always decorates the front window pane. This time, there were three hearts carved out of wood, typically the ones you would buy in a flower shop. A couple of months ago, I had spotted a series of three, little, coastal-style houses which roofs changed color, that he had put on display out of the same window pane. And then there were times too when he would display a set of three stone seagulls that seemed to be watching every move of curious passersby. That white house in the Auguste Latour Street has, in some way, stolen my heart, for there is something deep and enigmatic about it. I have never met the owners, even though they live only a couple of blocks away.

Moving on during my walk, I crossed a tiny bridge, mounting the once-operational railway trail that connected our village to several bigger cities until it was closed down and left abandoned, already more than 40 or 50 years ago. It now leaves the marshy soils to nature's *laissez-aller* and is often used, sadly, as a garbage ravine by the street neighbors. Man pays no respect.

While refocusing on getting my legs to move and support my body, I spotted an old man sitting on a wooden bench, bent forward, just at the end of the bridge. Next to him was his shopping bag out of which he had taken out two cans. I found it most plausible that he had come back from the main attraction of our little *commune, i.e.* the Colruyt supermarket, and, feeling a bit exhausted, he had simply decided to rest for a while before embarking again on his journey home. Or was he delaying his return on purpose, out of fear for his wife to scold him for whatever reason there might be? That, I will never know, but the truth is, I felt my heart break into pieces at the sight of the two cans beside him on that bench. He had already opened one of them, a tomato paste – unlabeled – and was now eating directly out of it, with his thumb, ignoring me staring at him. Could he be that hungry? Then why would he choose the tomato paste instead of a piece of fruit he might have bought too?

Or cookies. I did not dare ask him; instead, I smiled; he smiled back at me, convinced as ever in his perhaps soon-to-be social-media trend. Eating tomato paste. I admire his determination, his rebellion against social codes around food, for indeed no person ought to be frowned upon for thumbing out purée out of a recently bought can that has not yet reached the third plank starting from the bottom of the shelf in the cellar. So, *bon appétit* to him and thumbs up for breaking away from 'what shall the others say.'

An Active Volcano

I woke up this Saturday morning bereft of any feeling, of any emotion. Nothing, nada. The contrasting skyline with the one of the previous day was close to being breathtaking. A beautiful, deep-blue horizon welcomed the early morning sunrays into our living room, rendering shy and even more determined to struggle the little candles that seemed so desperate to shed if only a fluff of illumination out of their baroque *bougeoirs*. It does not last long for me to realize that nothing will make up for the void that inhabits shamelessly and quite disturbingly my defenseless body. I knew that nothing would free me from my incomprehension and (might as well say it) sorrow; nothing would trigger a sparkle, nor would I dare dream of getting some magic powder to dust off the settled anger and guilt.

Something did, however, provoke an inner eruption; an outburst so rare that I can count the times on just one hand, which, in the past, had solely been attributed to disturbances that affected my little sister. Just to be clear: you harm her, I will come after you, and bear in mind that even frail lambs can use their cunning to silence the worst of wolves.

This being said, it was not a protective bleat in this case; rather an inner bombardment of disbelief and stupefaction. Shock is not powerful enough a word to describe the burning energy that has suddenly gone wild, not finding any other way than to burst out of my mind by letting out flows of lava. The only difference being that the lava sliding off the volcano was not made of ashes from an infuriated Mother Earth, but of inner tears after years of successful attempts at escaping from my own self. My father had walked into the room by now, and I could already sense the tension that was about to erupt deep from the core. The trigger? The consumer society, with headquarters at our home.

Lately, I have been struggling with his behavioral pattern. Although many a man will probably argue that I peek too often too much into the habits of the *everyones* surrounding me, I cannot help but try to make my father (everyone actually) realize how frustrating it is to go about undisturbed in his/their fanatic consumerism and lure of materialism.

Do we need a ten-square-meter cellar full of food and beverage supplies, providing a somewhat ironical and contrasting view to the concrete war bunkers which had only been poorly supplied in times of war with cans of thick, cold soup or peaches in syrup? Do we need the two boxes of already-expired chocolate bars that you had bought months ago, arguing that their production would come to an end, hence hoping to enjoy the last bites of these sweet *gaufrettes*? While purchasing the last items, you had obviously forgotten that you would be off for a three-month foreign mission for work, with only home venues during weekends, and, by then, the very same chocolate bars had lost all their sparkle compared to the cookies and candies that you yourself had brought into our home from this or that *petite boutique* while traveling abroad. These are only a few examples of our stockpiles at home.

Please forgive me, *Papa*, but this is a battle that I can no longer fight. Even though it breaks my soul to capitulate before the impossibility to deviate from this compulsive buying and excessive consumerism (yours or everyone's), I have come to realize that there is a wall that separates us, a wall so great that it renders the war single-fought, only pursued by one battalion, the other being left unruffled, unashamed, and unworried. Always buying because, apparently, 'more' brings about even more. Yet, here I am, still fighting in an attempt to shake off even the lightest veil of what, to me, are considered inconvenient habits, especially in today's society. In vain. The only fighter had become the victim of his own weaponry being silenced off, but the energy I had used in the past to present arms had, by now, long deprived me of any force. An entente was not reached, an accord even less, but my body had itself decided to lay down arms. Instead, it had started its shutdown in order to prevent that any other damage be done to the soldier in his quest for greater human sharing and consideration, a quest against consumerism through selfishness, a quest against the comforting and reassuring certainty of *having*, in having not *enough*, but *too much*.

This very Saturday morning, I had lost any last bit of understanding I could have felt toward this 2.0 sort of 'waste,' and when I was furthermore faced to the unwillingness of my father to move his traditional nearing-closing-time grocery shopping to a mid-morning activity so that I could go with him, the lava had started to climb up, and it was a matter of minutes for it to explode.

Up it went when I saw him slowly opening his laptop to make an already-over-the-deadline bank transfer. Further up the lava went when I reminded him of my wish not to depart too late and head to the store, for I needed, indeed, to prepare the evening's dinner party that we were having, and despite it being small and *en petit comité* (just our grandmothers coming over), still, I wished to leave…well about now. Our organizational skills are as opposed as north and south, so here came the tears; they exploded from within. I felt helpless, and as I was unable to cope with the situation, so I rushed to Choupette, the little car that I use ever since my parents had decided to sell the white Fiat Punto that I liked so much but which would have been too expensive to maintain after nine years of loyal services to our family. This being established, I climbed in the car and behind the wheel I sat, uncertain and torn, nauseous at the thought of still being the *poète maudit*. Where to now? Where to?

The final destination of my car trip did not matter much to me, but I could not be on the run for too long. I suddenly realized that, sadly, I had nowhere to go, no way out. Perhaps I would head to the little grocery store then. I wanted to check for myself whether they had the special rice that I like to use for my paella dish. I had, indeed, promised my mother that I would prepare a paella when Oma and Mamiche would come over that evening. However, I did not find the Arroz La Fallera for my *paella valenciana*, and since I did not want to gear up back home, not just yet, I figured that I would buy some eggs too to surprise my sister still asleep when I had left, undisturbed by the morning volcano burst. At least she would be happy with a fried egg as a late breakfast. The storm was over when I parked the car back in front of our porch, because I knew my father was away by then…gone to the local supermarket. Without me, obviously. How ironical, perhaps even cynical. He had left only minutes after me. But, hush, for now. Hush. Let us forget about this, for there are things in life that will never change.

Drama Eruption

It is Sunday, and I woke up too early to my liking but at peace with my temporarily – although having already used this optimistic adjective for the last five years now – disruptive sleeping pattern. I was welcomed in the kitchen by two rows of five empty wine glasses, red and white, not forgetting the *coupes* of champagne, obviously. Unwashed. The green light of our dishwasher had probably just gone off, and some unused cutlery of our previous night's dinner party was left abandoned on the kitchen table. It looked to me as a battlefield of kitchenware.

I stored the first plates into the kitchen cabinet, making as little sound as possible, since both my parents and my sister were still sleeping. I took a deep breath and, feeling as empty and as fallen apart as the day before, I had decided that nothing today would trigger yet another lava eruption. I would try hard not to mind being reminded on a daily basis of the *petites habitudes* that I try to dust off the behavioral pattern of a great majority of people, starting with my father. Nor would I mind too much the food supplies that had been bought the day before, just enough to feed up a whole regiment of hungry soldiers.

I, therefore, solely focused my mind on adding some accessories to our breakfast table already set up. I took a soft-boiled egg out of the fridge for my mother so that it would not be too cold, the butter and *confiture* were out as well, and I checked on the gingerbread that I had made on Friday, making sure there was enough for my sister to fill her hungry or not-so-hungry mood of the day. There was. My grandmothers had only wished a tiny slice for dessert to go with their vanilla ice cream. Lastly, as I prepared my own oatmeal, weighing off the almond milk and cutting my grapefruit in bite-size chunks, I thanked the skies and life, for I felt blessed and loved, a little more than usual. How come then that one suffers so; that one feels as miserable and as hopeless as I do? Reality hits hard when one is reminded of the frailty of one's body, almost as if the lasting untamed and rebellious battalion were about to give up, but, then again…not just yet.

Stirring now and then in the sizzling oats, this time adding some water too because I like my breakfast to be mushy, that time adding bits of carob powder to flavor it all. Careful, I told myself. The oatmeal had almost burnt at the bottom of my pan. The truth is, my mind was already on the road to flashback last night when our grannies were over. It was just like the old saying, 'every cloud has a silver lining.' Yesterday, I had been shown evidence of its genuine authenticity. Or is it literary accuracy?

I wish not to recall into too many details the inner bombardment that went off the morning of our paella dinner party. I have moved on. However, despite the lava flows, and since I am a very reliable person, I had gone through with the meal preparations: chopping the white onions, preparing the saffron bags and heating the vegetable stock, crushing the cloves of garlic and peeling off some ripe tomatoes (six of them) as well as one red and one yellow bell pepper. As the day went on, I experienced mixed feelings toward my father; I did not know whether or not he had heard my point this time. It all seemed too soon, too easy to be true. He would not change his shopping behavior, and it was better to drop the issue because I do not have energy to spare.

Everything was about to change when my grandmothers arrived at 5:30 sharp that afternoon. The atmosphere was suddenly filled with love and care, memories and laughter, sweet and salty *mises en bouche* of the little *aperitif* that I had quickly improvised: crab toasts, mozzarella and olives, some cherry tomatoes with a fragrant basil leaf on top. It was all very simplistic, but where is the harm? While clinking our champagne flutes, the conversation took a Second-World-War turn, and both of my grandmothers ended up talking the whole evening about past memories of the *drôle de guerre*, as the conflict got to be referred to over here, in French-speaking lands.

From the pre-dinner drinks, we moved to the festive table that had been set up. I first came into the room with the hot seafood paella pan and let my mother in charge of serving the dishes, then came back with another, though smaller, pan, with the chicken version of this Spanish traditional plate that was being reserved especially for my sister whose seafood allergies I did not wish to awaken.

Once we were all seated (and eating), the story of little Cornell captured my senses, and I wish here to honor his soul. Sitting next to Oma, I listened with ears wide open and could sense the emotion in her eyes as she was recalling the story which I am about to ink black on white for history to be remembered forever. These are the lines as experienced by a little girl aged nine in the early '40s, when war had just broken out, on May tenth, 1940, to be precise. Here is how my *oma*, Jeanne, recounted it.

In Came... Cornell

Locked in an adjacent storage room, to the school's main entrance hall sat little Jeanne, stunned and unfathomed, punished by Sister Superior of the catholic nun school of Ruisbroek, a popular town on the outskirts of Brussels. She had been sent in isolation from her classmates in order to better reflect upon her sin, committed on her way to school that early winter morning of the year 1942, when the biting cold and damp air made her shiver to the bones. She had been walking to school with a boy her age from the same neighborhood, and since she was in good company, Jeanne did not fear the morning darkness. Back then, there were no streetlights, nor were there any lit houses on the 30-minute route to school. She would only trust her eyes, the same way a cat does in the darkness and guess her way through the still-narrow and obscure corridors that ran along the covered in frost maize and wheat fields.

Cornell was his name. The boy walking by her side, who noticed the cold that was harming little Jeanne's hands. "Put your hand in my pocket," he said naïvely. And so they walked, her hand in his coat's pocket until they arrived warm and sound for the eight o'clock start of classes, each in a different building. Harmless and innocent, or so we would believe these days, but in the '40s, they had just been found guilty of deep anti-Catholic sinning, at least in the nuns' opinion. They ought to be ashamed, punished even. Cornell was not their *affaire*; he was attending the community primary school for boys in another building. However, dear little Jeanne was to be summoned to appear before the court. Girl, what had you done!? Sister Superior could certainly not tolerate such transgression of the rule of God and so directly called the parents to the stand, her *bureau*, but to no avail, for they would not make the trip anyway, as Jeanne warned Madame Nun. Her insubordination cost her the deprivation of attending that day's classes and her being sent to a somber storage room with a tiny yet actual window out of which the little rascal swiftly and acrobatically climbed out, running home to her mother to confess her 'sin.'

No. This mischief would certainly not get the mother-at-home out of her daily chores and cooking. The girl's honesty and innocence were good enough a reason to trust her, especially since it was not the first time that little Jeanne ran home to get the unjust wickedness out of her heart, confessing to her parents. They were all ears to her cries and could only perceive a child's natural behavior in what the nuns had condemned and punished as open obsolescence and serious shortcoming, estranging the girl from God's path. She, rascal Jeanne, would undoubtedly go to hell, as professed by Sister Superior.

*

The paella plate half-full, I poured some more white wine in my *oma's* glass. Sitting right in front of her, was Mamiche, my father's mother and quite a character herself. Only after hearing such impiety, she herself argued that she had never heard such absurd a punishment being inflicted to a child. And by the nuns, what is more!

During dinner that night, I realized that my two grandmothers had grown up worlds apart. One was born into an honest working-class family, whereas the other one had clearly benefitted from a very bourgeois upbringing; her parents being famous and well-off traders from Hal, the 'city' as it was known back in those days, as opposed to the rural and popular town of Ruisbroek. Mamy, for instance, had never experienced cold while using the restroom, for even her grandparents had a toilet unit installed inside their house, *i.e.* one with a door and a water flush, a sink, and a bidet to add some comfort to the daily wash. Oma had, instead, been confronted with the freezing cold on her occasional night outings to the in-the-backyard-installed makeshift 'restroom,' if it might even be referred to as such. It was basically an open-air cubicle with a hole, topped with two wooden planks to place one's feet upon and a saloon door, resembling, indeed, the ones as pictured in genuine western movies or comically used as dressing rooms in vintage clothing shops. Sure enough, the parents would not let their children cross the yard in the middle of the night, especially not during (rough) winter times and certainly not when reminded of the war that was going on, a thudding, hitting silence whether it be day or night. Truth be told, at this point in the description, I shall confess that I did not dare ask about the use of toilet paper or chamber pots.

Moving from the saloon-like wooden restroom doors, my eyes were sparkling as I spotted the stapled pages of what seemed to be a diary, printed on thick, brown, recycled paper. The manuscript was gleaming onto the candle-lit dresser of our living room. I had, indeed, only just been handed the account of wartime stories by Mamy. Inside the blue-grayish carton folder was a chronological report of Mamy's family escape to France during the *drôle de guerre*. For two months, the family had left the bourgeoisie and their high-society lifestyle and had been taken care of by…well, rural people mostly, friends or relatives from clients of their *commerce* in Hal. And, so, even Many had experienced a little less comfort and splendor as her family was used to. Yet, they had the means to plan an escape outside of Belgium, which was never an option for little Jeanne's parents.

Memories, Past, and Present

Nowadays, this all seems surreal, especially as I am translating both my grandmothers' testimonies, one in Dutch, the other one in French, sitting legs crossed on the already-warm red-brick cobbles of the terrace, with only a small yet leafy laurel-like bush as sunshade. Sometimes, I even hear my next-door neighbors whining about the weather being too hot for this time of the year. Perhaps they are worried that their chickens, amongst which the famous queen Paola, might get sunburnt in their playground, for the yard had been transformed into a running-free terrain, reserving only a parcel or two for the vegetables to grow. A *potager* as they say in French, but believe me when I warn you not to eat the zucchini they harvest, for they are already twice the size of a ripe Halloween pumpkin. I am not fooled when it comes to cooking: the taste of the vegetables that my neighbors grow will be as bland as still water. Needless to say, neither will I buy any spare eggs from them.

It is a new day, and to my left, this early afternoon while on the terrace, I am delighted to welcome a second soccer ball that has joined the already and majestically installed pink one on the backyard bushes of my *other* neighbors. This one is of a bright yellow color with black spots and as synthetic a material as the ones children play with on the beach. Although I amuse myself with little things that I observe in my present-day surroundings, I also wish to give voice to memories of the past. This without risking, however, to lose my ability to write my own stories down for these times to be remembered too in the future.

So, for now, I am temporarily accepting the role of the storyteller, although bearing in mind that I ought to look for a project of my own…as soon as I can stand upon both feet without losing my balance too much. I still need crutches indeed, and the medical healing specialists are doing their best to untie this knot that inhibits any contact between the body and the mind, leaving the soul wandering about. Hence my wish to remember both the strength and determination of my ancestors, starting with their resolve to live freely and their struggle to reach France, somewhere in late May of the year 1940.

As I am about to unearth the secrets hidden in the recycled manuscript I had been handed over only this past Saturday, dozens of questions are suddenly invading my mind. I manage to say a little prayer in memory of Oma's father, Felix Ocula, a former combatant of the Great War, and one to remember Mamy's uncles who fought too against the *Boches* in the trenches, although, now, I am starting to wonder whether they had not been treated differently from the popular-class people that were called to the front, given their pertaining to high-society. I open up the blue-grayish folder, and inside is a letter dating back to Christmas of the year 2004, a letter that was addressed to one of Mamy's sisters, Fernande, the very one who was born near Jonzac, in France, when the Cornelis-Steens families were on the run.

In this letter, the late aunt tries to answer some of Fernande's questions regarding the circumstances of her birth. Said aunt, *Tante* Simone, remembers the May 1940 departure for the still-unoccupied French territory, a journey that would take the family from Normandy to the Charentes-Maritime department until they had reached a small village, the name of which she could not remember precisely.

The convoy would take the two families, all of Mamy's relatives (her father's side), over the Belgian frontier. Mamy was the second of an already-growing family that would soon reach a total of eight children, and Fernande (the fifth) was on her way, growing stronger by the day in the last month of Mamy's mother's pregnancy. Uncle Jean, one of the brothers of Mamy's father, Marcel, worked as an accountant for the Brasserie Pètre, a well-known brewery at the time. On May tenth, a Friday before Pentecost, there was unusual unrest at 5:30 a.m. The family woke up to hear the shootings nearing their city villa just outside Leuven, in Oud-Heverlee. Quickly, they had agreed to gather together in order to improvise an escape to France. It was better to leave while still hearing the firearms that were being shot, rather than witness the destruction they were about to bring.

The adults of the expedition would not leave, however, before securing their collection of wine bottles in the rainwater tank and seeing off Maurice who had been called to enroll the ranks of the Belgian Army. During the days following the German invasion, the family had witnessed the Belgian and Dutch governments' call for help from the English and French allies whose troops soon marched into the fields to protect the civil population from bombings. Some cities were already said to burn to ashes, forcing the locals to find shelter either by leaving their country, either by counting on a stranger's solidarity to welcome them into their homes. On May 15th, the Cornelis family reached the house of their closest relatives in Hal, and they all came quickly to an accord: start the engines of the Ford. They would be leaving that night.

They could not wait for too long, nor did they have the time to pack their personal belongings, only taking a bindle with the absolute minimum, perhaps a little more for Grande-Mamy, Maria Steens (Mamy's mother and my great-grandmother), who happened to be pregnant. Perhaps we might never know for sure whether the hasty leave was not, in fact, triggered by the sudden disappearance of their trusted midwife of the Hal clinic, Lady Marieke Stok. They had been told that she had fled earlier that month, leaving the family with no nearby hospital in case Grande-Mamy suffered from early contractions. Furthermore, they had heard that all medical personnel of the University Hospital of Leuven had gone on strike or were called away to the front, leaving the family no choice but to look for another hospital when little Fernande would be born. Hence, why not kill two birds with one stone (pardon the expression given the already-belligerent context) and escape to safer grounds? To France we go, then.

If that is a secret that will never be told, the Cornelis and Steens families did not hesitate anymore to switch their city *voiture* for the trunk of a truck that originally belonged to the Pètre brewery. It was an old Ford model of 1921, and all of them were struggling to find a comfortable position during their journey into unknown territory.

Their first halt *en route* was in the small Normandy village of Louviers where Grande-Mamy needed to rest, given her condition. The bourgeois families found refuge in a worker's house, the home of a widow. They stayed there for up to a month before continuing their driving deeper into the south. They were now approaching the village of Jonzac and decided to stop a somewhat four kilometers further down.

Upon their arrival, they would immediately take Grande-Mamy to a nearby hospital where Fernande would soon see the light of day. It was June 29th of the year 1940. Aunt Simone, part of the expedition, usually did not leave Grande-Mamy's bedside; she would only slip through the door in order to get some groceries from the *petit épicier* at the corner of the street. In her last letter, dated 2004, she recalls lending a bicycle from the next-door farmer, a woman she says. The periodicity of their shopping being frequent, the grocer suggested to take the ladies, both Aunt Simone and Aunt Germaine to see Grande-Mamy and to take her to their house for a couple of days or until she recovered from childbirth. Their staying did not last long however. When Fernande was only 14 days old, the Cornelis-Steens organized the journey back home, but, this time, by taking the train.

In the letter, Aunt Simone refers to their social status and to a thick envelope of money as well – the exact sum she did not wish to tell. They were, thus, all able to board the train wagon and were even amongst the first runaways to be heading back to their Belgian homes, although quite unsure and afraid of how destroyed or vandalized they might find it. She signed the letter with her own trembling hand, hoping she had provided Fernande with some answers to her questions and also wondering when her niece would grant her a visit during her next trip to Belgium. Fernande would, indeed, depart for another country, this time out of love, for she was destined to marry an Italian school principal and settle in a small-but-magnificent flat, a couple of footsteps from the *Città Alta* of Bergamo, in Northern Italy.

Reaching Out

The Cornelis having found shelter in a widow's dwelling in Louviers and them being lent a bicycle by a farmer's wife near Jonzac are only two illustrations of genuine solidarity. These are proof of the capacity of mankind to reach out regardless the differences there might be in their social statuses. It is, therefore, hard to envisage that, in times of war, social conducts and codes still might apply. Reaching out to those in need ought not to be some sort of regulation that one abides to under exceptional circumstances; instead, it should be a pure and genuine act of kindness.

Unfortunately, scores of examples of camaraderie thought to be exceptional in their nature or in their uniqueness (or ease) to be followed by the people of the world do not last long in time, especially when a semblance of accord or armistice hides just round the corner, leaving the actors to forget about the continuity of their good-heartedness. I wonder how or when we, all people, have become so self-centered, coming closer to the characteristics that are so commonly attributed to robots. It seems to me that too many of us are so busy with their daily, unquestioned routine or busy, trying to keep up appearances and sheep-follow the social conducts that they believe are pressed upon them, unaware of the danger that lures them into a trap until they have completely zipped up their souls from any emotion, any feeling, in short, any humanity.

I wish, however, not to draw too dark a picture of our human condition and ought to highlight the many hearts that have, indeed, reached out; they who helped and saved their peers in past or present times. Whether intrinsic to the members of the resistance in the Second World War or to all the other Cornell sweethearts walking about on the surface of the Earth, genuine benevolence and faith are as infinite a treasure to possess as the comforting and empathetic sparkle that I wish to spot in the eye of our neighbor, the *everyones* of this world.

Two nights have passed since the paella dinner took our family down memory lane. The pink soccer ball and its recent yellow companion still lay on top of the red Photinia shrubs in our backyard and an already-spring sunray is making my cheek blush. I am, again, sitting behind our open-curtain, large window pane, feeling the warmth invade my soul. The sky is as tranquil as ever, a deep blue color today, one that almost covers the white fluffs hanging here and there, disturbed only by the sound of a flying-yet-invisible-to-my-eyes helicopter.

Only days are left before the start of March, and I try not to flood too many interrogations into my already-encumbered and disillusioned mind. My wandering shadow remains, until this day, sheltered somewhere far into the fog and darkness of the woods, still unfound or avoiding to be, probably hollow, fearful, and shaken. My mind, however, challenges me constantly with not an intermittent but an incessant thinking process. It does not seem to stop spinning; turning in every direction, from the least meaningful detail to the utmost philosophical questionings of which I find myself the subject of.

I now hear the first gardeners trimming the hedges somewhere not so far away in the neighborhood, although not directly next door, in order for the properties to look neat and green and as ready as ever they will be, surely for the vegetation to better grow and blossom in the spring. As nature is starting to get ready for a new season, I wonder how we, as humans, can best prepare ourselves to embracing change. How does one find the sparkle that will eventually unlock the path, perhaps one that is buried too deep for him to find or one that is yet too soon for him to progress on and to grow as a person?

Nevertheless, I do not regret my blindly following the path that *I* thought was rolled out for me, *i.e.* a perfect schooling and academic background a 'perfect everything' that was achieved through endless hard working, inevitably bound to drive me sooner or later into the superficial shadow of my own existence, I must confess. Yet, I now spin, helplessly and uncontrollably, to the rhythm of my own misreading. How come that I cannot dispose of the blinders that I myself seem to have locked onto my eyes and which now prevent me from breaking free and walking to the light? Never lose faith, some say, but there are times that I simply wish to reply: faith also needs a little push, even if just a little sign.

Benevolent Mindfulness

My weekly visit to the therapist's turned into a heart-to-heart. As soon as I took off my military-green parka (obviously too cold for the season's temperatures, despite everyone saying it is surprisingly warm for this time of the year), I felt the tears already running onto my cheeks. There was no stopping them. I had not yet seated myself on the wicker bench that I sensed her compassion at seeing me so destructed, crushed even, disillusioned and helpless. No more. I said, no more. I cannot bear it anymore; the thoughts, the pressure, this tension knot that I feel is invading my brain incessantly. Sometimes, I wonder how my skull does not break under all this tension it has come to host unwillingly for the last couple of years.

Breakable. That is how I have been feeling for quite some time. Getting out of the car was not without effort, and I even struggled to climb the L-shaped wooden staircase leading to the front door of the therapist's. It was chilly at first, in the waiting room. Fortunately, I was quickly reassured when I heard the rhythm of the ankle-heel boots that my therapist wore that day. Clickety clack. This meant that she was soon about to open the door and lead me to the upstairs mezzanine where we would chat. I was only minutes away of freeing my heart and soul.

But am I really free? Am I? We have grown accustomed to the idea of freedom as it is defined in social or political contexts. However, not once have I pondered whether I had indeed freed my body, myself, my soul from the despotic and torturous rule of the mind. Or worse, had I really been free at any moment?

Although I remain rather insecure and unconfident about finding a genuine and comforting answer to these serious interrogations in the nearby future (why, let's hope so), I will, however, take the needed time to halt. So far, I have realized that I could no longer erase myself to such an extent; nor could I hide away from finding the peace that would eventually free my heart and bring comfort to my soul.

It was only yesterday that I wrote about my wish to see any sign, no matter how great or small. On walking into the living room this morning, I opened up the Venetian blinds only to discover that, in the flowerbed next to the window pane, on the outside terrace, there was a single yet beautiful, golden-yellow crocus growing savagely, undisturbed, and well-determinately in the middle of a heather plant. How daring. Yet, I admired the very wonder of nature, for the only crocuses we have been able to spot are growing further up in our backyard, meters away from this apparently alien species burgeoning out of adversity. I welcomed its uniqueness and its bravura. Clearly, this was a sign, meant for me.

The blossoming of this saffron-like-colored species came as a surprise into the otherwise-predictable morning stirring of my oatmeal. I had thus been blessed with a sign which I believe came directly to address my recent despair and sorrow. I will too, one day and probably when I least expect it, open up and free my body and my soul. I too will find the strength to overcome adversity and to grow regardless of the troubled marshland in order to blossom and spread the light. I too will find that sparkle. Eventually. Though, right now, I am in desperate need of strength and rest to better catch the magic of life when it finally sprinkles upon my way.

Present. The here and now. I need to forgive myself, my body; I need to sign an armistice and free my soul. Although I am fully conscious of the theoretical precepts, the guidance, and the advice that I am taught or given on a daily basis, I still tussle with the putting into practice of these founding principles. I also ought to make peace with the present. I understand very well that it is I and only I who hold the key to unlock the doors to a semblance of *entente cordiale* between mind and body; I myself hold the key, and only I must ask for forgiveness toward myself. In an attempt to be the 'perfect everything,' I have indeed completely effaced the sole person fighting for its existence, recognition, becoming, and deserving. Fortunately, just when I had thought that my inner light was about to go off forever, a little voice managed out a whisper: not in this present yet. You shall rise again.

Over the years, I had isolated myself from the *everyones* and *everythings* that I believed would or could harm me at some point. I was only focused on my working even more, my pausing getting scarcer, my effacement growing higher while my empathy and benevolence were reaching new levels of philanthropy. I had indeed nurtured this need to reach out to *others*, making sure that I most certainly did not reach out to my fragile soul which I had left deserted and eventually that I had come to ignore.

The present-day 'me' needs thus to find the sparkle that will stitch the heart, the body, and the soul; the three of them having suffered the disastrous consequences under the dictatorship of the mind. Therefore, self-love and benevolent mindfulness toward myself are the only sewing threads that can close up the wounds and heal the suffering. The scars, however, will last forever, but only by being scarred is one forced to pause to admire present awareness and time, sweeping away the sorrows of the past and blowing away the anticipations of the future. I have been wounded in the past; I am now suffering from these pains at this present moment, and I will be left scarred forever. Yet, only this present is mine, and in it I shall shine, find peace and heal with the strength regained and the love reconquered. I am the present, and in it I shall learn to live just as the yellow crocus has grown out of adversity.

*

The unavoidable freezing into the present of a burnt-out body, of a wandering, erased self, and a disillusioned soul is a painful, open wound that only time will finally heal. The mind, however, will still busy itself, for it is militarily trained to keep track of scores of interrogations and will not hesitate to let more-existential questions flood in. This sudden paralysis of the body renders me completely powerless and at my mind's mercy. I have grown accustomed to the increasing yet unfair sense of solitude that I experience, especially when being reminded of or when witnessing the lives as led by the surrounding *everyones* I meet, listen to, or read about (social media does play a significant role).

Gratitude, I believe, prevents many anxiety symptoms and can, therefore, be reassuring, especially to fear-frozen souls like mine. I find that being grateful soothes the fears that are buried deep within our hearts. It also rocks us, as does the sound of a comforting lullaby. Lastly, it encourages a thankful prayer that our loved ones are safe and sound from the very demons that our own body has tried so hard to annihilate in combat; they, at least, are not chased after. The warzone, however, is too wide and too deep for a sole soldier to march. We so ingenuously believed that the warm and golden sands would shape our future path, letting us shine along the way; but in fact, it now merely resembles a field of darkened and hardened ashes, and is as upsetting and unfortunate evidence of the self-inflicted damage we have done to our body as the chill and silence that are felt and (un)heard after a storm. The ravage is beyond control.

Nonetheless, I cannot help but hope that I will soon catch a glimpse of the ember that was left somewhere hidden in this dreadful and saddening canvas. I now see the remains of the fire that has consumed my body and the same one which had sent myself into the woods, seeking shelter, and that had precipitated my soul into forbidden foreign territory, one that is still inaccessible to me unless I know the key that would unlock the door without too much pain to be released. Neither my body nor my soul can handle a second turning.

I so wish that the day I reach the ember would near. The body has been dragging this shutdown for what seems like forever while the heart has been crying silently these last few months, and the soul battling its own hopelessness, sorrow, incomprehension, and despair. I have been roaming in a desert so long so that I sometimes catch myself thinking that I'd better close my eyes and surrender instead of crawling to the ember in the hope to catch a leftover sparkle.

Vulnerability, Perhaps a Key

Wind and rain violently hit our outside windows recently cleaned by my mother (poor she). They do, however, fail to blow away the thick layers of interrogations and apprehensions that coat the atmosphere, nor do they silence the fear or relieve the sorrow one feels. Wind and rain have, instead, come to represent what has been keeping me buried well into the depths of my rabbit hole where I have found it more reassuring to maintain this status-quo-routine existence in order to protect myself from any harm, rather than embracing change and giving a chance to future wonders to walk along my side.

From past experiences, I have learned benevolence and compassion, and I honor my duty to protect the *everyones* that I meet and care about and protect them from the potholes that I myself have come across my path. I am determined to achieve this goal and will forever find the strength in order to prevent everyone in general from suffering from the pains that I went through, from the wounds that I live by. Day after day. Many a man have taken advantage of my hard working (whether at school or at university), but even more hurtful for me was the stealing and the barefaced violation of my vulnerability. They all knew that I could never say no. And the worst part was that I felt I was obliged to them. I was guilty of my own emotional abuse, for I could not stand letting people down. So I said yes. Always. Until the body got the final say.

I have, indeed, always wanted to reach out to everyone until, unfortunately enough, I had only best succeeded at completely erasing my own person, myself, and to be honest, I have still no clue where to start looking. I am deeply saddened at the thought that I cannot seem to find my path – even though I do realize I might not be the only one in this case. I often catch myself halfway in my request to be given a sign, and signs do appear, they do, but I fail to interpret most of them, or so it seems.

While waiting, I sharpen my pencil and begin to write, for words might one day translate into signs of renaissance and indulgence toward others at first (obviously). Most importantly, however, I shall have to learn how to listen with a kind ear to my inner voice whispering: do not give up now. Not until love has found its way to your soul. If not for me, then the least I could do is owing this renewal to the body that I have nearly deposed, that I have fragilized by the missed coup.

Writing is liberating, indeed, but it also consumes the few strengths that I have from the encouragements I receive from family and a handful of friends. *Peu importe!* I hear myself say. It is my wish to echo the sounds of the unyielding soldier marching its way through the end of the battlefield. What brings me comfort day after day and fight after fight is that, one day, I too will hear the drums giving rhythm to past wounds in order for them to proudly and forever soothe the aching scars. This, in short, is what I am going through. And no matter how much or how little I prepare myself to hear a drummer boy in the background, my body still does not listen for long, and I find myself lost again. I really am. Although, being the perfect student in understanding all the theoretical precepts and the need to change from within, I simply have not found the key note that will help me practice in the symphony of life.

Patience, therefore, is a virtue, and there is a reason why I was halted at this point in my life, on December 14 of the year 2017. I could not go on like this forever or else I would have witnessed my own life passing by, with my shadow standing right on the pavement, looking haggard and not really living.

I need to change; my own behavior, the way I see things… But nor do I want to change too much. I want to keep the kind heart, the benevolent traits, the reaching out to others, the compassion, and the caring. I just need to figure out how to save a little time for 'me,' that other person that exists and wishes to be freed yet remains unheard and forgotten about, especially by herself. Hear me, please. As for the body… I shall admit that it asks for some kind of forgiveness.

Perhaps I am still too guilty or too ashamed to acknowledge the *coups* that the body has endured under my dictatorship. However, this burnout experience has now opened up my eyes, and I am deeply convinced that, sometimes, there is no harm in being vulnerable. None at all actually, because, in the end, I have learned over the last couple of months that one will never regret something for trying; one merely mourns the things that he or she hasn't had the courage to try. Showing our vulnerability and perhaps opening some wounds of the past in the process helps us to heal the suffering and to accept our scars a little more. The aim, though, is to bear them proudly without feeling even an inch of embarrassment.

Therefore, one shall not mourn the past, and I will make peace with my trying. For the last couple of years, and the many years before, I have tried to climb a ladder that was not mine to mount, and having experienced the view from the top, I suddenly fell off, only to discover that I really needed to climb a different ladder. Instead of the perfect academic and professional career, I had to face a tougher mountain this time, one that would enable me to grow as a person and experience love toward myself, acceptance of my body and compassion for it in my mind.

One deserves every step to be filled with golden-yellow crocuses, surprises, joys, first-light sunrays, and new things to discover. I am, from this present on, starting to realize that by accepting our vulnerability, we protect ourselves from a despotic rule of the mind that would send us back to our comforting and reassuring, workaholic lifestyle. But no. Not us, not me. Not anymore. Our vulnerability enables us to welcome the love and the confidence that we had been missing for too long; to welcome wonder again into our lives to laugh genuinely; to let our sorrow be consoled by *peu importe* who's sitting next to us; to trust again, although I am not quite there yet. Quite, mind you. Honestly, I still have a long way to go.

So, to all the people of the world, please do take care of yourselves. Really, I seem not to have a clue of how to take care of my own self, at least for now, and that is why I cling so much to taking care of others. I want to warn you about a person's strength of mind, despite the frailty of the body, for it can train its subject to almost self-destruction, to what I coin 'shadowiness.' Do not tempt it. Stay clear and celebrate the love and compassion toward yourself, your soul, your life. Tonight, I shall look up to the skies, knowing that there is a star shining for all of us to find our path. And I strongly believe that when that star be found, we will appreciate even more its sparkling, for it will illuminate both our days and nights, always and forever.

A Dinner Party

Sunday. Waking up this morning to the sound of a fierce wind banging onto the window pane made me appreciate even more the warmth and comfort under the sheets. The turning over onto my right flank welcomed the extra softness of the woolen orange blanket, the corner of which caressing the back of my neck. For only a second, I almost forgot to stretch out my arm to light up the screen of my phone, to check what time it was. I had a feeling that it was past dawn already, for I could hear that the streets were already too animated, the cars already passing by. We may consider ourselves lucky that we live a little off the main road. We only need to worry about the early cock-a-doodle doo from the neighbor's rooster.

Seven sharp. I am an hour late, perhaps more if I look back only a couple of months from now. I do not remember opening my eyes so late a time in the morning. I have always been an early bird, joining the chorus of the outdoor chirping when the sun is still too shy to come out. And, yet, the cold air of the bedroom is hitting my bare forearm, which reminds me quickly that I would better hide back again under the covers, safe and warm, even if just to disappear during the blink of an eye into the *One Thousand and One Nights*, the stories told by the me-version of Scheherazade.

These were the 60 seconds of fair and earned quietude that I have experienced at dawn, reflecting upon the previous night's dinner party which had printed lasting memories. The day before, a Saturday, I was a little anxious, for I thought my uncle and his family did not remember the invitation, the date and hour of which had been settled about well a month before. It was five to six that evening, and the sausage rolls had already been out of the oven for about ten minutes. Relieved was I when I finally heard the doorbell ring. Here they are, I shouted from the kitchen, still wearing my pink and flowery apron.

Ever since we were little, my sister and I have had a very special relationship with *Nonkel Join*, one of my mother's two brothers. We grew up with regular family gatherings; we always threw parties for the New Year's, for the Easter celebration, culminating with the summer traditional barbecue and ending with the All Saints Day's coming together. These parties were

196

always held in a different home, switching from one of my mother's three siblings to another. On my mother's side (Oma's), we were three girls and six boys amongst the grandchildren. The eldest was my niece, and my sister and I were the only 'little' girls left, numbers eight and six respectively on the children ladder, hence our being protected by the 'grownups.' The rest of the cousins were 'the boys.' My sister and I looked up to our nephews, sometimes not understanding their conversations or the thrill they experienced when all of them were gathered in the basement playing Ping-Pong. These tournaments would last to what seemed to us, girls, forever a time, so we preferred staying upstairs, next to the youngest of our cousins, drawing or playing with whomever amongst the grownups had volunteered to busy us for a while. All this to say that we have always had a very strong and close bond within my mother's family.

Within the 'grownup gang,' our uncle was the one who made us laugh so hard that we lost track of time. It was him who made us feel that those dinner parties would always end too soon, for he would still be admiring our polished nails well after dessert was served, or the new and *chic* outfit we had just received for the occasion. Nonkel Join was the 'fun uncle,' the one who would take us on his lap and play horse riding or who would lift us up and let us airplane-fly into his arms. He, the superman uncle, was the one who would come over for dinner, that Saturday night, and he was, truth be told, a little *en retard*.

I had already promised my mother that I would make the meat *ragù* on Friday, the day before the party, in order for the flavors to soak well into the Italian mix of meat, tomatoes, and vegetables. However, my recipe failed to meet all the characteristics listed in the official (and therefore traditional) ragù sauce (please do not say 'Bolognese sauce') of the Academia della Cucina Italiana. It would need additional pancetta to the mixture in order to qualify for authenticity. Moreover, I had secretly added a bay leaf or two…three even, only to enhance the tomato-ish flavor, but *hush*! That is definitely a violation to the authentic recipe. No one needs to know.

The homemade sauce having been prepared the day before, I would only need to oven-grill some *melanzane* or eggplants the Saturday morning, with a drizzle of olive oil and pepper (no salt). Finally, time had come for the *assemblage* to begin! A couple of lasagna sheets and some layers of sauce after, my heart was pounding from joy at the thought of the well-organized and on-time schedule of the day. The to-do list was almost all green-colored checked.

In the afternoon after lunch, I felt my throat thickening and my heart pounding. I dreaded the repercussions such dinner party would have on my body, on my sleeping, on my mind. It might seem all too exaggerated (or let us just say 'plain weird') to sense fear and discomfort invade one's body and take possession of the mind, overflooding it with thoughts and interrogations, anguish and panic. We had not hosted any dinner parties for the last year, save a couple of gatherings with our grandmothers, when they came over after a holiday or for birthdays. However, not once had we invited someone over, at least not since the day I crumbled to pieces in December, now a little more than a year ago. I thus prayed for my body to be lenient, forgiving; I prayed so that it would let me enjoy even if just a tad the important and well-longed-to company of this Saturday night (fever).

Fortunately and quite unexpectedly, my wish had been heard, and I had enjoyed the whole evening, not feeling this burnout preventing my every move. However, I shall be honest and confess that I did suffer from a headache when I hid under the sheets of my canopy bed somewhat too late that night. It did not matter much at this point in the evening to me, for we had already waved goodbye to our uncle and his family who were riding out of the front porch and disappearing into the streetlights' yellowness to find the way back to their home. It was one hour closer to midnight, and I could already find comfort into the woolen blanket I had vanished into. I whispered a yawning, then a peaceful 'thank you,' for it was the first dinner party that I had felt 'normal' again, not feeling any pressure from other people's gaze.

Never shall I forget the seven of us being gathered together around our living-room table, savoring the last droplets of lasagna sauce that were left on our plates. I shall remember, too, the laughing; a mixture of Tuscany past-vacation memories and future plans to buy a restored country house with a vineyard, somewhere into the hills of Cortona or Greve in Chianti; the exact location open to discussion, for 'the grownups' had not decided yet which *cépage* they would prefer for their grapes. Sold. I was, indeed, sold. Nothing could take this memory away, ever, for it was anchored well into the depths of my soul, only to be freed when in need of a little extra comfort and love; only when in need of something to hold onto when the giving-up blues would knock again on my mind's door.

Cycles

The teak side-table stands soaked wet next to the two sun loungers on the terrace, leaving only a puddle of rain mirroring the cloudy and gloomy sky. The morning breeze slowly blows away the gray pieces of fluff hanging in the sky, as if it were a contest to sort out which would be stronger to block the sun and thus letting a stain in this pale-blue shyness of a landscape. I wonder whether this too is a trick of fate; a reminder that even the early spring temperatures that we had experienced only a week ago – allowing us to get rid of our woolen jumpers and socks while bathing onto the sun-side terrace – are nothing but an ephemeral souvenir of short-lived peace and tranquility.

The naked hedges, the abandoned branches over the grasses on the lawn, or the battered watering can that had been knocked over by the last two nights' stormy weather are all proof of the parallel between the cycles that govern both nature and mankind. Whether it be called hibernation, pause or distress – the latter concerning especially the many of us who are suffering from all sorts of aches and ailments – this parenthesis between closure and blossoming, between halting and thriving, is core to nature's renaissance as well as man's newfound soul. The only difference perhaps lying into the almost perfectly scheduled spring and summer interludes, whereas I have been waiting for the last 26 years for a lotus flower to overcome adversity and for the petals to start opening… I wish spring would start for me as well.

This involuntary yet compulsory coming to a halt has nonetheless exposed the many fears, doubts, and questions that have inhibited the flowers to paint my landscape color bright. I will tell you the story of a little girl who had been focusing all her attention and strength to her growing up to be a responsible and intelligent young lady, but whom, alas, had spent all these years locked into a prison of her own making. She had effaced herself from the outside world and buried her soul deep inside, leaving her body to its own devices, until devices there were no more. She had grown accustomed to pressuring herself in the pleasing of the *everyones* around her, making sure to never fail anyone or anything, hence being the perfect *everything* that would, at last, wander lost into the oblivion of her soul. How then was she to break that cycle that was preventing her from rising from the still-burning ashes? When would she break free and hear her own voice? How far would her inner light spread the spark that had been secretly buried deep inside? When would she live? Did she know how? Could she learn?

This girl desperately needs scissors to break the spell. This state of enchantment had not been dictated by fate, nor was it the result of any punishment for any sin whatsoever. Instead, she had deeply rooted these *traits de caractère* into her behavior and even deeper into her heart and soul. Although her humanity was noble and laudable, it was also very destructive to her own blossoming and living. This girl utterly convinced herself into knitting what seemed to others the perfect life, yet failed to prevent the needles from being tangled. That was, until the woolen ball of her own creation had started to suffocate her soul, leaving the body crumpled and the soul unheard and ignored. Scissors now she needed most, if not to untie her from her knitting, then perhaps to hear the snap that will ignite the living.

Ashes

Repent and believe will be my first set of keys to open Lent. Today, I shall, indeed, receive ashes not as a symbol of penance, rather as a visible sign for grief. Although the blessed dust will not be distributed by a priest or a pastor given my shut-indoors case, I will still welcome prayer and faith; I shall ask for forgiveness to my body, but most especially to my soul. On this Wednesday, 46 days exactly remain before the Easter celebration. Today, mankind is reminded about humility and sacrifice, and we are all invited to embrace the power of reflection and mercy.

For the last several years, I have almost burned myself up. I have seen dust from up close, and it is from these burning ashes that I shall find the wick to light up the candle and spread the light from within out again. I shall rise and spread the spark that has been imprisoned for too long. I wonder, though, if it had even gotten the chance even just once to find if just a slight passage to shine in past years. Sorry. Truly, deeply sorry I am.

I seek forgiveness because the woolen ball that I have been knitting so perfectly and candidly did also prove to be the best weapon to encourage the *coup* toward my own body and self. The irony is that one does not need the outside world to order his or her soldiers to march toward the victory of a near self-destruction. I do repent the knitting of this ball into which I am now suffocating, yet I need to undo the threads myself in order to reach the purest kind of wool, and then only shall I find a semblance of comfort in my heart as well as benevolence for my soul.

However, I also believe that I have been blessed, for this compulsory standstill will only last for an interlude of time before I will be opening up and blossoming genuinely. Upon repentance and belief shall I step forward onto the path for enlightenment and growth.

Whether this year or next (or any as a matter of fact), Ash Wednesday will always remind me of Madame Josiane, my primary-school religion teacher. I can still see my eight-year-old self sitting on a school bench that had been displayed in a U shape that would allow the teacher to see us all and to welcome a certain fearlessness or openness into our conversations. Madame Josiane liked to stand center-stage and encouraged her pupils to speak out, to listen and to be heard, yet insisting on values such as respect and politeness. Although Madame Josiane did not interpret the Gospel with the same distance as our Church priest, Père Ignace, she could instill the Catholic principles in our hearts, and only later would we know the true meaning of her words; only when growing up would we recall her teaching and her guidance. And if I were to choose one memory I wish to cherish most, as if to honor her classes, I would undoubtedly pick chocolate. Yes, you read this right, chocolate. It was she who made all her 28 pupils believe that from Ash Wednesday on, all of us had to give up chocolate as a symbol of fasting, a sign to open Lent and to wait for Easter to celebrate renaissance and, let us all be honest here, stock up on (and indulge in) the well-deserved and long-awaited-for Easter eggs, whether milk, dark, or even the not-so-fancy *praliné noisette*, all would do to feed the most *gourmands* among us. Only let us forget about the liqueur-filled chocolate eggs; they are only part of the Easter-basket décor in order to be given later to our grandmothers, for their sweet tooth also deserves a treat or two!

Time in a Jar

The chocolate eggs and Easter bunnies have made their majestic entrance in shops big or small, invading the décor and making sure to guarantee quite a peculiar contrast whether they are being displayed between the fruit and vegetables on special offer this week or between the half-off fish fillets. The latter would have been on display for too long a time, and, now, the shopkeeper is hoping to sell them to I don't know whom. The worst thing that could happen would be for the buyer to refreeze these fillets after purchasing them, 'to keep them fresh' or so he would like to think. I will just pray for this not to happen. Store-bought fish is seldom 'fresh,' in the sense that it has usually already been frozen before, and I would certainly not recommend to anyone to refreeze (without cooking) any sort of foods that have previously been frozen. This matter being clear, I find myself in the different sections of the store, walking past this combination of tastes either too sweet or too sour (the fish, again, please!). I wonder whether it is not too soon a time for the Easter treats to be on sale, although I shall admit that I would like to stock up on a jar or two in order for all of us to find some sweetness in our lives, so that we can come at peace, close our eyes, and breathe.

Far from being a meditation guru or a yoga gymnast (maybe I ought to), I sometimes wish that time would come up wrapped in containers or jars from all shapes and sizes. I would buy time for the people of the world to reach out to their fellow citizens, their peers, their friends. In our 'fast and furious' society, time has too often served as an excuse for not engaging into a collaborative or participative structure of society. Well, time or fear, pick one, for fear is also to blame. The latter often causes a stir in (political or community) discussions about solidarity and assistance.

Therefore, I would be willing to buy us some time, although not before checking its own kind of nutritional facts. On the back of the jar, I would be pleased to read that time is made out of love, respect, tolerance, freedom, solidarity, relief, compassion, benevolence; ingredients to which I would add a drizzle of joy, genuine smiles, and sprinkles of both earnest – and fairness of its recipients. Time in a jar would absolutely not include self-interest, egotism, violence, malice, or any other additive that would only spoil its authenticity, falsify the laudable intentions both of the seller and buyer, and destroy our own good nature and kindhearted sharing.

From the early stages of life, we have been drilled for speed whether at school – mixed together with an undeniable fierce competition between learners, pupils, and students – or in any other environment that we find ourselves driven into: at the gym, when we go grocery shopping, when we are traveling, when…everything. We hasten ourselves out of fear of running out of time. Hence the inevitable potato chips that goes down the wrong way, it getting stuck in the middle of our throat and eventually making the unfortunate victim cough so hard that aside from blushing, now ends up crying too. Cheers to puffy eyes afterward.

Instead of near-death by chocking, why not teach the benefits of time? Hasty decision-making, impulsive behavior, lessening of panic and heart attacks, plummeting of stomach ulcers and spasms are only a few examples of the importance of pausing, even if just to close your eyes. One might as well breathe in and let the oxygen freshen up one's thoughts. And breathe out again.

The adding of a time dimension to even the simplest of actions opens up a whole new sense of freedom; it offers a most singular and exceptional perspective from which to paint one's landscape of life. It uses only the most precious mosaic to make for an unprecedented patchwork. For instance, while walking briskly to work, many of us are often busy checking the time almost every minute or two. We tend to keep our eyes on our feet moving on the pavement, somewhat absent-mindedly, and realizing too late a time that we had better avoided the half-a-sandwich leftovers we came across half-crushed and soaked in last night's rainy storm. Adding a time perspective, that same person would most certainly 'walk' to work, yet, instead of looking face downward, he would lift his eyes up and contemplate hither and thither, the little things, trivial perhaps to some, but worthy of interest, only waiting for somebody to notice him and appreciate their being part of the scenery and their role in sustaining the mere act of pausing. Break. Break free from the society-instilled brisk walking and engage into the observing and the contemplating each step of the way.

International Women's Day 2019

Early dawn will paint the sky rosy wild and will make you shine throughout this day all sunny and bright. Forget to look downward and lift your head up high instead. Let your spirit admire and contemplate the little things while your soul catches you smiling for even the slightest nothings and unknowns. Today is March eighth, and as you breathe in, you shall remember that on this International Women's Day, you shall be empowered with a source of adrenaline and a gorgeous-yet-ingenuous smile. Spread your spark and reveal your true self. Do not hesitate. You can always find a way later to let your eyes wander about the stars. Until then, the star itself will guide you and will shine its light and magic upon your person. I have faith. So do you. Yes, you do. Happy Blossoming to you all.

Mind

A peaceful and comforting bamboo-flute Asian music is playing somewhere in the background, although being spasmodically interrupted by the ever-coming-back advertisement for yet another online pharmacy's cosmetics or medicines. My now five-year-old computer renders the mouse clicks slow, and it takes more than several seconds to switch screens and press 'ignore' the ad. Perhaps the computer is not to blame; I suddenly realize that it is my mind that has become slow in motion. I'd better get my reflexes checked up. Never mind, I tell myself. Back to relaxation with meditation, calming and soothing sounds of nature. It was bamboo flute, actually. Perhaps I ought to get my brain scanned.

I wonder, sometimes, whether I share the same traits as panda Po's when he is taught by Master Oogway that the "mind is like this water; when it is agitated, it becomes difficult to see. But if you allow it to settle, the answer becomes clear."

My mind is still wrestling, hence how can I expect it to benefit from the 'time dimension' I most dearly and sincerely wish everyone to find? I might consider the need to take a lesson or two of T'ai chi ch'üan, long for tai chi, the Chinese martial art with which we are confronted when watching the *Kung Fu Panda* movies. Even though I have no intention whatsoever to participate in this elaborate training, I do believe, however, in the power of these exercises and in the physical techniques taught by traditional masters in order to improve both the mind and the body's functioning. I wish I could find the strength that I know is buried deep within myself to reach the same levels of focus and calmness that panda Po has ultimately found after his many ups and downs. Key to the philosophical cultivation of inner strength is, I believe, benevolence in its purest form, straight from the heart.

Yet, in order to care for the *everyones*, one shall first need to take care of his or her own body and free his/her mind of the violent storms ravaging the soul and crushing his/her ability to listen to the heart's own crying. Tai chi is said to fill up and cover the potholes left by stress on both the body and the mind in order for the path to be rendered even and smooth.

Unfortunately, as I look at my trembling fingers struggling to keep up pace with the words storming out of my head (for there is, indeed, so much left to tell), I believe I shall first attempt to hush the never-ending flow of fears and thoughts that have cooled the waters too deep from within, preventing warmth and light from sailing in. The time has come to allow some benevolence toward myself.

Disruption

The first buds are sprouting up on this stormy Sunday morning of March. I wonder how they still manage to hang onto the branches of the trees and how they keep their pinky-rosy *fond de teint* so blushing alive, although being swept from left to right at a hundred or more per blowing wind. A cat troika is playing out there in the flowerbeds of our yard, and I can already hear my mother's irritation for the damage and disorder of their 'scrubbing' in the lavenders Or was it in the blackcurrant bushes? No sooner had she grimaced than the dark-and-white-spotted cow-looking cat had disappeared under the bushes and into its safe haven. The coward. Or better said, what a pussy.

The stormy weather brought on more wind and rain throughout the whole day, culminating well into the afternoon as rain and hail seemed to match the newfound equilibrium of the skies. Such violence or nature's tantrum swept most living creatures off the ground as well as the unfortunate and obsolete objects that one randomly leaves behind in the yard during the winter months, only to discover them back, covered in moss, when spring knocks on the door. Branches had, by now, been flowing hither and tither, the pink and yellow soccer balls had been dethroned at last, yet the lovebirds, a couple of pigeons really, seemed not too disturbed in their cooing. Why would they? I admire and respect their poise, the elegance of their crossing the neighbor's rooftop as if entrenched in the slate. I cannot think of any other reason than their own conviction that the storm will pass eventually, although not as quickly as it had shaken us out of bed early at dawn.

Even so, waking up in the middle of a storm, only to wander further into a tempestuous painting of nature's own *chef d'œuvre*, is a trick of the artist in his attempt to add a brand new and original mix of colors on his palette, with great care, that is. Some painters will certainly need a little more time in their trial-and-error sketching in order to find the matching color that lightens up the portrait that he has been working on for as long as his footsteps have marched in and out of his *atelier*. Others, on the contrary, are content with very little. It is possible that most people are, indeed, satisfied with the standard palette and that these are comfortable in the conventional uses of the pencil. They would further argue that it brings them the reassurance and self-confidence they seek: it prevents them from overthinking and micro/macro-analyzing every possible and impossible situation that might or not arise. Nevertheless, the automatization and depersonalization of their painting might, in the end, not receive the desired or hoped-for appreciation, not so much from the public, but rather from their very own soul. Therefore, instead of hushing off the voice by ignoring the array of bright and unknown colors at their disposal, all artists and all living selves ought to take a moment to stand still and contemplate the view in the making in order to fix the 'getting over the edges' before the painting be spoiled forever.

As tempting as the trivialization of daily life might appear for stripping the mind off its thinking processor, I have always known that I was going to be a misfit, a social outcast, a black sheep. I certainly do not endorse any sort of standardization, nor do I favorably back the roles of society, the media or social networks in the maintenance and perpetuation of stereotypes, but I believe, indeed, that it was never meant for me to fit into the same framework anyway.

Ever since I was little, I had a feeling that I was the odd one out, and never have I managed to find comfort in my being different. I was surrounded by blogs, social media, family, and friends, all kinds of actors of a larger society whom speak in favor of one particular image which is to be copied endlessly. In their expectations of a 'good life,' I saw the image of a girl, growing up to become a good student, partner, wife, mother, friend, and employee. A good and perfect living being. When lucky enough, that girl would meet a high-school or college *beau* and swiftly board the ship of daily routine, ironically coined *metro, boulot, dodo* in French, or just subway/work/sleep, day in, day out. It would not get any fancier, save some all-in prepaid holidays perhaps and the weekly visit to *belle-maman* for the family gatherings, the culmination of a drained and indifferent existence.

I was bound to drown even before getting aboard that ship, whether it be a yacht or a raft. Unfortunately, I am still floundering into troubled waters, trying my best to keep my head above water, recalling to pinch my nose when the tide is high. I have been engulfed before, and I am still trying to emerge.

Although it might prove difficult to add clairvoyance as a new feather to one's hat, one can still find certainty in nature's cycles. Calm will come after the storm, as does the blossoming after the leaf fall and the deep-blue sky hiding behind the darker cloud puffs. I, thus, have faith that this storm too, no matter how close to the tempest that has been destroying me nearly to the core, will at last die down and the quiet will eventually return.

How fascinating and thought-provoking a statement then, especially since my night rest had lately been all but a haven of peace and tranquility, weatherly and emotionally speaking. Last night for instance, when the clock had just rung the stroke of midnight, the wind had indeed come up, feistier and more determined than ever it had been for the past few days. As if even nature had known that *more* was coming. To me.

As I listened to the sounds of nature from my canopy bed, my feet got in a tussle with my woolen-knit blanket. It was a stormy-yet-not-such-a-cold winter night, and I felt too dizzy and obviously not clear-headed because of the frequent middle-in-the-night wakeups. Suddenly, a flash of lightning had lit up my bedroom, and I was wide awake. My heart was immediately filled with joy, and I could only welcome this rare and spectacular white brightness into the room. It only lasted for a couple of seconds, but there were the longest and the quietest since I cannot remember when. No time to think; here came the loud and greasy clap of thunder that would signal the end of the childish wondering as to where the lightning had struck… The only reply that I could think of was that this thunderclap must have hit somewhere not so far away from me, even though I had wished that it would have enlightened my thoughts tonight, and perhaps that it would have healed me from within with its starry lights. Somewhere or sometime in the past, I had, indeed, lost the grip I thought I had on a reality that was already slipping through my fingers. I had not seen the burning out coming, yet I wished I had heard the first crackles.

I am now listening to the thunder drifting away before it disappears into the night. Early dawn is nearing, and I count the minutes before I hear the rooster's crowing. These are the moments during which I let my mind slip away from any source of anxiety, from any deep questioning about the meaning of life and from my inability to fit into a reality that seems 'okay' to most actors in society. During these brief yet precious minutes, I let my mind dust off some old memories in order to relive a certain event or situation, to experience and revive it again, but this time making sure I do enjoy the feeling, the comfort, or the happiness it ought to have brought me in the past. I shall confess that I feel saddened at the thought of not being able to seize the day, as they say, when the day presented itself. Therefore, time has a special meaning to me, from the moment we open our eyes to the morning shower: priceless remembering. Even though it be only in thoughts, the memories are set alive without the fear and the panic I might have felt in the past when unfolded in their original context. Dawn sweeps the fear away.

Time Machine

For the last year, especially since the flame had started to flicker and the light to go out, I have been traveling into a past capsule more often than I can recall. These *voyages* are not intended to be nostalgic, nor are the travels tinged with any darkness or gloominess. I only wish to embark on a journey during which I can remember things without fear. I, thus, travel to memories from the past, because I wish to fully enjoy the goodness, the peace, or the pleasure of key events; I wish to contemplate, whether it be a feeling, a smell, a detail, a change in the packaging of the cookies I used to like, a *trait de caractère* of a certain somebody, anything, really, that makes my mind sail back and forth, or shall I say 'swing' from past to present day. I cross over the bridge of time in order to find the peace that I ought to have found years ago already. I am, therefore, very thankful, and I consider myself blessed, for I can unlock in great details the box of *souvenirs* that I have been assembling ever since forever. This is the treasure I cherish.

On most early wakeups, I prefer to open the sweet jar of childhood memories rather than risking any leftovers of the bitter or sour-aftertaste marmalade from my high-school and college years. It is not so much that I did not mix *any* good ingredient to the recollections of my teenage years; quite the opposite actually. I do recall *many* 'spoons' of genuine laughter, true happiness, savory Italian or Mediterranean dishes, shared joy and flying butterflies in the stomach when the cute Italian waiter had smiled after presenting the *piatto di spaghetti* in front of me, with me being extra careful not to stain the blouse that I was wearing or leaving the restaurant or *trattoria* with *salsa di pomodoro* leftovers (left and right) obviously stuck on both sides of my mouth. Back then, my worst fear was that I would leave a restaurant, grinning from ear to ear, only to realize later that a big and nasty leaf of parsley had found a rather cheap accommodation, right between my front teeth, suddenly making me regret my choice of *spaghetti alle vongole* right away. Because yes, pasta with clams is traditionally served with freshly chopped parsley, to the great chagrin of absent-minded gourmands.

Overall, I sometimes travel back into my teenage and young-adult years, but I am constantly reminded of the fear that had started to settle deep down. I am, thus, often a defenseless spectator of a painful reality, for fear has now come to tackle the muscles, preventing me from moving as I wish. Ultimately, this paralysis has found its way to my heart and has gone straight to my soul, rendering me bereft of any emotion, any benevolence toward myself.

Childhood memories are therefore sweeter to travel back to, and even though I have always been a bit of an anxious kind, the kid that I like to remember could still *feel* and *fully appreciate* the little things. For instance, back in primary school, there was a vending machine with a choice of four cookies and one strawberry yoghurt-based drink, the latter being far too big for a child. From time to time, my father would hand me a one-euro coin right after he had dropped my sister and I off in the morning and that he had accompanied us until we had safely found our way to our respective classrooms. We were, indeed, always late for school, and the children had already started to take their seats, so he did not want to see us running alone through the playground. This coin, that both my sister and I had received, would either be spent the very same day or would be secretly kept in a little side pocket of our schoolbag. Until that one day, when we headed out of the cafeteria after we had emptied our lunchbox (and showed to the supervisor standing at the doors that we had indeed eaten our sandwiches and that he made sure we had not left any crumb uneaten) and could spend the coin for a dessert of our fancy.

Back to our tête-à-tête with the vending machine. The French dairy company Danone had launched an irresistible and savory chocolate and-vanilla pudding, or so it seemed from the advertisement that appeared on every television in-between cartoons during the children's late-afternoon programming. A first layer of dark chocolate was covered with an intense vanilla cream, but since the former did not appear right away, any hungry gourmand was facing a dreadful and tough decision: shall he dare mix the pudding layers…or not?

Judging from my personal experience of the *Danette* (for that was what the pudding was called and still is to this day, even though the array of flavors has increased tremendously with a caramel or even a cappuccino version these days), I considered the options and made some sort of compromise. First, I would carefully have a spoonful or two of the vanilla top-layer pudding and while digging the spoon for a third catch, I would glimpse some chocolate spots that had started to appear right in the middle, making it henceforth possible to have a little bite of that as well, although without mixing it altogether, at least right away. It would only take me one taste of the chocolate mixture further, for me to decide to 'go wild' and mix both flavors in the *petit pot de crème*. "We're going in," I hear myself say.

However, I need to confess that no sooner had I stirred the chocolate-and-vanilla layers than this dessert had in fact become less appetizing than I originally thought it would be. How I wish I had bought the Prince cookies now; these round, crispy, chocolate, cereal cookies presented as a sandwich with a delicious chocolate-hazelnut paste in it. And, bonus, the ones from the vending machine were the extra-large bags with not one, not two, but four – yes, four! – whole-wheat *galettes*! Every child would first bite off the top of the round cookie in such a way that it would reveal the chocolate paste stuck on the last wheat cookie of the sandwich piece which would inevitably go spongy and damp because of the licking-off of all the chocolate-hazelnut mixture with the child's tongue! Long story short, the cookie was eaten in three different yet savory steps: first the top cookie layer, next was the licking off of the chocolate (and saving some for later, on both sides of the mouth, *bien-sûr*), and, finally, the munching of the last (if not broken yet) cookie. The vanilla version of this cookie existed too, but that would just spoil the fun, right? All children's hearts shall surrender.

Besides bringing back to life memories from the vending machine, I would like to point to the person or place-specific types of cookies. Those we would eat only in certain places, at appointed times, at a specific person's house. Who then has not a favorite treat back at Granny's? Interestingly enough, this peculiar cookie (or sweet) was like the hallmark of our visiting that particular person, in my case, Mamy's or Oma's, my two grandmothers, during school holidays. We would have *this* kind of cookie at Mamy's, but *that* kind at Oma's. And never ever would we switch habits or eat *this* at Oma's and *that* at Mamy's. Not once. Ever. If bananas, canned vanilla-rice pudding, Jaffa cakes and homemade *crêpes* or *crème au chocolat* were always on offer at Mamy's place, we would have the Nic Nac (topped with sugar), the Marquisette cookies (basically, a delicious and very sophisticated butter cookie whose edges are covered with dark chocolate glaze), the Napoleon or Chokotoff candies, and the chocolate seafood pralines at Oma's. How I like to indulge in these tasty moments. They remind me of the warmth and comfort one could find at one's grandmother's house. I would gladly learn about your person-specific cookies too…

And yet, here I am, writing about the *gourmand* that I used to be while I think about the milk chocolate Mignonette of Côte d'Or that I was bold enough to have with my herbal valerian tea yesterday evening. I did, however, regret it later during the night, for the cramps and reflux rendered the sleeplessness rather unpleasant. Look at the bright side: I spent most of the remaining time before pre-dawn reading and getting lost into every word written by the great Sebastian Faulks in *A Week in December*. I realized that in this piece in particular, the author had adopted a different style and approach than he might have in his masterpiece, *Human Traces*, one of the works I admire so and one that indeed belongs to my personal and all-time-favorite-books ranking. One would not believe that it is possible to end up reading at night because of having indulged in chocolate. Yet, here it is. Proof.

A Different Kind of Disorder

The calendar is hanging on the makeshift pin board in our kitchen, left from the Italian-brand, overpriced, vintage refrigerator. The page has just been ripped off, and the date announces that time is nearing to ready ourselves and welcome spring. Yet, as I look up at the sky, I see a low depression threatening the otherwise-tropical climate that had flown over Belgium earlier this year. This morning though, nature had decided it would color the landscape rainy and gray. The puddles have already become a source of 'more and merrier' for the kids to play, and their splashing in the water has quickly become a bit of a disaster for the parents in their many attempts to wash off the deep-encrusted mud onto their children's shoes. Umbrellas are the 'it bags' of Belgian streetwear; whether it be the automatic (when functioning) pocket umbrella, the classic canopy one (black for the elite with a leather handle to match the designer suit of its owner), or the fancy bubble one with its *en vogue* spherical shape, all have become what sunglasses are for the Italian populace, a basic commodity turned into a lifesaving – stay dry – item. The time has thus come to welcome rain, these droplets of happiness and love.

The chilly weather appeared to have altered the awakening of nature after its winter break, although a break there is not, since the sap of the trees hides away deep into the roots, only to spurt out reinforced, sweet, and warm with the first warm sunrays. When spring has arrived, flowers will announce nature's renaissance, and leaves will turn again into a beautiful emerald green. But not today. The daffodils are being swept from left to right by an unforgiving gust of wind, and, deep inside, I can feel my own helplessness battling against winds of anger and sorrow. I look at the view, not the one in our yard, but at what I have become, wondering what I have done to myself. The petals I have almost torn off, and here I am, waiting for the wind to fall…

The home-interior version of potted daffodils have little merit to show off their sunflower yellowness. These little bell plants have just enough water and are treated with great care by my father who is the only one who seems to remember to water them. They are standing with splendor and pride on the low wall between our kitchen and living room, all yellow and bright.

The daffodils inside and outdoors offer, thus, a very contrasting landscape, yet a complementary one I shall add. I cannot help but look through the window and fall quiet, still. My mind is carried away by the softness of some piano notes playing in the background, a YouTube suggestion for relaxing music (Celtic as it appears). Perhaps my soul feels closer to the outdoor-living flora fighting off the bitterness and vehemence of the capricious weather conditions. I find it hard to be inspired by the comfortably installed flowers behind me, for they have not experienced adversity, nor are they facing any challenge whatsoever. They have been purchased only to decorate an otherwise-boring room. They are thought to add this touch of liveliness that announces a too-early attempt to hang on any type of Easter decoration. Rest assured, for I do not intend to let the kitschy chicks or chocolate bunnies invade our home. I have, however, no objection to buying some chocolate eggs and filling them up to the rim of a giant bowl, tempting the innocent hands of passersby who will obviously indulge into the devil's chocolate-candy nest.

My hands, however, need to heal from the deep cracks brought about by these biting winds and cold air. Since Lent is not even halfway through, I still have a couple of weeks left to figure out how I will unwrap these mini chocolate treats from their paper envelope and make sure that I pick the right flavor among the mix of colors. I do not wish to end up chomping on the only one in the basket that has been stuffed with liquored marzipan or a too-bold version of pistachio and hazelnut *praliné*. Please just give me a double chocolate filling. Simple is best.

Lent is also a time to reflect upon our life, our values, our love and care for others, but also the good treatment to our own selves. Over the months, time has changed me the same way as the winter season announces the rebirth of life and the renaissance of one's faith into future prospects and petals blossoming. Be it for the transformations or the revolutions affecting both mankind and nature, all of us have the power within ourselves to add colors to our palette. Art can heal, for it does not follow the same severe-ranking appreciation that applies to banking and financial products. We might be the victims of social pressure, but let us not forget that art too is oftentimes underrated. So, who are we to determine the value another person's 'worth,' as if he would be creditworthy, penniless, or bankrupt? Instead, why not use art to open ourselves up to different cultures, different horizons? Why not let art speak for us so that its coloring and light can reach out to others, in desperate need of a soothing voice or just of someone who would listen to their own voice?

Perhaps that is the reason why I value art so much. Any type actually, for it releases a unique and liberating power that ignites a flame you did not know was still alive and burning. For instance, I believe that art can indeed be found in the mere activity of reading, since it welcomes an absolutely remarkable and picturesque world of imagination as well as personal interpretation. Moreover, even though only the eyes can actually see, the emotion itself is felt deep within the reader's heart. The same inner peace will later on radiate its warmth and light onto the outside reality; it will spread amongst the audience.

To tell the truth, I sometimes wish I were able to sketch how and what I feel, simply because writing about it does not seem to be enough, at least for me. There is no chance one can write the full extent of his or her emotions and experiences. Nor is it possible to print on paper the extent of our inner pain and suffering. Any artist writes down only half of the tenth that he wishes to tell the world. But, again, that is the stark reality anybody seems to be confronted with for we all face our own hurdles.

Personally, I find that writing alleviates my pain, and I see it as a way to overcome obstacles, my very own hurdles. I, thus, write bits and pieces here and there every day or whenever I feel that putting words onto paper can heal the wounds a bit more…until the typing on my computer pumps up the little energy I have at the moment and forces me to click on the button 'save for later.' If only I were 'safe.' Why did this happen to me, again?

Away with self-pity! I hear my mind saying. The wounds of the past have raised yet another curtain, one that I did not dare open sooner. Recently, I have come to realize that the burnout *mise en scène* was actually the *décor* for something greater, something deeper, something that would save whatever was left of 'me.' I had completely erased myself. I had been ignoring my inner voice. Until December 2017 when I was forced to press the pause button.

It was then that I decided to take up writing as a means to listen to my inner crying. I did not dare talk about this secret wish that I have; the wish to edit or even to publish my own words, my own voice. I am too scared to be disappointed, however. I fear the consequences of what a possible rejection could have on the last hopes that battle together to keep me alive and well, even though I am on the verge of falling into despair. If I accomplish this dream, how am I going to keep strong, for I would have shown my most vulnerable side in my writings? Then again, deep down, I know that I nourish the wish to help other people who are struggling too, to reach out to them, the other souls that are on the verge of effacement.

One area that I would therefore like to research is how a burnout experience can trigger a still-unfamiliar and seldom-talked-about eating disorder. Sometimes referred to as *orthorexia*, the obsessive and uncontrollable need to eat only healthy and strictly healthy foods can quickly become a loophole for highly sensitive people that suffer from the all-time classic 'what would the others say or do?'

I believe, indeed, that when a person is physically frail and emotionally fragile, a forced house warrant or any compulsory break from his or her daily (destructive) routine can lead to an increased need to control things. Since said person no longer understands the body or its (failing) responses, he or she will turn to whatever topic of interest is at hand, in this case, food.

However relieved a person's entourage might be at the sight of his or her finally escaping the workaholic pattern that had nearly annihilated his/her existence; growing concern is being expressed about the new 'hobby' which is paradoxically escalating until it quickly turns into a compulsive obsession. In the case of food, the victim realizes the desperate need to control the food intake and to raise awareness about the origin of the ingredients. Moreover, it turns out it is easy enough to provide with the rightful argumentation for this new behavioral yet obsessive pattern: by being selective about the food and by setting very high standards about either the consumption, either the dietary patterns one wishes to follow, a person feels he is finally taking care of himself.

Hence the choice to opt for the most nutritious and most powerful diet possible in order for the body to recover more quickly: proteins, lots of good fats, vitamins B9 and B12, a bit of zinc here and a pinch of iron there, all is meticulously verified to ensure that the mind, too, is relieved.

Unfortunately, by making sure the body won't collapse, the victim falls into the trap of the disappearing self. One is swirled up in an automatic routine, controlling everything with the same frenzy as the one he or she had used in the work sphere until now. Nevertheless, the burnout reality came as a siren call that the same way of functioning had indeed been devastating both for the body and the self. So, by adopting the very same characteristics of the workaholic/behavioral pattern, only to implement them onto this newfound interest in food (in our case), is twice more devastating for both the body and the self. The former is required to function with little place for fun and near-zero 'comfort' munchies while the latter is excluded little by little from social events and gatherings with friends, since it has become an imposition to hold the reins, oversee and execute everything, especially when *others* are looking, the exact same people one is so afraid to disappoint.

Writing about this part has been especially painful for me. Please know that my intention is not to scare people off, quite the opposite actually. I wish to raise awareness about the danger that looms like a shadow over the (sometimes too late in time) burnout diagnosis. Once a person has experienced such a humiliating collapse and what seems to him/her like a personal affront, it is essential that he or she be supported by different experts (doctors, therapists, psychiatrists) and, perhaps, most importantly, by family and friends. That way, the lost soul is less likely to transpose the destructive pattern onto the new reality he is facing. I thus wish to encourage the world to take the time to pause and embrace every moment, because once the wheel has stopped spinning, it is difficult to get rid of the dizziness. The body never forgets a trauma. So do not let it happen to you nor to anybody. Beware of the alarm bells. Let them not ring. Not once. Ever.

Energy

Circles, spinning, all around. Purple and dark at first, then Saint-Patrick Irish green and navy-blue ones. Small and insignificant in size, although these circles quickly become thicker and fuller before they grow even larger and take too much space. Suddenly, they disappear from some radar in-between my closed eyes, similar to red bullets showing live air traffic onto the tracking flights dashboard of some government facility. The circles, where did they go?

Laying onto the table in the therapist's mezzanine, I feel I am only a short distance away from the healing hands that are lingering above my helplessness, my incomprehension, my sighs. I am short of breath, but gone with the flow is the tension I had previously felt in my muscles. I cannot feel my body anymore; I seem to be floating. I am suddenly aware of her hands being near my head, without ever touching it. I feel a strange-though-very-real, even palpable, flow of energy finding its lodging in the frontal lobe of my head. I breathe out and hear a peaceful heartbeat. A deep-purple color starts to spin and turns darker and darker – it is almost black now – as the hands capture the pressure that has been locked since forever in my brain. It feels like a magnetic field coming out of its hiding place, appearing right behind the eyes, and up to the center of my head it goes until the pain is almost unbearable.

For several (what seem to me like interminable) seconds, that tension or this new sort of headache is too intense, too present, too hurtful for the eyes. I keep them closed, but I also fear that by not acknowledging the pain, these light bulbs will forever go on and off like car turn signals, eventually driving me crazy. I am afraid that, unbeknownst myself, I will let the strain glide away and that it will hide back into the deep corridors in which it has been squatting for years now. Unwelcomed, yet very present indeed.

"Almost there; toughen your way through it," I hear myself whispering while laying on the makeshift-massage table, covered with only one towel, always a dark blue one. Three small books are supporting my neck and serve me as a pillow. "The pain will soon go away." At last, I sense a shadow disappear from above my eyes, and I know that the therapist is now gently removing her hands from the energy flux that has been hovering above my head. It does not feel as a current of air or a draft better, nor does it resemble the passage of blowing wind. But it's right here. I feel something, a tension, a force; something is lingering for a while inside my head, then it vanishes, only to invade my throat, leaving me gasping for air but for just a second; I cannot breathe. My throat is thickening, and something is strangling me from within. Luckily, it vanishes in the blink of an eye, and I manage to take a deep (well-deserved) breath. My eyes are closed, and for the first time since arriving here, I notice the smell of the welcoming and comforting atmosphere created by the open-log fire whose ashes had been burning for hours in the downstairs' office room. Breathing in, one more time. All right, see you next week then!

Emergence of the New Season

Night and day will be of equal length for the spring equinox marks this very peculiar day. A Tuesday, this year, will celebrate the Earth's equator passing through the center of the sun. I like to believe that this new energy will empower all the people of the world to embrace the changing course of their paths.

The first day of spring will, therefore, symbolize the revival of strength so that one can take up one's journey from where one had left it or change its course and hence come as a symbol of the resurrection of faith and the celebration of hope. On the human scale, our inheritance and our different backgrounds will only add up to the knowledge that we acquire step by step and to the teachings that we share with our peers. Heritage being greater than the sum of its parts, mankind ought to remember the past, but the wounds must serve as a reminder of how not to get our fingers burned. In the present, mankind shall live in solidarity while paving the way for future generations to follow the footsteps that have thus been engraved in respect, tolerance, benevolence, and sincerity.

The incredible balance between Earth and Sun occurs at two regular times every year and reveals the entrance of new light and life on Earth. Whether it happens in the spring or in the fall, we are all facing change, and it is up to us to decode the wisdom and the meaning behind our personal journeys.

Evidently, this year most specifically, I wished to believe that March 20th would be a turning point, one of the many I have hoped for. Instead, I realize now that after a two-week respite (the ski-resort holidays at the start of February) during which I had felt that I was crawling back up and almost escaping from quicksand that had been swallowing me up, the tide has engulfed me even deeper than before. Consequently, I was forced to welcome back the unrequited visits and the lasting stays of headaches, toothaches, never-ending nightmares and a hyperactive brain, acid reflux, and too-often too-early wake ups, mostly at around 1 a.m. if it be not 2:43 a.m. or 5 a.m. again.

This year, in short, the spring equinox shook me to the core as if I were suddenly aware of the damage suffered. It breaks my heart when I am confronted with the level of destruction that my body had undergone and as I face the almost-perfectly accomplished erasing of myself. However, through adversity I shall rise, and I can't help it but smile, for as I am writing all this down, I can spot a greasy pigeon that is swinging up and down on the same branch of the wild pine trees that are decorating the backyard of our neighbor. Up and down, unceasingly. At least someone is having the time of its life!

Burning

Needles. One of which got stuck in my hair, as it has already happened during my past visits for acupuncture. Breathe in and out. Great, now there is also one needle that remains fixed into a painful area of my right ear; it is not the lobe though because the fat it contains would prevent the patient to actually feel the sting. Instead, I feel a prickle in the helix, that bony part going from top to earlobe and resembling the Andean Cordillera on the South American continent, by meagre means of comparison with the human ear. Do not worry; I did not know a thing about ear anatomy before looking it up just now.

When all needles are in, an infrared old radio box is placed under my neck, serving me as a pillow. I wonder whether the waves it sends are immediately transmitted to a portable computer or any other machine that is carefully monitored by the doctor from his consulting room next door. I try to relax and close my eyes, but I am half-sitting half-lying on an uncomfortable and wobbly chair. It smells of disinfectant, cleansing alcohol, and after a quick check on what – to me – looks like a baby monitor but, in fact, is some sort of remote control for acupuncture practitioners, I am slowly rocked and transported away by the healing background flute and bamboo music, the same C.D. that has been playing over and over for years now.

When the door closes, I quickly glance at my watch to check the time, for I would not want to fall asleep while the doctor enters back, finding me slobbering. I know I have a 20 or 30-minute rest in this dentist's chair, covered with a light-paper seat cover. The tiny room I find myself in only has one other stool, although it had disappeared under my green parka coat and the shredded tiger-printed scarf, the latter I have been meaning to knit back to life, but that is when I take up sewing classes. By then, I will probably have bought another dozen, and we will be celebrating the first half century of the new millennium.

It is rather chilly, but the rabbit-fur sleeveless cardigan that I had bought on sale two years ago brings me sufficient comfort and warmth. Finally, I look around one last time and cannot help but compare this austere chamber to a forgotten unit of a typical, obsolete, mountain chalet. The heating is at least 40 years old, the patient's chair is rudimentary, and its basicness sprains the eyes when one thinks of the latest zero-gravity, deluxe, air-massage chairs in other consulting rooms. It does not even look like the Rosita lazy-boy chair from Joey and Chandler in the Friends series. That one was only broken at the very end.

Yet, for the next 20 or 30 minutes, I know I will sometimes open up my eyes, half asleep, only to check the time and close the shutters off again, being swept away to the rhythms of some Native-American or Tibetan musical waves. I am aware of the needles again. Although their healing effects are perhaps not visible to the naked eye, I am the living proof of their powerful stimuli to trigger a responsive reaction from one's immune system, for, even now, as frail and physically beaten as I am, I do not catch the colds that are running the streets, nor does my sister's coughing or phlegm destroy the last ramparts of my body's army defense. I know these somewhat-unconventional treatments are beneficial in the long run.

Unfortunately, the needles did not put out the fire that was maliciously burning inside my already-bloated and fragile digestive system. I have been used to its *à la carte* functioning, choosing from among a menu of dislikable symptoms and, depending on its mood, picking cramps for starters or ending with pops of air exploding within my belly and aching as though a block of concrete is inhibiting the pressure to lower down.

That night, after the first of the twice-a-month acupuncture session, I woke up in cold sweat at 11:54, just before midnight, hunched up and in pain. It took me some time before I realized that I had never experienced such a sharp inflammation. I was on fire, from within I mean, starting at the back of my throat but really reaching the 'heat' point in my belly, right under my stomach and deep into my bowels. The clock stroke one, two, then three in the morning until, finally, I could stretch out my legs at 3:43 without worsening this discomforting and sharp flame that had set me afire. Gastritis, the doctor said, before warning me about the stress issues or anxiety I still struggle with: the clock had almost struck a stomach ulcer. And the worst about this new chapter of the burnout experience is me having to give up coffee and avoiding anything too sour. Exit fresh tomato sauce. I need to figure out how to let go. Quickly. I need a plan. Even if only for coffee and pasta sake. I cannot let them down.

I would like to add, perhaps as an aside, that treating inflammation, any kind really, without the use of traditional medication is not as great a challenge as one might think. I would first recommend a healthy routine. One can, for instance, rely on the intake of fresh fruit, wholegrain foods, and leafy greens. A switch in habits can also prevent many little scratches: let us start with dimming the light or activating the blue filter on our cellphones; let us continue with quitting the H-24, staying connected at any hour of the day, or for the bold ones amongst us, resort to homeopathic granules and round tablets that taste bland but have a therapeutic benefit in time. Perhaps the only inconvenience of the latter experiment with regard to the healing of inflammation and headaches in general is the taking of the homeopathic little candies one hour after your meal, or leaving a 20-minute-fasting break before munching again. This requires, thus, a little bit of organizing, I shall confess.

Lastly, I recall both my doctor and my therapist sharing with me a secret ancient recipe to ease inflammation: one ought to put a raw slice of potato on one's tongue and let it melt slowly until the patient's patience is up and he or she finds oneself chewing on the starch which interestingly enough appears to be blending tremendously in the mouth.

Unfortunately, I could not only rely on magnesium vitamins and other nutritional supplements that are served as side dishes with most of my meals. Not in these acute gastritis circumstances. I needed what water is to fire: an immediate solution that would allow me to breathe again, without experiencing pain. So, I was ordered to swallow a ready-to-drink jellified product, some sort of gel made of licorice and 'amla,' the latter being another berry, not a Tibetan dried fruit this time like the goji berries that I mix every morning in my oatmeal. The amla is actually an Indian gooseberry that I had never heard of, said to relieve stomach cramps and to appease the digestive process because of its high fiber nutritional value. To top it all, this thick, jellified, compote tastes of raspberries; a flavor I do not specifically wish to last while climbing up the staircase before going to sleep. Or trying to.

Burning, Day After

The next morning, I was tempted to open my eyes to the rhythm of carnival drums. At 6:45 on a Sunday, the *Gilles* – famous for their impressive hats with ostrich feathers in Binche and other carnival cities all over Belgium, their faces covered in wax masks and their traditional costumes meant to scare off winter – were already out in the streets, the drums beating, their clogs dancing, and their baskets filled with (ripe) oranges ready to be thrown to the crowd later that day.

Every year, the procession starts at three or four o'clock in the morning at the house of the eldest Gille. The performers collective share the same tradition since the Middle Ages and would not, under any circumstance, miss their glass of champagne and a plate of oysters, for that is their breakfast before the day's parade. The first of many others to follow (most of which including bubbles though). If the oysters are swallowed up in no time at all, the drinks are plentiful, and as the day goes by, champagne is traded for Belgian first-price-category beer. The merry souls will walk through the streets behind a fanfare meant to ward off the evil spirits of the winter and burn them down at the end of the parade, when they make their entrance into the village center, happily welcomed and cheered by the crowd who also came wearing their most ridiculous costume. Little girls are disguised in witches if they do not choose to wear their Disney uniform or their mother's wedding dress, whereas the boys prefer to look like their favorite superhero or the latest knight or cowboy model they have heard of at school.

This startling décor means that Easter is fast approaching and that the chocolate-egg hunts are almost back in vogue again. Yet, not before the Gilles's noisy clogs have burned the gray landscape of the previous winter months. The dancing and cheerful playing make me reflect upon my own imprisonment, my own winter break. A change is coming, of that I am sure of, but will it for the better?

That morning, hearing the beating drums in the background, I was trying to figure out an answer. I chopped my red grapefruit into bite-size pieces until my eyes were thrilling with joy to discover this new crop from Florida, that we had purchased only the day before at the local supermarket. I was looking forward to the difference in taste and texture between the Spanish variety that I had been eating until that day and the yet-to-try Florida grapefruits.

It was only after I had heated my oatmeal and weighed down the fresh bee pollen out of its frozen container that I could sit down at the breakfast table and bring the first piece of fruit to my mouth: savory and more than satisfying, I might add. Perhaps I was in a too-happy mood, for I boasted about the deliciousness of my morning fruit-bowl routine, showing my mother how shiny red and incredibly fresh the fruit was, the savor of which already dripping from my watering mouth. And gone was it!

After only two spoonfuls of carob powder and goji berries oatmeal (with extra egg, mind the protein addition), I felt like an inner fire was destroying the upper part of my stomach. I know of past experiences of cramps, headaches, bloating episodes with the occasional constipation; but this was an unprecedented category of pain, an unknown to now sense of suffering. Surely, there must have been an explanation. How then am I to fight back when the fire is already ravaging the center of my upper belly, at a crossing between the stomach and the duodenum, most of the times even launching an attack on the upper bowel? Minutes later, I felt the cramps getting more intense, and there it was, the bloating I mean, right on time in my lower bowels. All of a sudden, the stress levels were all desperately ringing; it was too much for me to handle. What was destroying me from within? Tell me, please. I was begging, "Put me out of my misery."

Truth be told, when one is faced with such helplessness, or when one's sensitivity has already been challenged too often over the last months (years?), one cannot prevent the tears from falling down, for that is the only source of relief. Their warmth and sweetness offer better comfort than the rival bombing of anger that would only make the headache worse and the heart melt down till just a crumb. Why? I had already given up on coffee, was grapefruit next? I swear (please excuse the language) that if pasta and salmon are on the list, I might jump into giving up food altogether. What left is there if one cannot eat what one fancies most?

My dearest wish today is to rediscover all the flavors of the artist's palette without any hatching. Not one. Until then, dear Reader, please go fetch that *piatto di spaghetti* you have been craving for and make sure you treat it with a sumptuous yet authentic sauce of your choice. And, for heaven's sake, do not pass on the *dolce pensiero*. Indulge in something sweet, something that makes your heart melt. Happy pasta to all. I dare you.

Audacity

Or the lack of. From somewhere hidden in a corner of my mind, I must retrieve this shameless chutzpah, the access of which I have never unlocked. I have never had the nerve to stand firm, to be determined or have a real sense of myself. Some are born confident, sometimes even *dikkenek*, as they say in Belgian slang (referring to one's growing neck by incessant and continuous bragging); others are more discreet. It does not mean per se that they stay in the background of the picture; they simply prefer the quiet modesty over the empty talk.

As the months are passing by, I notice that I still have a long way to go. The ground still needs to be laid, whereupon the foundations will be built later on. However, as high as this mountain may seem to me, I ought to look back one last time and congratulate myself for my traveling on until now onto a bumpy road, the exit of which I am still trying to catch the sign for. I will then enter the beautiful world of living a carefree life.

How I wish this were true. Talking about exits, I remember a hilarious anecdote from when my American family came over, almost ten years ago, about the 'exit' signboards on European highways, all in a different language each time we travel to another country. We were driving at 130 km/h on our way to visit the Roman remains of Trier, in Germany, when my aunt spotted the first of a long succession of *Ausfahrt* boards, the German equivalent of 'exit.' For a while, my aunt (one of my father's sisters) had been asking my American godfather which '*ausfahrt*' we ought to take, as if it were the obvious English word for it. We all laughed in the car; we being a bunch of cousins in our teens, first because of the resemblance of the word to our poor childish and preposterous imagination of the verb 'to fart,' and second because of my aunt's confusion and persistence in using the German word instead of the American one. Funny I should think about this again while writing this piece about self-effacement.

Later on during the trip, we literally landed up in the middle of the *Hauptmarkt* (the main center of medieval Trier), and before visiting the Roman gate, Porta Nigra, we could walk through little stands with local products on display, among which, it goes without saying, beer. That last one was a subject for discussion, for when my cousins read the German sign, *Bitte eine Bit*, on a tent with beer *en degustation*, they immediately queued up, happy to try a sip of lager in a country in which they would not be fined for drinking under the age of 21. They were both almost 16 and 18 years old and had found out that they were as such on the threshold of the legal age to drink (in most European countries). Cheers to them, or better said… *Prost*!

Beating around the bushes, I was previously writing about audacity and how I have been lacking of it since forever I can remember. Not once have I experienced a what-I-call 'red-carpet moment,' *i.e.* when you are at the center of the spotlight, but instead of becoming petrified and feeling your dress giving up to intense sweating like the Niagara Falls, you are proud, confident, and relaxed. Nothing can spoil your entrée, nothing can ruin the image that you have of your perfect self, the very one that you have been searching for while standing in front of the mirror and powdering your nose one last time, even though it is already pink-pale and free of any visible (with a magnifying glass) blackheads. You have reached a balance between composure and the needed *élan* to walk proudly and self-confidently. Everyone, save me. Not once. I would be standing in the backstage area, a bold runner-up if need be, not showing her uncertainty and fear. But the fear of what, exactly? What fear has been destroying me to such an extent?

I could not find anything to reply when the massage-therapist asked that very same question. The one I call Marraine la Fée, my fairy godmother, holds a very special place in my heart, for I trust her with my life. Actually, to be honest, it is my body and my soul that have come to trust her more than the despotic and destructive rule of my mind over the years. I do believe in her somewhat untraditional (at least to our Western-society thinking) healing powers, although she is a certified, Chinese, medicine practitioner.

I know her skills; I have read the Yellow Pages. She tries to kindle our subconscious, to 'feel' what is invisible to us in order to create inner ways, thanks to which we can be fully aware of the environmental factors that surround us and consequently influence our every move or being. She tries to stimulate (or boost) a patient's self-confidence by making a strength out of his or her sensitivity and intuition. She is a godmother with a golden heart, but I must warn you, for she is not easily fooled. I cannot thank her enough for her support and the care with which she is treating me. And this aside, from the tissues that she hands over to me when I end up crying in the chair – suddenly noticing only then that she had traded her magnificent, vintage, oriental rug for a petite-size one, less wooly and impressive. "Oh, Child," she would say, "the old rug is at the dry cleaning's." Phew, I thought she had gotten rid of it. Such a relief.

While she closes her strappy sandals and adjusts her hearing device, she asks me not to speak, for she cannot hear me when she is bent over, with her foot, one at the time, on the stool while she reaches for the straps and closes them up. *C'est parti.*

Let's go. And so I tell her everything, all the daily anecdotes that make up for what, to others, is described as the normal way of life, but in which I always seem to perceive a tension to a certain level, low to high, depending on the day, the lack of sleep, or the type of activity we are referring to. I have come to realize that I am very sensitive to the surrounding factors or the context in which I have landed up, whether it be a particular day or not. Overthinking might be seen as a quality to some, but I can assure you that I am fighting day and night with this enemy of my own making. I have mastered the art of feeling responsible for *the everythings* of *the everyones*. I thought I was meant to take up the role of housekeeping governess, anytime and anywhere: at school, at university, then at work, and especially at home. I enjoyed the self-righteousness as well as the self-satisfaction of things well done, of helping out, of reaching out to others and hence preventing them from experiencing any unhappy of unlucky event or feeling. Unfortunately, I got carried away from my own journey toward finding inner peace, searching for myself, knowing my own likes and dislikes, or merely how to travel on my own and live. For all these years, I have erased myself in order to pursue (or achieve) something bigger: pleasing others, the *everyones*.

In our everyone-is-watching-you society, how can we expect to harvest self-confidence while all eyes are connected, everywhere? From social media to the fashion runway, from the new trending super foods to the gym membership, from the competitive systems devilishly elaborated and followed by schools to the even worse job interviews during which one is asked to hand in a top C.E.O. with 20 years of experience (well, at least) resume instead of the self-degrading academic career with the extra summer job. Perhaps society, too, ought to add the time variable to its unhealthy, unbearable demands. Just a pinch of time. For human beings to retrieve their continuous search for inner growth, at their own pace and with the additional push for those of us who got a pebble in their shoe. Please, just, *"Listen to the wind of your soul,"* as Cat Stevens would sing.

No. As Simple as That

A green woodpecker shamelessly disturbs two pigeons fighting under the apple tree in our backyard. The early damps of dawn have lifted long ago, but the grasses still have that translucent sparkle when the mid-morning sun shines directly upon them. As April Fools' Day is nearing, the temperatures are still too chilly to venture outside without an extra layer, yet one feels the back getting warmer and itching uncomfortably because of early signs of perspiration (why the extra layer again?), before the body shivers when crossing the threshold leading inside the house. The vanquished pigeon escaped its opponent's pecking by flying off and nestling onto the green bushes separating our house from the neighbor's. The proudly crowned gladiator continued to circle around the apple tree for a while, probably enjoying the reward of the love of a female pigeon. This is nature telling me somehow that spring has officially arrived into town.

Whether sparrows or robins, I am sitting in an audience of nature sounds and chirping birds, although not without the occasional roar of a passing-by car or the two-tone nee-naw of an approaching ambulance, probably speeding up to reach the nursing home in time, only a block away from our house. The first buds make a timid appearance on trees, bushes, and in flowerbeds, while tulips blossom in pale-pink, off-white, and apricot dresses. But most wonderful of all is the deep blue sky, bringing comfort and warmth to the tired souls and bodies, damaged by months of winter break.

With this new light and shine, I almost do not feel the headache that has been bursting my skull ever since I woke up this morning. I almost forget about my quivering legs, unable to hold the weight of despair and incomprehension, tumbling now and then, while the soul whispers slowly not to give up and learn to say no. It all starts with a 'no'; no to erasing myself further, no to shattering this body anymore. It has suffered enough.

April 1ˢᵗ, 2019

April Fools' Day has arrived, and a beautiful sun welcomes yet another week in my quest for hope and self-care. Leaving March behind, I have wished for things to start to change. I have wished that I would try to recognize the signals and that I would listen to my body, especially since the gastritis episode that is still giving me a hard time and that has deprived me from my favorite breakfast recipe.

This year, April first will be happily recalled, for I have three positive changes to pin onto my personal agenda. Firstly, I had to give up (temporarily, mind you) my delicious and savory breakfast – the one thing I looked forward to each morning, behind pasta and salmon – my grapefruit and egg/carob/goji oatmeal. However, after a week-and-a-half of testing with apples, pears, and cinnamon, I have finally found my new spring-season *petit-déjeuner*: May I present the blueberry-goji oatmeal (using almond milk) topped with cut-in-half, fresh, Portuguese raspberries. *Una bomba.*

Second piece of news and not the least, I have decided that I would treat myself a cup of freshly ground black coffee even though I felt the stomach burns coming back after having my instant oats. I did not press for a double coffee serving, but I could not resist any longer, especially since my mother was sitting next to me at the breakfast table in our kitchen, having a sip of her coffee, to which she adds a lump of sugar and a splash of milk. And trust me, the burns were worth it all the way. After a ten-day break from coffee, I was as thrilled as a little girl while holding my lucky mug, the one I had received on my tenth birthday when I went out swimming with my classmates on a Saturday afternoon, somewhere mid-September. Our hairs were still wet and our eyes red, save mine which were sparkling when I opened the present that I had just received from my *petit amoureux*. It was a mug with tiger prints on it, and in it was a little cuddly tiger. For years, I had prohibited anyone from drinking out of the mug; instead, I saved it in my bedroom where it stood on my bookcase as an invaluable and irreplaceable work of art. I did receive it from my first boyfriend, so no trespassing!

The last surprise came at a little past 11 in the morning, when I opened the fridge and took out a soy-milk yoghurt, quite spontaneously, to start 'snacking,' a habit I have been trying to take up from time to time without ever being successful in making it last in the long run. I officially make the wish to find the courage to continue and to last. Pinky promise.

Long story short, it does not matter how many changes one is willing to welcome in his or her life; it all comes down to a good night's rest. It may seem trivial to some or even preposterous to others, but I have not had a decent night of sleep since quite a long time, years to be honest.

Nevertheless, I need to confess that last night was unusually peaceful for me. Even though I cannot, yet, enjoy a straight eight-hour snooze, for the first time in weeks, perhaps months even, I could go back to 'sleep' (defined for me by a constant state of watchfulness and alertness, although the eyes are closed). I woke up several times during the night, but this was a first success of getting back to closing my eyes. This has seriously been a very interesting experience, one I had looked forward to for too long a time now, one I dared not hope for to happen anymore. I was pleasantly surprised at how changed a mind and body can be, how light they can be, after a good night's rest.

Obviously, this enchantment could not last, for the next night, I could not get any sleep. Any as in none, *nada, niet*. I heard my father fill his bathtub with probably too much (hot) water and no foam, and I even chatted with him about the books he had received that day from a colleague, both of them sharing a literary interest for a certain Italian author, the name of whom I have forgotten. Still, my day had been rich and fulfilling. So I did not mind not being able to fall asleep and lying in my bed with a copy of Isabel Allende's *House of The Spirits*. I cannot recall the last time that I did not suffer a headache, or the time I could enjoy some reading on our terrace with a view on our backyard and through the fence, directly into our neighbor's chicken coop, watching Paola and the other gals run free.

True story though, for only days before, two out of the four hens had dug under the enclosure separating our yard from the neighbor's vegetable garden, or what is left of it, since the chickens trample on the plowed rows of potatoes and peas. On a Saturday evening, I was checking the roasted fennel with salmon fillets that I had put in the oven while my parents were toasting on the well-deserved weekend break when the weekly chores are all crossed in. Check, check, check! I had to gather my strength not to open the oven before it beeped and so steal a taste of the Scottish salmon I had bought earlier that day on the market. I am the only one in the family who likes the totally harmless white matter oozing out of the fish fillets as they cook, and probably the only one who knows that albumin, as it is called, is merely a coagulated protein that leaks out because of the heat. My sister, though finding these white bullets rather unappetizing along with the grayish or darker 'stuff' beneath the fillet when cooked skin-side down, is nevertheless very thoughtful and saves both on her plate for me to nab while we sit down and have our family Saturday night's dinner. How thoughtful of her. She knows me too well. She would do just the same thing with leftover pasta sauce, for she knows that I like to steal the celery out of the tuna-pasta sauce. And since she eats only the pasta, I have volunteered to empty her plates by all means.

All this to say that we were about to have dinner that Saturday night when, all of a sudden, my mother blurted, "There's a chicken in our *parterre*! Oh no, wait, there are two of them!" It took two pairs of hands to lead the deserters back into their coop and a grateful smile from our neighbor to make the dish even more deserving while we giggled, looking from out of our kitchen, amused.

The Following Day: Me in April

It is day two of April, and I have just had a soy-milk yoghurt and chamomile herbal tea. Midday was nearing, and I still had not chosen a snack since breakfast at eight this morning. I did not wish to break with my new resolution of 'happy' extra snacking. Baby steps, some tell me. I know. So, do not expect me to have a second mid-morning breakfast or to prepare myself a crunchy peanut-butter sandwich (I like almonds but, really, cannot enjoy the taste of peanuts). It has been years since I have lost the habit of eating between regular meals, and it will take some time to be at peace with the extra food (and bloating). Hence my pride while savoring the last spoon of this late-morning yoghurt, at almost 12 o'clock really while I know that I will have lunch at around 1 p.m. In the olden days, I would never have munched on something so close to one of the three regular meals a day, simply out of fear that I would not be able to finish off the plate. It is a small victory for the healing 'me' here, but one out of many more yet to come, or so I hope.

The truth about a burnout experience is that the inner burning is both self-devastating and physically destructive. The consequences, both the open wounds and the apparent scars, can, unfortunately, only be assessed (and addressed) on a case-by-case approach. Indeed, every burned body and soul face their own demons and each subject fights tooth and nails (if any left) on a unique stage, in a deserted terrain, at their most vulnerable time. To be honest, the uniqueness of the pain and the individuality of the recovery process make the journey deserving for every lost soul, for us really, because we are all given another chance after getting our fingers burned. We will try now not to make the same mistake twice.

So please, meet me. I am a 26-year-old burned body and self, still fighting her way out of the flames that are burning inside. The gastritis episode was yet another wake-up call that I cannot continue any longer in the (almost successful) destruction of my body from within. The wounds start to show too much on the outside; I am frail; I have no 'gazelle butt' as I like to call it; I am uncomfortable wearing pants or sleeveless tees, the latter because my arms are too skinny and the muscles (or veins) show. Furthermore, I am constantly battling against bloating and stomach cramps, headaches or migraines, insomnia, and I do not know how to hide these huge panda rings under my eyes. Lastly and perhaps most importantly, I am the prisoner of an incessant vicious circle of self-degrading lack of confidence and body shaming.

Nevertheless, who would not be completely at a loss in this new Photoshop, filter, and cut-me-off society way of thinking and people's reproachful glancing? Georges Orwell's *1984* might have been adapted over the years, only, this time, the people that are indeed watching our every move may not be 'real'; they are merely a figment of our imagination. I believe that social networks, the media, and our H-24 online status to the once-great World Wide Web has triggered a shadow pressure and a constant state of anxiety or vigilance in our minds. Since we know that our every saying, moving, or being can be the subject of the next hoax, we automatically feel restrained in the discovery and the developing of our self, and, consequently, we tend a little too much to stop listening to our soul. We fear what others might think or say. For the sensitive people among us, this is a battlefield in which we are deprived of our own weapons and onto which we will have to fight the fiercest enemy of all: our mind. And believe me when I tell you that this fight is going to be long and an arduous one, for we need to release ourselves from whatever grip others might have on us. Only then will we be free. Freedom of the mind is a personal trophy awarded to the self-liberated souls from society serfdom.

Ghosting

Eventually, one comes to wonder how this invisible pressure to which he himself only appears to listen to has succeeded in casting a disapproving spell onto the burned soul. Although many a man will have little difficulty in sweeping away any form of criticism; others, however, will display a great sense of trouble and will experience discomfort at not taking too seriously these (oftentimes) destructive, analytical, social skills uttered by their peers.

I had once read that there are three ways of looking at or thinking about a person: first, there is the image that others have of the person that we are, and the more they come to know us, the more they will be able to sketch a precise landscape of both our personal and professional behavior. Secondly, there is the real you, that 'presence' or the space that you occupy onstage. This is the apparent human being that is standing, both feet within our society; the being that is in fact bereft of any judgmental (especially personal) opinion. This is, in short, matter made of flesh. Lastly, let us not forget that we, ourselves, also create a positive or negative persona in our own minds, a 'somebody' that takes over our world and that reigns over both our body and our soul. This shadow being that exists in our (shall I dare say) imagination will influence our moving, saying, and thinking, regardless of the damage it can trigger sooner or later. Unfortunately, when damage there is indeed, it is almost already too late. Just when that third image dominates most of our thinking, then we have become, without us noticing it, an easy prey for ghosting. Self-effacement only takes seconds to erase a self while the soul will seek asylum somewhere deep within out heart. The more we wait, the more difficult it becomes to unlock the door to free ourselves from our own destructive spinning wheel.

I now need to confess that ever since I was little, I have been working very hard to please others and to never let them down. I wanted everyone to be proud of me. Sadly, for me, this invisible pressure that I have been referring to has never ebbed away, quite the opposite actually, for it grew stronger by the day up to the point that I had erased myself completely from my own world of imagination and from the social landscape. I had lost my freedom to simply exist.

On this day of April, I enjoy the pleasant company of the sun peeking through our kitchen window, and I feel how its warmth caresses my left arm, the only one exposed to the sun while sitting at the breakfast table. The morning light also brings a new sense of comfort which encourages me to finally admit to myself that the burnout 'tragedy' did not break out as a consequence of my one-year-long professional career. On the contrary, this tumbling down was merely a siren call issued by my body after years of self-inflicted torture, peaking with the very (or too) strict food diet that I had decided to stick to in order for the body to last, always a little longer, always with more protein and supplements, until it collapsed on most of my returns home while waiting for the subway. Except that one day in December 2017 when it was one time too many.

The energy I thought I could find in highly nutritional quality foods no longer sufficed to tone down the pleas of the soul. Hence the reaction of my body to spare me from the rule of the mind. In my case, the burnout has saved me; it has come (unwanted at first) to protect the life that I was slowly effacing while being at the service of others and living under the command of this invisible pressure that I had come to know better than my own self, and, that, I feared more than anything, more than losing my own life.

Divorce

Any separation epitomizes a turning point in one's life, just when, quite suddenly and perhaps unsurprisingly, that person finds oneself at a crossroad. It does not mean, however serious the case, that he or she is willing to accept this new reality that is changing his or her life. Yet, there is little one can do, for one way or another, the future looks uncertain indeed, and there is no possible way back. Pedaling in reverse would only bring more damage, so the only way is forward.

Nevertheless, some of us need a little more time before taking their first steps onto a still-untraveled road. The fear of change, be it for better or for worse, will influence their choice to stay with both feet firmly stuck in the middle of the traffic circle, unsure. Unfortunately, one grows accustomed to this status quo. This standstill has the advantage of leaving the passenger undisturbed in the backseat and eventually offering an invisible yet secure cell out of which he is now afraid to come out. Opening its doors would simply mean getting out of his comfort zone and risking his life. But isn't that what we are supposed to do? Only by stepping out of our safe haven will we be able to free ourselves from our inner fears and so allow a first communion between our body and our soul.

It is easier said than done, and I am myself trying to step outside those brick walls that I have built over the years. Until this day, I lack the energy to hold the hammer that would tear the outer walls all down. I know the plans and the drawings by heart, for I have been the architect of the comfort zone I have been assembling in order to protect myself, always a little more, not from the outside world (there are no sharks or bears in Belgium, nor are there dinosaurs wandering about in the streets), but protect myself from the invisible pressure that has been following me everywhere I go.

This shadow has become the voice of inner destruction and self-effacement to the benefit of others. To the rule of the shadow, one must add the pervasiveness of social media and their reported side effects. It is increasingly difficult not to compare yourself to others, not to lower yourself down, not to…and so the list goes on.

These ought to be the architectural precepts of any growing person, and I know them well enough because I am the first person to advise *the everyones* about *the everythings* that can alter their lives in just the blink of an eye. Sadly, I have still to find the pencil to pin them onto my own sketch and apply my precious counselling to my own self. I ought to at least try to erase the stains that have hindered my building process for too long. Not all stains are bad though, for they leave a mark behind which there is always a lesson to be learned. My first move will be coffee. I want to break free from the gastric reflux, and what other way is there than to drink coffee and enjoy every single sip of it? For the last couple of days, I have been training my mind to welcome back coffee into my organism. The body shall not fear it anymore, not after full 13 caffeine-free days. This is such a relief, even though, truth be told, I was not really given the green light by the medical team; instead, I have just decided to ignore the burns in the morning and make an effort: one coffee, one only, as a means to open the gate to inner confidence. I shall not yield to any pressure.

Although an indistinguishable crack at first, the damage later grows into a split, then a clear-cut break until, finally, a separation is yet but inevitable. At this time, one already knows it is too late, and depending on both the gravity and the scale of one's self-neglect, he or she will continue to ignore the siren calls and will increasingly turn a blind eye as the awareness of his/her poor condition floods into the mind.

The greater the problem, the more time we need to collect our thoughts together before we undertake a certain course of action. I was saved by my godmother who connived with Mou, my mother, in order to take me to a psychologist who would eventually slap me in the face with the terrible diagnosis. I did not know at the time that I was about to start an adventure, a healing process, of which I did not know anything about. The following week, the family doctor ordered the house arrest. It was mid-December, 2017, yet I had known for three years that the car that I was driving was set in reverse. It was about to crash, and that very Thursday, it hit rock bottom. So, please, do not wait any longer. Do not burden yourself with dread, for you are the only one who will shatter and disappear into dust. Life ought to be lived, not borne. Get yourselves out there and risk a life worth living for. Otherwise, how would you know that rain can be warm and sweet if you do not step outside and feel it for yourself?

Over the years, my faith has kept me going, and whenever I felt the bricks of hope starting to tremble, I would rely on the bedrock of faith. It forces a needed halt in the midst of the quake so that we can listen closely to the language of our soul. When doubts are flooding in or when anxiety rushes in, take a moment to close your eyes and breathe in. And out. Faith will meet you right when you need it most. You know you can let go. Embrace this time and make it yours; there is no need to save face in front of others, not now that you are alone. Mind you, I said 'alone,' not 'lonely.' Try to cherish this 'me time' and to welcome this new sense of communion. There is just you and the prayer that you are addressing to your soul.

For the last couple of days, I seem to have accessed a new level of my recovery. I have come at peace with certain *traits de caractère* that I do not wish to change about myself. I will not give up benevolence, nor will I stop reaching out to people. I will not break from the healthy lifestyle I have grown used to, although I will loosen up a bit. I will rediscover a palette of tastes and flavors that I have been restricting myself from. Moreover, I wish to help people and contribute to a general awareness about the dangers of setting yourself on fire in order to please others or to meet unrealistic social and beauty standards. I also wish from the bottom of my heart to find the light that would ignite my inner smile, the one that I have lost several years ago with the Salamanca experience and that has been missing for years. This is the promise I will try to fulfill without ever destroying myself to such an extent.

Several days ago, I was up in the middle of the night, reading into Isabel Allende's *House of the Spirits*. I could relate to one passage in particular which reminded me of my father's speech to me a couple of months ago: *"You're a hopeless loser, Son. You have no sense of reality. You've never taken stock of how the world really is. You put your faith in utopian values that don't even exist."*

I shall confess that this felt odd as I was lying down in my *baldaquin* false king-size bed. I shivered with cold and had to pull over my extra knit blanket, the one that Mamiche had sown when I was little. The sole reply I can think of today is that I have grown being all too much aware of the dysfunctions of this world, of the disguised evils of today's society, of the lust for power and the increase in egotism while we tend to forget about solidarity and communion. A person's grandeur as such does not depend on his fortune or height; a person's generous heart is, in fact, modestly hidden behind his will to invest his (full or spare) time in the emergence and growth of his peers.

So, instead of launching the first-ever foldable smartphone which would only be bought by a fraction amongst the wealthiest people on Earth, would it not be more sensible for market leaders to participate in the development of phone lines and internet access for the people who *still* do not possess a cellphone or who *still* have no free access to the worldwide web? Perhaps, the empowerment of the erroneously called 'lower classes' amongst the world population will contribute to their rallying up to the middle classes so that, together, they will back up the technology-enthusiast leaders who, in turn, would see their profit skyrocket because of their new audience supporting their solidary policies. See? Everybody would win from it. I simply cannot understand this burning need to unveil yet another technological eccentricity – a *foldable* phone, really? – while a great majority of the world population is waiting for insight and knowledge to be spread and backed up financially. Grandeur, in this case, would be listening to *their* ideas and implement them depending both on the context and the needs of that country per se, not the benefactor's country of origin. The time has come to put an end to any type of conquest; let us start with a different approach, one that encourages solidarity over serfdom.

Is believing in and imagining a better world utopian? I would rather think not so, otherwise the very foundations of humanity are bound to be torn down. As I was busy working my way up to a burnout, I could only think of following the path I thought was prearranged for me by I don't know which superior force. Whether fate or a simple electrocution of the soul, my body shut itself down, and although the first months were filled with paperwork, distress, more paperwork, and the constant need to fight against social stereotypes about a burnout reality (no, it is not the same as a depression), I was later on forced to admit that I had never really lived. My choices and decisions had always been made and taken based on what was accepted or acceptable by society at large, or they depended upon the *bien vu* attitude, that invisible pressure I felt was looking down on me constantly: *what would the others think or say?*

Little did I know that I would soon find out about the divorce between my body and my mind, a split triggered and *mis en scène* by my soul, perhaps as a way to avenge itself or merely because it could not find another solution to save the life that I was destroying and the body that I had come to abandon and was consequently bound to rot because of lack of care and interest…from its host.

The months following the 'curtain fall' that fateful Thursday, mid-December, 2017, were extremely disturbing. From one day to the next, I was thrown into a new and feared reality: being a recluse. Within weeks, my condition had even worsened, and until this day, moments of normality are scarce. It does not matter how many times I keep telling myself that the very concept of 'normality' is devoid of meaning, bereft of any sense. What falls under the term 'normal behavior'? What defines a 'normal reaction'? Who is to judge about the 'normality' of people, and why are we so frightened by what others think of us? Who is behind this culture of competition and examinations during which we are asked to prove ourselves, our worth, our value, our intelligence? And who considers himself sufficiently and superiorly skilled for him to categorize one of his peers' intelligence whereas the latter can show in many different ways and not only by solving impossible Pythagorean mathematical problems. Unfortunately, for many of us, the world is not ready yet to bring up their children by encouraging their unique talent, whether it be artistic or simply an uncommon one.

Personally, I have suffered greatly from the supposedly accepted social codes. That is, until I had erased a great deal of myself and finally succumbed to woolliness. As a result of the painful divorce between, on the one hand, the protective approach adopted by my body with its shutdown and, on the other hand, the pervasive pressuring preferred by the despotic mind, the soul had eventually ended up wandering about in the unknown, sometimes stirring a tantrum when it felt that danger was nearing.

After the first months have gone by, one starts to admit that there are limits one cannot trespass. I had slowly come to realize that I could no longer keep up with that permanent servitude that I had come to impose on both my body and myself. Although the very recognition of the mind's dictatorship might be considered a step forward, the recovery process is a far cry from gearing up; the latter rather suffers a standstill during which one's mind acknowledges the need for radical change, yet it is not ready to sign the ceasefire. Not yet.

During months, I would wander about between the awareness that I could not drive in reverse and end up in any worse condition than I already was and the freeze in which I had imprisoned my body into, submitting it to a strict routine, monitoring my every move, my every thinking, my every reaction, my every least thing, every hour of every day. The bubble I was living in as a recluse was obsessively figured out in every possible way, so much so that I had literally not a second left to think about getting to know my true self nor to listen closely to my soul. Every minute was closely monitored and scheduled, out of fear that change might worsen my condition. Little did I know that the absence of change might eventually destroy a person too.

Nevertheless, I was never the 'stay at home in my washed-out/worn-down sweatpants' kind of burned self (or patient). I do take a shower in the morning, and I have three decent meals a day, which I prepare myself rather than go for the easy (sometimes unhealthy) takeaway; I still care about food, and I am still 'presentable,' and by that I mean that I wear clean clothes and that I do brush my teeth. I would hate for people to think that burned bodies just veg out in their couch, that they binge-watch television or the latest Netflix show or that they spend the day doing absolutely nothing except stuffing themselves and going to sleep. And being irritable on top of everything, I forgot about that one. Needless to say, I have no stereotypes whatsoever about people going through a burnout or any kind of illness. I actually prevent myself from reading books about it, and I do not participate in group discussions I come across on Facebook. I strongly believe that every experience is unique, that every road to recovery is personal, and that every battle is fought privately.

Furthermore, I must warn you that the burnout sticker that got stuck onto me was not the greatest evil I was confronted with. It was merely the trigger for a compulsory further and deeper questioning of what I had done to myself and *what* I had become – mind you, not *whom*, but *what* – *i.e.* a shadow devoid of the most basic human personality traits. I did not know who I was; nor did I dare to dream about any future prospects. I could not picture myself crawling into a future for which I did not even have the strength to look forward to. That certain was I that the paralysis had already crossed a (sensitive) boarder from which the way back would ineluctably prove to be Machiavellian. I had lost the dignity to be an active member of this society. Shoo now, shoo the serf; get your fork and start your own revolution. Be the Marianne of your life; fight for liberty and reason and free your own self.

Marianne's Day-to-Day

I have now made peace with time, as I understand that only patience will bring about a first wave of behavioral changes (for the better). Practically speaking, my days were still scheduled around the same (military) drill. I would open my eyes after a night of combat against dizziness, aches of all kinds or insomnia. At some point, I would get bored in my bed, and after having checked my phone on the nearby bedside table to reassure myself that it was morning yet, I would activate the Wi-Fi and scroll down the newsfeed on social media to discover the latest talked-about recipes or I would fall upon the profile-picture changes of one person or another.

Later, at around seven and long after I had heard the rooster's cock-a-doodle-doo, I would find it 'late' enough, indeed, to start making some 'noise,' *i.e.* little sounds that are typically associated with a person's showering and getting ready in the morning. All clean, I would walk downstairs to prepare the *gigantesque* breakfast that I always treat myself to, even though I had to adapt it, since the gastritis thought better of my food choices.

On weekdays, my father would usually sit a ten-minute-*ish* with me while he swallows (stopwatch by hand!) the honey, apricot jam, and Nutella, store-bought, white-bread *tartines*. He would check his watch then, only to make sure he could scoop out a mixed-fruit yoghurt (sugars and additives included) and a seasonal piece of fruit, all this in a record-breaking time because he still wants to catch the 8:30 a.m. train to his office in Brussels. More often than not, he would run onto the platform only to face the facts and opt for the later convoy. Luckily for me, I am merely a witness of this breakfasting against the clock, for I keep myself busy, preparing my own oatmeal bowl which I will force myself to eat peacefully. The important thing is to eat it all, no matter how long it takes.

So, here I am, sitting at the breakfast table. I still hear my father shutting the door and making certain that it is locked by pulling at it not once, wait for it, but up to four times. I should not worry about the keyhole being broken, I tell myself. Instead, I open my computer and load the emails I have received, most of them spam newsletters of which I am too lazy to unsubscribe. What a bad habit; I should slap myself. Just indulge in the porridge and try to act normal. Enjoy breakfast, I hear myself say.

By the time I spoon the last oats out of my bowl – some 30 minutes later – the coffee beans are being ground, and I steal some dried cranberries or raisins that I keep in the cupboard just for the sake of having some morning ritual. While sipping the first drops of black gold, I switch back to my Outlook page which I have customized in pink. I would discover the email that my mother used to send me (almost on a daily basis, save for weekends obviously) from her office in Brussels. She knows that I am waiting for her 'news of the day' message filled with anecdotes from the 6:42 a.m. train carrying either the sleepy commuters (sometimes not that excited to be headed to work), either the last tipsy party animals who had been waiting for the early (or late) train back to their slums. And just when they would snuggle up and go to sleep, my day on the other hand would kick off and *comme d'habitude*, I would already be ignoring my body's aches. What has happened? I seem to have long lost the habit of feeling any sort of pain, or any…emotion.

Still at the breakfast table, legs crossed, the coffee mug on one side and the jar of honey on the other, I would soon find myself organizing memos and paste them on the 'schedule for the day' that I plan out in my head. Another habit of mine. I would not sit still for long because I cannot stand that the dishes – and, by this, I mean the pan that I use for my oatmeal and the tea mugs of the night before – would rot in the kitchen sink. Hence my automatic response and switching into gear by cleaning whatever utensil or pot that cannot be put in the dishwasher.

What next? How can I make myself useful? These are the questions I ask myself in the morning, out of fear of falling into the great cliché of stay-at-home, sick people. Instead, I play Cinderella, despite the evil eye of my therapist watching over me. Break free from the depersonalization of yourself. Live your life, they say… Or try to figure out your likes and dislikes. "Another day, perhaps," or so the mind replies. There is some ironing to attend to. Indeed, if there is clean laundry left from the weekend washings, I would head to the garage and spend one or two hours folding and ironing my father's shirts, towels, or pairs of socks, finding sometimes a lonely one amongst them and knowing exactly that the twin and matching sock would not be retrieved any time soon.

Further on in the morning, as the clock strikes 11-ish, I would typically head to the kettle and make my first cup of well-deserved chamomile tea. The second one would follow at least one hour after lunch. How curious though, when I come to think of it, as I am writing this down, that ever since I was little, I had (have) been living based upon a 'work comes first, the reward later' pattern. I would always need to make myself useful at first in order for me to sit down and enjoy reading a book for instance; well, that is when my eyes are not too tired and my body not too exhausted from that self-imposed military schedule of the day. Growing up, I would first study and do my homework, and only when I would consider it finished would I allow myself a break one episode of a children's program. The problem of this behavioral (and authoritarian) pattern, however, is that as you grow older, so does your workload until you find yourself at university, faced with the inevitable truth: there is always something you need to work on, whether research for a paper, preparation for your finals, searching for job opportunities. I did not see any time for pausing into my timetable. On top of that, I also had to live. Well, guess which I had given up… Sadly, I have not managed to find any rest since, and, even now, I still have to learn how to stop, how to say 'no,' or just how to pause and breathe in. And out again. I will be fine, I know I will…but I'm not quite there yet.

Next is lunch, and I would take some prep time which always involved the weighing of the salmon fillet and the rye *tartines* while the broccoli would be steaming and the computer ready for a 20-minute Netflix series, only on weekdays when no one is home. Of course, the meals I 'enjoy' most are the ones that are shared; I do not particularly like sitting alone in front of an episode of *Friends* or *How I Met Your Mother*, for it reminds me too much of the *kot* years, the Salamanca breakfasts, or the Mons evenings spent alone behind a desk while working on translations, making and studying vocabulary lists and, of course, (reluctantly) welcoming the endless stressing out. "You, chicken!" as I would say.

During the first months of my house arrest, the salmon, *crevettes*, or sardines would be digested during an early afternoon walk, mostly around the block, as part of the ritual that I had obliged myself to maintain, and this every day at the same hour in order to remain active, or at least keep up appearances that I was. However, my legs have become too frail and are unable to support my brisk walking, yet my mind seems more determined than ever to keep pace and ignore this torturous and vicious circle that I was spinning into. I just would not listen to my inner crying.

Three, two, one step, and, finally, I would be back home. What a challenge, indeed! Now I definitely deserve another chamomile herbal tea even though I feel more like dropping onto the couch, on the verge of passing out. If reading became unbearable for the eyes, or if the storyline was impossible to follow anymore, I would try to sweep away the black lightnings, those 'flashes' that I have suffered from for some time. When successful, I would try once again to make a siesta. Alas, more often than not, the lightnings struck so hard that even closing my eyes was hazardous and painful.

Luckily, my mother would come home from work between 5:30 and six o'clock in the evening, and she would help me out of the sofa. I am somewhat ashamed to admit that I could no longer move out of the couch, so heavy I felt. I did not weigh much though, yet the body seemed glued to the leather sofa. She sometimes had to carry me so that I could stand on both my feet, and whenever I felt the least loss of balance going through my veins again, I would collapse. I found comfort in knowing that I did not need to go far, since my favorite spot was only a few meters away: the kitchen. Dinner preparations were in order by then, and I would melt into my personage, aka the cook for the night. For the next two hours, I would disappear into another world, one in which I could not feel anything, one in which I enjoyed the cooking, the mixing the ingredients, the spooning into the pasta sauce, the counting down to sharing our meal together. I felt alive again, even if just for a brief period of time. *Bref*, I would feel whatever is closest to an 'ordinary' life.

All this to say that living at home and trying to kick off the road to recovery when your body and your soul are burning is no meagre a challenge, quite the opposite actually. Shoo the image of the depressing sweatpants and the ransacked house; I have become the guardian of neat and clean, startled at the sight of my father's coffee cup, messy breakfast plate and knife, the latter being covered in crumbs of too-sweet apricot jam and Nutella (don't even get me started about the discount honey which, in fact, is merely a mixture of sugar and artificial flavors, home to Chinese laboratory bees). But no need to worry, I will clean it up.

Unlike other burnout warriors, I was not defeated by the overload of work, neither by the dissonance or lack of qualifications. It was not the new job that pulled the trigger; the wound has been open ever since I can remember. Sadly, I will have to admit that my own personality, my character, my being and acting, all have dug this hole so deep into near-destruction and self-effacement that it will take boldness, strength, and time to close it up, if ever that will be. Deep down, I know, however, that the imprint, the scars, and the stains shall remain forever.

Spontaneity

Unrestrained and lighthearted. That is exactly how I felt after breakfast on the sixth day of April, a Saturday was it. My head was clear, the headaches nowhere near, and the hot coffee taste was still lingering until it sweetened my soul. Warmth and comfort, sometimes, take you by surprise when you expect it the least.

Sitting in front of me at the table was my sister. She was home for the weekend with a long-awaited-for additional day off work on Monday. Earlier during breakfast, she had determinedly expressed her wish to go and see an exhibition and spend the rest of the day in Brussels. I notice her puffy eyes, probably from the lack of sleep. Finally, she gives in to a yawn as if suddenly aware that she could climb back into bed, since she was still wearing her pajamas. Never would she have believed the following momentum of spontaneity, never would she have thought this was even likely to happen. I told her that I would go to Brussels with her, that I would try an outing for once. It took a few seconds before it finally kicked into her brain, and next thing I knew, she was ready for takeoff. It almost felt like we were going on a little vacation, just the two of us. As sisters do, though not when the little one is to drag her bizarre old granny out of the house. To be honest, I won't mind if you would think of me as a hermit. No offence taken. None.

All jokes aside, I was indeed going on a little escapade. I had had enough of my own self-degrading routine, my lack of listening to my soul. It is one thing to always take into account the fragility of your legs, the bloating, the pains, the evils, and the aches. Yet another thing is the realization that the art of quitting any ordinary activity out of mere fear (of change?) is even more destructive to your soul than the actual running of a marathon and its consequences on your body, despite it being at its lowest.

That morning, I was struck by lightning and, thus, decided to challenge my body in order to bring some comfort to my soul. It would be safe enough, I knew that, and I was thrilled to risk an outing, the first in a very long time. The last one that I recall was a little reunion before the Christmas holidays with my two best friends, one of whom has been living in Sweden for two or three years now and has found happiness in the great wild North, having swapped her casual sneaker shoes for moonboots until finally giving in to the sexy, outdoor, hiking shoes. We had met at the Central Station in Brussels but did not walk further than the little café/restaurant on the corner of the street where we decided we would stay for hours while talking and drinking chamomile herbal tea (for me) and what ought to have been hot chocolate with a cookie, even though the milk had been served too cold to make the sweet cocoa beans melt, and the absence of cookie was rather unfortunate and unpleasant, considering they had charged us too much already. The joy that filled my heart at seeing the three of us together again, like old times, could not hide my deepest cry: both of them knew about my 'condition,' but I could not tell them anything about me. I felt guilty, and, honestly, I was also suffering from a cold and, well, not feeling too well. For a change.

That reunion was months ago, so there was no need to be afraid. Astonished yet delighted at this sudden and quite spontaneous, totally unexpected decision that I had made, my sister mounted the stairs two by two, perhaps to make sure that I did not bail out. She must have been in such a hurry, for she asked me several times whether her makeup was properly applied and whether her hair had not suffered from an *Einstein-esque* electrocution. No, Honey, your hair looks just fine, it hasn't…fried. Yet (and, now, I giggle like a silly girl).

Luckily for us, the weather was clement with the whole hair situation that day, although not so much with our geo-localization skills. We ended up confused and lost, walking in the opposite direction of the Place Sainte-Catherine where we were headed for lunch. My father had volunteered to drive us to the capital and had dropped us at the next red light on our way, where, for the first time in quite a while, I felt the adrenaline in my stomach as we opened the doors, passenger's side, and stormed out of the car, just in time, before the lights turned green again. Close call! Off he was for his 'chores,' as he likes to put it, although admitting that he enjoys spending his day going from one store to the next or gardening or ending up at the *pépinière* to buy more plants and vegetation for our backyard. Let us put it this way: my father is best pleased when he can chicken run from one place to the next.

Here we were, left stranded on the pavement while I zipped up my handbag. We marched our way through the *Galleries du Roi et de la Reine*, a covered passage hall where chic boutiques and chocolate houses fight for the least square meter that appears to be left. My eyes were opened in awe and admiration before the Easter-decorated window displays, but we quickly regretted our slow pace, for we ended up lost in the middle of a group of German tourists taking over whatever little space there was left between the central corridor and the covered terraces of the coffee houses and *petites épiceries*.

My eyes were spinning around, not sure where to look: up, left, no, right… There were too many details I had forgotten about and too little time to save the pictures in my memory. The overwhelming parade took too much of a hectic twist, and on the count of three, my sister and I promptly deviated to the left, a hasty decision that made us almost collide with two Asian tourists wearing (to my great surprise, or shall I say disbelief?) slippers – the rubber ones by all means. The ones you would normally wear around a swimming pool in order not to slip, even though the wetness of your feet is bound to make you skid sometime along the race, if you had not already lost face because of the clack that your own footsteps noisily leave in their trail. Everyone has noticed you now, there is no doubt about that. So, yes, that kind of slippers.

Hence our flight to a secret haven, the one place where you lose yourself amongst the scent of new paperback collections, the silence of curious readers discovering the summary at the back of a signed (or not) edition, and the awkwardness of first-time customers ill at ease to speak in English to one of the aproned store managers. We entered the English bookstore. It was not as calm and tranquil as other times I had been there, for there was a man shouting on the phone, asking why his mother had to send him out to purchase a book that she did not remember reading but felt sure she had read *somehow*. He mentioned some book titles while eyeing the shelves and even seemed proud of himself to exhibit his anger and confusion while dialing his mother's number again (she had hung up on him apparently, now who wouldn't?). This time, he had lowered his voice, insisting that *Daddy* get over the phone. The man, although huge, looked like a motorcycle cop in his late 40s, wearing his black, leather, biker jacket and holding his helmet under his left arm while his other hand was busy holding (breaking) his cellphone. He was, in short, the perfect personification of the old bachelor still living with his parents, although haughty and disrespectful. The disturbance would not last long, however, for the man had soon decided to leave the supposedly already-read book on the shelf and set off, politely saying goodbye to the cashier who was astonished to witness this sudden rush of smiling from this peculiar customer.

Back to our own book picking, my sister and I spent the next hour submerged into a tidal wave of books, a torrent of highlights and prize winners, and a sea of edible wonders directly imported from the Anglo-Saxon world, ranging from the comfort food pantry to the special tea collections, all of them on display right next to the Penguin random house mugs and the Jane Austen cotton-tote bags. We had entered the Waterstones bookstore of Brussels.

Spending some time amongst thousands of literary pieces, memoirs, comics, city guides, magazines, and peanut-butter jars (with and without crunchy lumps, mind you), we detoxicated our body from the agitation and pressure that we had felt earlier during the Saturday morning hustle and bustle, so typical of a capital city.

As we pulled the glass door, we walked past a rotating stand of newspapers, and I could not help but notice the English version of a Chinese daily mail among other copies of German and French intellectual gazettes. The carpeted floor gave off a dusty smell, and there was an unavoidable dryness in the air which was certainly not rectified by the air coming out of the heating system that always seems to be preset on 'high' in any bookstore around the world.

When we headed out, it was already past noon, and my sister feared that the end of our little *sortie* was near. Deep down, she knows that it is still too soon for me to resume any normal Saturday outing, so I could not help but blurt out: "Come on, let's go eat." She froze for what seemed to be an endless minute, giving her just enough time to recollect her thoughts until she gave away her surprise, rapidly followed by a childish excitement. "But… I didn't think you would… I mean… Are you sure? Are you feeling okay? We can ride the subway if your legs are too tired. I won't mind, I promise. Wait, is this for real?"

It was. I had decided that I would ignore the urge to pee and try to condition my brain so that it would support my body, at least until we had reached the burger tent on foot. That is when we got lost in our very own capital city. Nevertheless, the 30-minute detour was enough to whet our appetite and fully enjoy our posh, comfort food. After the December 31st episode during the Christmas village market and the salmon burger, I was ready to freshen up this burger adventure. Take two of a happy meal.

I had not noticed right away that my sister's face had changed when she opened the menus, for she had spotted the changes made for the spring-season options and stopped at one in particular: the disappearance of the sexy salmon and spinach burger. A classic. *My* classic, actually. Mayday, mayday.

Although I must confess that I was a little panic-stricken at first, I regained my composure almost as soon as it had left. I need to change, I told myself quite spontaneously, to which my sister had the most fitting reply, quoting the *Mamma Mia* movie: "It's an adventure, Harry, it's good for you." I could see how proud she was of me that I would choose something *different*. This meant that I would get out of my comfort zone. Furthermore, I had always wanted to try the Portobello mushroom burger, but I never did opt for that option, because the salmon always hit first in the charts when I frequented the burger tent. This time though, there was no fish alternative to the other meat burgers on the list;

there was only the red-bean and soy vegetarian burger, but as you may know, I am not *that kind* of vegetarian, since I am not the greatest backer of plant-based and fake-meat alternatives. I am merely a person who swears by a Mediterranean diet, and, by this, I mean that I endorse the Puglia or Campania recipes which are mostly based on fresh-caught fish and seafood, little pasta here or there, and grilled vegetables (use extra virgin olive oil; please do not sabotage the ingredients!). There is nothing I can do to my disliking how meet tastes, both red and poultry. It is not as if I were allergic to animal proteins, that is just for cow milk or lactose I suppose; I simply do not enjoy the taste of it, nor can I appreciate it as a connoisseur ought to. So why waste both time and money on a burger that would be left stranded on the plate? I might eat the pickle though, I like it. But, again, it has at some point come into contact with the meaty sauce. My sister would be of no help, for there is no way she can eat two burgers, even though it is surely not a lack of desire. Challenge…unaccepted. Portobello it is then.

We did not have to wait for long before our orders arrived: classic *meat lover* for her, Portobello and grilled bell peppers for me. Except that I could not find any grilled vegetables, only a timid three or four leaves of baby spinach and the giant mushroom, obviously. With eyes up to the ceiling, the waiter brought the plate back to the kitchen, sermonizing the chef for this quite-unfortunate oversight. The second time was a charm, and, at last, I could bite into the unknown. Here was change, and I was embarking on a new journey of flavors. Once again, the adrenaline was running through my veins. I had kept my eyes closed as to better savor every bit of this new mixture of lightly heated-up ciabatta bread out of which the olive oil was dripping, though not too much, just the right amount actually to keep the fingers moist and let the customer the pleasure to lick his fingers off in secret when he had secured a safe perimeter out of sight of any too important a person's reproachful glance. Eyes talk apparently, so I wanted to make sure I was in no one's nearby radar.

This new burger renaissance enabled me to make peace with an old habit of mine to control every possible detail about the contents of my plate. I still need to break free from the very selective and restrictive list of places that are deemed safe to go eat, at least by the very critical me. I thus proved that I could swap the usual salmon and veggies bowl that I have for lunch almost every day of the week (sometimes switching to sea-bream when bought fresh from the market and frozen the same day in our freezer in the cellar downstairs, only waiting to be baked sometime in the week when I am out of salmon). What can I say? It felt like doing something extreme, out of the ordinary, like when one goes bungee jumping. Eating the Portobello mushroom burger symbolized more than a plan B after your first option had vanished; it represented the crossing of a new boundary, the trespassing of a new frontier for me. I had, in short, exited my comfort zone. Aces Alice…aces indeed.

Later on in the afternoon, we walked to what could be considered the Upper East Side of Brussels, the Sablon, a part of town especially coveted by antique and art dealers before colliding straight with the Palais de Justice at the end of the street. I wondered whether I would walk past a lawyer wearing his gown, but my sister warned me: they are not supposed to wear it outside the courthouse, perhaps so as not to attract attention or simply out of fear of reprisal which, to be honest, I can understand, for no one would particularly like to be thrown rotten eggs at his just-returned clean laundry and fur, black overcoat.

We ended up in the Pain Quotidien to sip (unsurprisingly) chamomile herbal tea – although I spilled most of it because I could not handle the tea pot, so clumsy was I, dead with fatigue – and a citrus lemonade for my sister who took a slice of cherry crumb tart too. I felt blessed, sharing the crumbs with her, sitting at a table normally set for six at the back of the veranda, safe from the rain. Time had been on my side until that moment, but as I lifted myself up from the teak chair, I knew I would have to unlock some hidden motivation (and strength) in order to walk the way back to the Gare Centrale again where we would wait for the train to take us – almost – home. My mother would then catch us at the station and drive us back home, exhausted though happy. I could not have dreamed of any better first outing. And, you know what? Sometimes it is okay to feel worn out; exhaustion can be liberating in a way.

An Upsurge of Spontaneity

Waking up that Sunday morning was not without effort. I bore the remnants of ghost-past exhaustion and welcomed back, unwillingly though, the headache hammer which seemed to have retrieved its favorite lodging. I could not move much that morning, nor could I withstand too much noise or talking around me, for my ears were sensitive and ill-prepared for any first scan or analytical study of spoken words. It was a 'leave me alone, don't expect me to chat happily' kind of morning. Words would, thus, simply wander about in my head; the mind being unable to treat any type of information let alone make any sense out of the spinning words.

Lunchtime arrived sooner than I had thought, and I was relieved that I could disappear again into my safe haven, a.k.a. my kitchen. There was a leftover of French fries from the doggy bag we had asked at the burger tent, and I reheated them in a frying pan along with a turkey schnitzel for my sister. I, of course, would treat myself to a beautiful skin-on Scottish salmon fillet with broccoli, peperoncini, and a steamed jacket potato topped with some genuine *fleur de sel*, the one from Guérande, located southeast on a map of *la douce* France. I feel no shame admitting that I was most pleased to meet the salmon again at healthy/favorite plate o'time.

As the day went by, I finished the book by Isabel Allende, and I cursed myself for not having bought the copy of *I Know Why the Caged Bird Sing* by Maya Angelou the previous day while I was at the English bookstore. Instead, I had decided to set it aside (save some money) along with another book on my sister's reading list because she wanted to purchase both books with a gift card that she had received for New Year's from her godfather. Since she did not carry the gift voucher in her purse that day, she decided it would be better if she just set the books aside and handed the card to one of my parents for them to pick them up during the working week when they make time to drop by the store, voucher in hand, *cela va de soi*.

After dinner that night, the most unexpected event happened, one that would be engraved in our best memories of family nights in. There was a spontaneous decision and shared laughter, accompanied by cheerful clapping of hands and a series of spur-of-the-moment giggles. We all took our appointed seats in our sofas – the big, vintage, three-seat couch being used by my sister and I (we do need the extra space) while the matching individual leather armchair of this two-piece salon set is already shaped to fit the contours of my father who does not seem to be bothered by his sitting on the cushion instead of putting it aside. Last but not least, my mother would squat the baby fauteuil there is left, the one that is closest to the mahogany coffee table and, strategically speaking, the Easter chocolate egg basket which, obviously, is not empty, considering we are nearing the end of Lent and hence approaching the egg hunts and possible binge-eating on sugary treats (and indigestion).

With the four of us nestled in the *salon*, my sister tried to conceal her annoyance at my father's gaucheness in his handling of the remote control as well as in his (impossible) quest to find the title menu of the D.V.D. player. We had indeed decided, quite spontaneously, to watch the *Mamma Mia Two* movie that we had purchased months ago, though the copy remained intact with its price tag and plastic wrapping, left forgotten about in one of the D.V.D. drawers in a not-so-frequently used room upstairs. Movie night.

It might seem trivial to some, but to a burned self, watching a movie can prove to be very draining. The biggest and most unexpected surprise, unseen for years, was perhaps the fact that I did not mount the stairs at 9:30 p.m., hence breaking with a granny routine of going to bed at a somewhat 'premature' time as some would consider. Not tonight. I would sit and watch the movie. I wanted to feel again what it was like to stay up 'late.' So, it was well past ten indeed when I finally succumbed to fatigue, yet I was thankful that I had been able to follow the plot through the end, although not quite fit actually to continue to sing along with the Abba songs.

We were all enjoying the musical atmosphere that rejuvenated our souls and drew us closer together. That movie had come to epitomize the reunion of a lost past tradition of movie nights in, of the four of us sharing the same childish innocence and glee, of clapping our hands and smiling like we were allowed one time more on the merry-go-round. I, thus, found myself smiling one last time before closing my eyes and going to sleep. Cheers it is; to spontaneity, because although it destabilizes and undermines a burned-out body, it also ignites even if just a shadow light in the lost corridors of the soul. All there is left to say for me is that it is actually nice to feel alive and to forget, for however brief a moment, that I am actually not doing very well, no. Not yet. Soon, I will be reminded of the creaking of my right hip, the dizziness and fatigue, the bloating left by the indigestion of adrenaline peaks, or was it the peak of fear? Fear of the unknown, fear of the evanescence of time? I wonder.

Ephemeral

For some time now, although quite unbeknownst to me, I have been surrounded by both quotes and works of art by the great and inspiring Frida Kahlo. She is one of the gurus whom my sister has come to be fond of, so much so that she cannot pause the reading of her biography. As a result of her 'while-in-the-subway' reading, my sister has been sending me screenshots of excerpts that she believes affect me directly. This time, however, I am the one who comes across a passage that strikes me most, and I kneel before the artist's words: "Nothing is absolute. Everything changes, everything moves, everything revolves, everything flies and goes away."

What I have come to learn in the last 14 months is that hanging onto 'forever' as a notion of time is only twisting the knife deeper into the wound. I have, so far, failed to understand why human beings in general always seem to try their best to hold onto the chimera that something, mostly a positive experience or situation (or even love), can and does really last forever. Many amongst us take for granted that there is, indeed, a never-ending thread that is attached to a precise needle which we use to knit our lives perfectly fine, without ever skipping a button. Nonetheless, given that we are all surrounded by counterexamples of the everlasting period of time of any kind of state or being, why not give up once and for all the excruciating pain and disappointment that we inflict upon our minds by our constant gripping to this illusion of permanency?

To tell the truth, I think we are driven by hope; the hope that something agreeable can and will last forever, at least for as long as we need to hold onto that particular event or situation. Yet, every day, life has proven unfair to nurture such hopes, perhaps this is for the best too. Until now, I had always believed that I would follow a path that would be shown to me through whatever possible signs which I would also be interpreting while on my way. These might have come to me in all kinds of ways, whether a hint, a highlight, or even a blow, and I would have found a rational explanation to all. I shall confess to you that I strongly believe there is a reason behind the hurdles we hop; that there is a smile behind any tear, both the tears of laughter that run down and the silent ones that have taken to the cheeks to demonstrate against helplessness, desperation, and confusion. Still, they shall not be defeated.

Growing up, I had the little girl's dream to marry (at a decent age) and have a family of my own while switching from superwoman at work to busy-mom and wife on the home front. I had a plan, a luxuriously elaborated one, designed with finesse up to the details. In order to stick to my road map, I first needed to have good grades, starting with a school report of which my parents would be proud of and, later on, a university degree with high honors and, what is more, an additional diploma too, because, well, *why not*? The last stop would be the finding of a job that would provide me with a sense of fulfilment and a means to give back to the world what it has so kindly given me, whether it be the teachings or the lessons that I have learned. Sadly, that little girl had not expected she would fall off that train of thoughts, let alone that she would break into pieces as she hit hard to the ground and, thus, be forced to abandon her preset itinerary. Instead, she hit the emergency brakes.

For as long as I could go to sleep at night with a possible fast-forward scene of imagining my older self in an apartment, at work, walking head high into the streets with stiletto heels and blaming herself for wearing them on a rainy day (typical, right?), French-kissing an Italian fiancé, although never quite realizing how 'a man like him could possibly be interested in a girl like her.' These were the scenes that would make me fall fast asleep and send me away on innocent dreams. Unfortunately, once I had arrived in Salamanca on February sixth, 2013, I stopped having these secret (healing) conversations with my mind. Instead, I would soon learn how to fight tension knots – although not being very successful, as you might have noticed. I had lost the ability to project myself into the future. I had stopped picturing myself into further times. How was I supposed to interpret this sign – the end of one's life and growth visualization – as the beginning of loss, as the disorientation of my soul, as the emptying of myself, or as the start of disappearance into self-oblivion?

Back then, this felt as failure and defeat. I found myself guilty of breaking with my expectations, my hopes. Therefore, I supposed that the only way out was for me to dive head first into the impossibility of letting myself down, *i.e.* hide behind work and more work until work was all that I had come to live for. I would not be vanquished this time, and, so, as from my arrival onto Belgian soil again on June 16th, 2013, I decided to lock myself up into the research work that I had been trusted to undertake for a professor at university whom I did not wish to disappoint. I gave up my summer holidays in order to better reach that goal. I had nothing to lose, for I had already lost the lightness of being and was madly driving into the bustle of inner fighting. I switched gears, never to let go of the gas pedal.

In hindsight, I realize that despite the fact that the siren calls had been playing loud and clear for some time, I had simply decided to ignore them. What was I thinking? These signs would not disappear that easily, for they had come prepared into the battlefield: they had quietly but surely taken advantage of the first aches, the lack of self-care and the rise of low self-esteem. They later took advantage of my lack of benevolence toward my body, which, consequently, always put my head into more work, more servitude until, finally, there was ever less of *me*. For years, I have denied myself any benevolence, any gratitude, any love. Until the forced shutdown of December 2017, I preferred to ignore those signs, those siren calls from both the body and the soul, because as the months were passing by, I had gotten increasingly afraid of my stepping backward. I had lost 'where' *forward* was headed. I could not see it anymore, nor could I prevent the nightmares flooding in and disturbing my sleep pattern. In the end, I came to think that there was nothing more that I could do to the micro-siestas of the night; that I was condemned to wander through the days like a phantom errs through the night: hollow because of lack of sleep and the dreadful weight of headaches and emptiness. Who was I, and how could I have gotten so deep in the marsh? Guilty again: I got more scared by the day. I knew I was not *completely fine,* and, let us be honest, who would not find refuge in work, the sole plan or road map that had not shattered?

Vongole Veraci

Perhaps struck by a sudden wish to go back in happier and worry-free times – I shall never find out why I reopen the souvenir box over and over again – I have bought earlier this morning two nets of *vongole*, or clams for the food lovers, of one kilogram each. It is Saturday, and this only means that market day has arrived. Mou and I braved the bitter cold and had decided that the just-above freezing temperatures would not hinder our walk or going.

I had been waiting for a while at the fishmonger's stand until, finally, the ticket number echoed in the chilly air, announced loud and clear by the captain himself. He is not really a captain at sea, but the cream and navy-blue, woolen garment he was wearing would perfectly match the thick, yellow raincoat typically worn by fishermen. I myself suddenly felt nauseous because even though my mind was picturing the boat entering harbor, my senses were capsizing, as I could only smell the roasted chickens that were spinning on the wheel right behind me. Fortunately, I could focus again on the fish auction going on that morning, a bit further in distance than the North Sea's docks, and my eyes were, again, possessed by an inexplicable attraction toward the catch of the day. The Scottish salmon was as beautiful as ever, skin on *bien sûr*; the soles (mind you, not flounder, for there really is a difference between a sole fillet and a *filet de sole-limande*) were waiting for me to be taken back home – maybe next time? – the shrimps were almost sold out and their neighbors, the scallops, were not in fashion by customers. Last but not least, the *branzino* or sea bass was eying me, for it already knew it had conquered my heart and saved my soul from the dullness of industrial fast-food fish one can purchase at the supermarket, if fish it truly is.

Back home from our fishing, I cannot quite describe the overwhelming suspense that has found lodging into my stomach, although it being quite a positive new experience I might add. The excitement seems to be powered by a fair amount of once-thought-forgotten adrenaline, accompanied by colonies of butterflies flying ecstatically through my body, enjoying their newfound freedom as they are acting as a unique gear that fuels me from the couch and deep into the kitchen pots. The smell of freshly crushed and chopped garlic cloves calms me down and takes me back to a safe haven of peace and quiet, far away from the torturous shadows that had once sealed a deal to always pressure my soul.

Unlike the soul, and not quite convinced that the body is any better shape, the *vongole* are safe, of that I am sure of. I cannot help it but take one more look at them while they are bathing into a 20-percent of pink, Himalayan, concentrated, salty water before I will let them rest in our refrigerator, covered with a wet kitchen towel, on the second counter from the bottom. Sleep tight for the next two to three hours. The *vongole*. I hope they enjoy this Jacuzzi treatment for the next couple of hours, for it will take some time for them to flush out any remnant of the sea, whether sand or an unfortunate rotten comrade, unable to adjust to its new environment and determined not to end up between (and spoil) the flat parsley and the hot chili peppers of the sauce. Long story short: *Sta sera mangiamo un primo di spaghetti alle vongole.* Dinner is served.

It was now half past seven, perhaps a bit later, because my father had only just returned from the weekly grocery shopping, and the moment of truth had finally arrived. I opened the lid and was immediately reunited with past memories of our sharing *spaghetti alle vongole* with our friends on the Italian seaside in Lido degli Scacchi. Olio, aglio, peperoncino e prezzemolo. Simple yet authentic tastes. Simple yet genuine. Simple, just like that. Like Italy: *un mondo di sapori con pochi ingredienti*, a whole world that is opening to us with only few ingredients, yet the love and care with which they are prepared reunites us all around the dinner table. What is food if its taste cannot be shared? What if the love cannot be spread? One can spice up a meal with dozens of tricks and countless of additional pinches of *this* or *that*, but never will one feel the same warmth as that which is brought by the comfort of being with our loved ones. Cheers and *buon appetito* to all.

Asparagus Are in Season

Tuesday night or *martedì*, and I am looking at my cherished, Italian-made, one-pot inox saucepan, the one we had received from the very friends we used to share our spaghetti vongole with on a yearly basis. A not-so-out-of-the-ordinary day one shall say, unless it were for the pasta that is now boiling (that is always a milestone, mind you), and the chef's eagerly waiting for the alarm clock of the oven to beep. Time is almost up.

Only when I hear the piercing beep will I rush to the sink and drain the perfectly golden al dente spaghetti. I shall toss them right into a colorful yet simple, vegetarian sauce, save for the anchovies, but, then again, there are only two of these fish fillets, and they are chopped into pieces so small that they have melted into the clear asparagus jus and yellow bell pepper sauce. Two only, yet they turn even the most boring dish into fantastic fireworks going off into the delicate palates of whom is *précieux* enough to appreciate a pinch of authenticity and a dash of Mediterranean *folie*. As I open the lid to unveil the *piatto* ready to be served on a Tuesday night, I whisper slowly to myself that food is too often depreciated, even trivialized to such an extent that one tends to neglect the emotion that these simple-to-more-elaborate-flavor combinations awaken in both the body and the soul. There is never enough pasta.

Cooking, therefore, is a three-time living emotion, for it buries the cherished fragrant memories into the past; it unlocks gratitude and thankfulness in the present time to share; before it unleashes a sudden moment of folly at the thought of sharing the same food with our loved ones on whatever appointed date in a near or not-so-near future time, a moment for reunion whether planned or spontaneously left hanging in the air until serendipity strikes and gets the four of us together again. Hence the no brouhaha, the no chichi nor bells and whistles into the elaboration of any meal whatsoever. The only thing that matters is pasta, for it has the power to transform even the most basic (boring?) night into a *One Thousand and One Nights* tale. So, which one will you tell?

Symbols

Palm Sunday has officially welcomed, or so we hope, the last chilly – freezing in the morning – and rainy day of the season, but, most importantly, it has cut through the ribbon of Holy Week and has unveiled yet another time to celebrate peace, resurrection, and love. The Easter festivities are just around the corner, and I cannot help but remember the processions that are about to take place all over Spain for what they call *Semana Santa*, Holy Week to us.

I recall one very particular procession, the first that I had ever witnessed. It was back in the Salamanca days when my parents had just arrived to pay me a most-needed surprise Easter visit. It was somewhere in mid-April, and we were back in our room from the daily wandering about the streets, our feet hurting and not quite recovered, our minds still a little struck at the many paper towels that had been thrown to the ground by hungry customers. These *servilletas* would not be swept away by the *pinchos* or *tapas* bar tenders, at least not before closing time, and would thus leave the place a pigsty or a not-so-welcoming mess for the next wave of starving tourists, waiting at 5 p.m. for the 'night shift.' Poor them. If only they knew the kitchens do not open until 9 or 9:30 at night. Around the Plaza Mayor, we had indeed spotted while peeking through the windows of the bars and restaurants, the bits and pieces of *patatas bravas* and *croquetas* left stranded, uneaten, waiting to be trampled on by the crowd on their way to get their next tapas order. At least the house pets will be pleased with the Spanish twist on their otherwise-dry kibble food.

The hotel that my parents had booked was located in the southern part of the city. As we headed back from the underground car park, we were caught in the middle of the procession. It was so stern that it literally gave me goosebumps. I was not so much stunned by the gigantic Virgin Mary with Child that was being carried by a group of eight or ten men, yet I was rendered speechless by the traditional costumes they were wearing, reminiscent of something *bad*. Hence my puzzlement: on the one hand, I had come to admire the strength of these men for having to carry such enormous structures or life-size crosses on their shoulders; yet, on the other hand, my face went blank at the solemnity of this religious act, too quiet for me to merely stand there, feeling somewhat uncomfortable, watching the Ku Klux Klan lookalike white or purple hoods and robes marching past us.

After these confusing emotions had melted down, I suddenly remembered the shopping bag that I was still carrying in my hand. Truth be told, I really could not wait for the 'clan members' to walk past the entrance of our hotel so that I could climb the stairs two by two to try on the just-purchased pair of Minnetonka boots. This expensive present was given to me by my parents, for they knew how hard it had been for me to live abroad, especially sharing a cubicle with a destructive narcissist as best friend.

During the Easter break, my parents had, indeed, witnessed the final straw. It was the day I showed them around in the apartment we had been renting, and as I opened the door, I discovered that the one time that she had decided to do the laundry *herself*, she had put one of her purple gym tees together with pale-colored tank tops of mine, turning them into a horrible turquoise mauve. They were hanging in the entry hall, ruined. Perhaps it was not such a great idea to show my parents the apartment that the two of us were sharing with a Canadian student and chickpea addict. Juanita, if you read this, please know that you were my lifejacket more than once, and had you not been our roommate, I think I might have exploded earlier during our semester abroad. I take the opportunity here to thank you for your true friendship, your wonderful presence, and your thoughtful efforts.

Moving on from the terrible sight of mortified knit tops, I locked the door and headed into town with my parents for a shopping delight. I had spotted the five-layer fringe soft-suede boots ever since day one on Spanish territory, when walking to the university campus. The store was located in a side street of the Plaza Mayor, just before the frozen-yoghurt and ice-cream shop. The corner boutique had quickly become the must-peek-into-the-window-display stop on our way to class. And there they were, standing beautifully among summer wedges, stiletto heels, ballerinas, and moccasins: the Minnetonka high boots, sold at 180 euros the pair. Obviously, I could not afford them, for I had a very strict and exhaustive grocery-shopping list that I had decided to stick to, because I did not want my parents to pay for everything. Whatever was left at the end of the month was not to be spend on frivolities. There is no need to worry though, because I always bought just enough food to cook with, and I could always manage to bring some decent dinner together, even indulge in a little piece of chocolate for dessert, but only one at the time when I fancied a sugary treat.

Those months abroad, we did not eat out, nor did I spend money on student parties (I was never a party animal anyway), but I did use my savings to buy a three-month unlimited access to the gym pass for the bargain price of a little over 200 euros, if memory serves me well. This was the only luxury I had allowed myself. This being said, it comes as no surprise that I found myself jumping in the air as my parents brought me to the store for me to try the boots on. Was this *for real*? After a little check for size and care (I was afraid they would not 'acclimatize' to Belgian weather), I left the shop ecstatic and as proud as a peacock, although leaving out the vanity and arrogance typically associated to the use of this particular idiom.

Bref, I was nuts about the purchase, yet this was nothing compared to the symbolism of these fringe boots. They were my freedom, my first something to hold onto during this dreadful experience. Three days later though, when I waved my parents off, I believe the tears ran off my cheeks for what seemed to me an endless amount of time. Little did I know that I would never fully recover from these months abroad and the dire regime I had survived to.

Although it still hurts when I go back down memory lane, I am blessed now with the warmth of a refreshing yet timid sunray that encourages the chirping of the birds and the breaking out of spots on the almost-packed in-green bushes of our backyard. Holy Week has arrived, and grateful we shall be.

Oh Holy Us

Girls, when they are little, are desperately excited, for they simply cannot grow fast enough and become part of the small group of young women they look up to, be it during family gatherings or the annual school party or even the countless other events and daily encounters where children mix with grownups. But do not be shy; we have all dreamed of "13 going on 30," only our fancying started at age five or six. Mine did at least.

This New Year though, I would embark on the 27th year of my existence, meaning I am only three years away from what the little me thought would be a perfect life. I would have it all. I would lie if I told you I were not filled with dread at the sight of what I might have become by then. I cannot picture me *at all* because I have absolutely no idea of the most important Ws: where (add location?), what (add any activity), (with) whom.

As I have no other option but to have faith in the long recovery process of a lost soul and an almost-beaten-to-death body, I see the little girl I used to be and I try to remember her dreams. On this day especially, I recall the big family reunion at my uncle's for New Year's Day when little children were playing around. There was a dinosaur in the game, chasing after two princesses (obviously) and trying as best they could not to bump too often into the adults, seen as standing obstacles. We, on the other hand, were too busy talking and sipping champagne (water for me) to notice the kids stealing all the chips and appetizers.

It was one such event during which I was reminded about my own time when I wished nothing more than filling my mother's bikini tops and fitting into her wedding dress that sadly had no veil with which I could play. We switched turns with my sister, playing Carole and Corole, two maidens ready to spend the next hour or two sitting on the staircase with our legs hanging and using the step right above the one we were sitting on as the desk of our (imaginary) school bench. Other days, we would dress up and save the world, impersonating Alex and Clover from the Totally Spies series, missing an extra playmate to be Sam. Never did our 'games' reach such real-life experience as whenever we played at Mamiche's on sunny summer days that we spent at her apartment because we were too little to stay home alone. These were the rare occasions when we were allowed to wear heels, even twice our then-shoe size. The clickety-clack on the floor and on the outside slabs leading to the three garage boxes appended to the main building was happily welcomed, as it represented both the urgency and the gravity of our rendezvous to save the world.

While wandering about in these childhood memories, the toasting of champagne glasses brought me back to this day's reality. Here I was indeed, standing in the doorway between the kitchen and the living room, trying not to lose my balance as my nephews' children were playing and probably looking up, this time at me, the grownup. I was suddenly aware that I was part of the small group children look up to. Our generation had somewhat unexpectedly become too much aware of its adulthood, of its having crossed that bridge, whereas the grownups that we used to look up to back in our childhood days, our uncles and aunts, had now acquired yet another distinction in our minds: they were sages; standing out by the wisdom they have acquired from their life experiences. The Goldilocks were running lose as I tried my best to decipher their game. Of this, I am absolutely certain: the little man was a dinosaur pursuing second-generation cousins wearing tutus and princess costumes. And just when I wondered who would win and who would be granted a consolation-prize kiss from the princesses, I saw three pairs of deep-blue and wide-open eyes, all staring at me, unsure whether to show me the greasy bowl of paprika chips or their healthy companions, the olives. One of my nephew's daughters had suddenly appeared to me as the little girl I used to be, when it was I who was left scared and reserved when asked to talk to grownups. Reminiscent of my own shyness, I smiled at her and simply said: "I will only take one, one green olive," (although I really prefer the black ones) and next thing I know, I was putting my hand proudly (or was it approvingly?) on her head so that she would never forget how special she is. I did not, however, tell her what I had secretly wished for: that she would never know the same battles as I have had to fight, many of which are still going on to this day. I wished that life would treat her well and right with poise and composure.

She was long gone before I came to my senses. The innocence in her eyes made me realize that when I was her age, I would always be looking up to the people that were surrounding me. Unfortunately, this habit has always proven self-destructive for me and did little to actually boost my confidence. Growing up, I did not belong to those popular girls that never seem to doubt about their walking, their talking, their being; the very ones that never seemed to be panic-stricken by a pimple outburst or shameful rings of sweat under the armpits that you, unlike the dolls, try as hard or as best you can to conceal from your classmates' direct field of vision, especially when raising your hand to answer a question the teacher had just asked. Unfortunately, for our species and especially true for the pimple-sensitive and sweaty subjects that were not spared by puberty nor by the hectic commutes once they would have secured their first job, we live in a combative society, one in which each and every single one of us is tested, whether conscious or unconsciously, and in which our own peers are both the predators and preys of the game we are forced to play. One remark only: we have all started with a different set of rules, with different cards and with inequitably distributed jokers. Yet, no one seems to care, and certainly not the ones benefitting from any advantage, whatever it be. So let the dice be cast.

This fear of others and the too-early an-age awareness of what *others* might think or say started in kindergarten, when the other kids were out playing saving the world whereas I stood there, mending and folding my classmates' socks and scarfs. Even back then, it seemed that I liked things to be neat and clean. I wanted the Miss to be proud of me. I could not deceive my parents, and, soon, I found myself locked in this vicious circle of efficiency and performance. I was aware of the poison that slowly but surely ran through my veins, until it filled the wounds left by lack of confidence. I could find refuge in work, and the more I did for the others, the less I had to think of me and that haunting, invisible pressure. The latter I had myself enforced upon my mind, but how was I supposed to know that it would gain control over my body and try to get rid of the soul?

To tell the truth, I have always wanted to please others, for as long as I can remember really; I chose to make myself useful to others, to make others, they again, proud of me, hence my not-so-personal decisions, for they were always made in line with social pressure and standards. Creativity and out-of-the-ordinary-ness are quite a hazardous battlefield, one where the mere act of crawling cannot prevent the mines from exploding in your face. If you are lucky enough to make it to the finish line and enter the safe zone, you might have earned some respect and possibly have won the admiration of your peers.

However, many among us are still fighting with their best soldiers on the front, not for themselves, but merely to win sheer approval (or recognition) from their peers. One day, those people, too, will shine through their difference, their talent, and their uniqueness, but until that day has arrived, they are locked in a cell of their own creation, tortured by their thoughts and desperate by the questions left unanswered.

So, is it really *our* fault that we have erased our own selves when one considers the growing-up process as a challenge given the circumstances, *i.e.* finding your place in a world of testing, comparison, performance, and velocity? What has happened to finding our inner peace, our purpose, our future? What happened to becoming a better person, reaching out and listening to our peers, regardless of our academic and professional careers? We all exist as a person, and it is unfair for those of us who still believe that they have to deserve their place into society, obviously *en accord* with whatever they have achieved so far. Meritocracy, in short, has condemned too many souls, but the day they shall rise, they shall shine among the stars and be freed from superficial artefacts. Hopefully. One day.

A propos, do you not find it ironic that our society is increasingly locking everyone in his shell by encouraging self-absorption and self-centeredness which started, for as long as I can remember, with the use of head and earphones at the turn of the century, instead of the 1950s' radio transmitters that could make a whole household dance to the rhythm of cold winter nights and summer, bistro-themed barbecue gatherings or dinner *al fresco* parties. It thus looks like technology has been withdrawing mankind from Aristotle's description of the human behavioral pattern, that 'man is by nature a social animal.' So why does society evolve into such inhuman a form of organization if it proves to be devastating and simply unnatural?

While I see the first fireflies flying the nest on this beautiful spring Thursday, a sparrow lands on a crooked branch of our burgeoning apple tree. The rising temperatures and the mounting morning sun make me wonder why we, the people of the world, are so desperately focused to reducing everything to solitude. I realize, indeed, that activities or habits that used to be carried out in groups are now only aimed at single beings. For instance, I think of how a radio program used to bring people together, or how dining out would draw families together, or even how telephones and social media were meant to ban physical frontiers so that people could stay 'in touch' wherever and whenever they wanted.

Nowadays, we need 'people management skills' to reach out to our peers. The radios have come to be considered vintage or are merely purchased as home decoration since one does not find the time anymore to pick out C.D.s from an open display, preferring the tracks to be randomly selected by a music software and not minding titles and artists, not quite listening neither, yet not putting it down, for it creates a certain *ambiance* while your friends are over. A party mix, they say.

Next in line are the night outs. Here, too, the reality is quite different than it used to be – and I am only referring to the tidal wave of changes over the last two decades. The last time I went out eating in a not-too-fancy restaurant, I was struck by the great majority of families letting their children be glued to their tablets and smartphones, sometimes so young of age that I had to prevent my jaw from dropping to my waist, although, oftentimes, I failed to hide my astonishment. I am afraid it is indeed easier for parents to lock their children up in their own bubble, for they can at last enjoy that lovely *tête-à-tête* they have been longing for, making sure not to leave out the hashtag 'couple goals' from their social-media status update. Click: #dinner with the kids. Parenting goals. So obvious.

Speaking of posting pictures and status updates, I believe there was a time when social networks were supposed to keep people connected anytime, anyplace, no matter how far away they were from each other. But then, why do I have this weird feeling that these platforms only encourage egocentrism and hauteur through this new fashion of 'posting' messages and pictures only to increase one's chances at self-esteem and selfish pride, especially since the person behind the update is actually counting the like, love, and wow emojis?

Telephones, on the other hand, have greatly improved over the years, and they have even 'lost their lines.' Although I must applaud the ease with which one can now travel everywhere with a mobile device within reach, some a tad more expensive than others I dare say, the wireless system seems to have rendered people *less* communicative than before. A true fact it is that we are always 'available'; yet more often than not, the profile activity silences us from real verbal communication, and we find ourselves the builders of an invisible frontier.

I find it ironic that my grandmother succeeds in filling entire pages of communication bills with numbers going from her best friends' living just several blocks away to her daughter's in the United States whom she calls once a week either after 5 p.m. on weekdays or any other time during weekends, when long-distance communications are free of charge, at least according to what is written in her phone-service contract, negotiated with one of the two Belgian giant providers. I shall not digress here on the duopolistic market situation preventing smaller actors from taking a seat at the big boys' table.

Our generation, however, has come to loathe talking over the phone, giggling even when we have to leave a message, not sure how to handle voicemail. We, thus, prefer for our fingers to suffer from early arthritis as a consequence of our frantic typing out on a virtual keyboard with blocks of letters too small for our thumbs, until we inevitably end up taking twice as much time to send a piece of information whereas it would have taken us less than a minute if only we had called or left a voicemail message over the phone. But this, of course, would imply direct contact with the recipient. Instead, we can also choose to leave a forever-long voice message on WhatsApp. If these are only a few examples of how increasingly *solitaire* we have become, I cannot help but wonder why human beings seem to lose little by little their ability to talk, to hear their voice and make it heard at the same time.

To bring this little *pensée* to a close, I must highlight the apogee of this gradually becoming inhuman behavioral pattern: While society (and by this, I mean the partakers, the *I*s and *we*s and *us*'s that, together, make for this human association of common interests and ends) draws human beings further away from their communicative features and their personal interactions with one another, which is also largely encouraged and applauded by technological innovations and leading tech-industries; the work environment, *au contraire*, insists on communication skills and interactivity, team work and team building, 'afterworks,' and open-space work environments. Again, I find that ironic, yet you cannot say that I did not warn you about the consequences: an ever-increasing number of lost souls, wandering about because they do not fit in this make-believe.

Egg Hunt

Crunch crunch… It is that time of the year again, and here is the *croustillant praliné* sound of the hazelnut filling of an Easter egg. As you go about your egg hunting, I hope you fill a basket that opens a world of sweet and savory wishes. Mine would be for you to find benevolence, peace, and, most importantly, love. Add a touch of *je ne sais quoi*, that little something that makes you special, that makes you sparkle, that makes you wonder, that makes you want to live life to the fullest. Curiosity and awe are key to unlock the dearest treasures within our hearts, so do not hesitate to stockpile on both. Happy Easter to you all. Always.

One

I believe we all have a unique quality that not even the roughest tide can sweep away. We can waste time and energy, trying to run away from it, or we can accept that *trait de caractère* and embrace it, for we have the power to turn it into the first stone that will pave the way for our future path. I believe, indeed, that we, as human beings, all have a little something that makes us who we are, that separates even the most similar-looking-like twins and distinguishes them from their resemblance or train of thoughts. And if all human beings are born with the same capacity for love and benevolence, it is, however, to each and every single person, to develop the very qualities and *traits* that he or she most wants to be associated with, known for or compared to, because (let's face it!) our society is always about comparison and competition, so we might as well use it to our advantage.

Unfortunately, for me, the qualities that I had come to cherish and to live by almost blew me off my course. I had become increasingly anxious, and, at the same time, I was emptying myself from any benevolence toward myself.

Today, as a burned-out body and soul, I am often chased by dreadful thoughts which I can no longer sweep away. Some are related to the people living under the same roof as me. My parents and my sister are the ones that are 'stuck with me' most of the days, although my mother – dear Mou – feels like a hopeless spectator standing still at a terrible front, unable to participate in my personal battle against this shadow, this pressure, this despotic mind of mine, yet always on her knees to pick up the pieces hither and thither around the quicksand. If she could, she would glue the pieces together, although, right now, it looks more like a labyrinth of vanquished dominoes. Instead, she just tickles my hand when I have one out of so many sleepless nights, because I do love a good tickling, especially in the palm of my skin-crackling hand or on my wrist. These mother-loving strokes remind me of a childish laugh I used to have when she blew hard in the neck or on my belly to make my sister and I giggle one last time just before kissing us goodnight and turning on the musical night light which is now hidden somewhere in the attic among the boxes that we never open, probably broken by the differences in temperatures of the seasons (and years) passing by.

Struggling souls will surely wonder how thankfulness and gratitude can be expressed not on a daily, but rather on a forever-lasting basis, for it does not seem fair enough to kiss or hug your family and utter a sheer 'thank you.' Those are the people who pull you up when you have fallen down. So I wish there were something I could do to show them how grateful I am; how much I value their endless support and prayers, although I would not be offended were they to sigh at my umpteenth *why me?* speech. I must drive them nuts sometimes (most times?), pardon me the language register.

Whatever to Stay Alive

There seems to be no logic at all in the burned-out episodes of my life. I sometimes feel like they are streaming it online while I would be watching it from the outside. I still do not belong to this wrecked body, this lost soul, and this flame that has burned out. I am losing patience to see the light be reignited, only, this time, never to be blown out again.

We are nearing the busy month of May now, a rather festive month shall I say, for it starts with Mother's Day and ends with our mother's *actual* birthday. In-between are communions, confirmations, middle and high-school parties, Ascension-Day, and the perhaps or perhaps not following bank holiday (for the lucky ones, not the self-employed). Anyway, *sicher ist sicher*, May always comes with its share of surprises, its still-chilly (if you wear ballerinas) mornings and too-hot-for-your-trench-coat afternoons when you get out from work, until you arrive safe and sound at home, yet with a buzz in your left ear because you merely forgot to put down the air conditioning system and there has been just too much cold air blown into your face while you were driving in your car. Long live the month of May.

This year, on the second day of May, my grandmother, Mamiche, is heading straight to Leuven to have lunch with three of her close friends whom she met years ago when she still lived in this Flemish city center as a housekeeper at the service of a professor and priest. I remember him simply as The Professor. And for cheese, because when Mamiche would babysit my sister and I when we were little, we would hide back in her skirts as she was bringing the professor's lunch: a plate of smelly (half molten) cheese, a *délicatesse* some say. I admire my grandmother's willpower, her energy, and her strength, even though she also tells me about the so-so days she has every now and then. Yet, not today. The party will meet at 12 sharp in the Italian restaurant Mamma Mia in Leuven, where the four of them will order one pizza each, whether *romana* or *napoletana*, I do not know, for there is a difference indeed in both taste and structure of the pizza, depending on the *pizzaiolo*'s preference for a thick or thin crust. The *romana* is my parents' favorite kind – it has a somewhat flatter dough, is a little more baked, with superficial charcoal-colored crusts – but the *napoletana* is said to be the original one, for only in Naples was the pizza born, with ripe San Marzano tomatoes and mozzarella cheese, cooked soft and tender with a thick (still tender) crust. Oh, just so you know, if you wish to offend Italians, try and put some pineapple on your pizza… You will think twice about ordering it next time. Mamiche is safe though, for she always indulges in the *quattro stagioni*, perhaps because it reminds her of Vivaldi's Four Seasons?

It, thus, comes as no surprise that I look up to my grandmother, for she has genuine gumption, while I am merely a wandering shadow. The only real thing about me are the dry hands on the verge of crackling, so much so that one could use them as sandpaper to make wood smooth, even reaching an almost-polished shine. So while some are happy, eating pizza with friends, what does a shadow do to spend the day?

On most days after breakfast, I would find a little cooking atelier of my own. I would quickly clear the table and get ready to either bake a cake or cookies for my sister, either meal prep for my grandmother, this time, my *other* granny, my Omaatje, because she has been an absolute lover of the meatballs in homemade tomato sauce, and I cannot wait to give her more (it is, for one matter, a very comforting freezer-friendly meal).

Cooking has, indeed, been my loophole, my safe haven, my gateway to a better-feeling self, although it be only an ephemeral state of being. I could not tolerate the despotic mind to rule over my body and soul, especially right after morning coffee and honey o'clock a time. No, I shall not surrender to a new invasion of thoughts. Some would go for a yoga break; I, instead, choose to cook and thus spend the morning 'busy bee-ing' in my kitchen. I am proud of the knowledge I have gradually built over the years, both in nutrition and food pairings, although a little less proud when it comes to my own flexibility in testing and meal prepping *for me*. I have, without a doubt, the most complicated and fussy palate, or is it the mind, really, that dictates our food behavioral pattern? If the latter turns out to be true, then I am not out of the woods yet.

This reminds me of my last visit to Mamie Rose, the massage therapist. She said I should not be afraid of food, for it has never killed a soul. When one comes to think of it, it really has not; our eating pattern, on the other hand, is the real culprit. Take the McDonald's timeless, original, classic hamburger for instance. It is said to be 100-percent pure beef (the origin of which being somewhat blurry), topped with a slice or two of pickles, onions, ketchup, and mustard. All of it is held together in a sweet bun-kind-of bread. Yet, the old classic has never killed anybody. That hamburger has nothing in itself that could kill us immediately upon eating it. The consumption of too great a number on a too-short period of time, however, will unleash an unhealthy eating pattern ruling over your reasonable mind and effacing the healthy diet you were supposed to follow, if only merely to belong in this body-shaming-driven society.

If the hamburger and French fries will surely satisfy the delicate palates of scores of party animals after a night out, pulling in the drive-thru at five or six in the morning, I myself will not join the merry men and women queuing. Food per se has no license to kill, but I know my mind has been playing tricks on me from as early as the high-school-drama years or rather the hide-yourself-and-eat-your-lunch years. The mind later increased its hold on my body, and I continued to erase myself further during the Salamanca military experience; a time when both the food purchasing and the consumption of it were closely monitored. Until this day, I still do not know how I could have been led by the nose by my at-the-time best friend. The grocery shopping was to be done on a weekly basis, always sharing the food we had bought instead of buying our own preferred products. Moreover, since my morning cereal was more expensive than the bread loaf she would have with Nutella, I was expected to share the weekly cost of bread, even though I did not eat any. Some say a flat-share is about compromise, but what do you call it when one side is being oppressive and the other is being pulled underwater? A tyranny?

After I came back, I started to control my own food supplies; I wanted to make sure I had enough of my favorite foods. The grip, however, quickly turned into a compulsive habit of controlling the whole food chain: from the buying, the meal preparing, and the dinner eating. When I landed in June 2013, my body experienced a short period of time that I call 'rejection,' a time during which I simply could not eat anything, for there was a horrible tension knot that only grew larger and larger, and the mere fact of drinking would result in cramps and the swelling up of my belly. A very disappointing experience, especially when you are traveling with your parents on the Amalfi Coast and that you cannot indulge in the scores of delicious specialties of the trip. This could not last and, fortunately for me, I was saved from thinning down to a too-much-alarming state during my second year into my master's degree when my family doctor put me on a high protein (and high fat) diet. He saved me. Take One.

Take Two of the rescue plan would be launched after the additional diploma in management, and the one year into the labor market. If food saved me once before, I hope it will not mind this one more…

To bring these memories to a soothing close, I must confess that my eating pattern irreversibly changed once I had no other option but to monitor my three meals a day and divide them into protein tables, calorie intakes, fiber, vitamin, and carbohydrates labels, all the while making sure that I had – day in day out – enough fuel to keep the basic functioning alive and well. In other words, that I would not thin down anymore.

Whereas some would think that a cheat day (or week) would do the trick to gain the extra weight, I could not stockpile on food, despite my best efforts. Digestion got increasingly more difficult for me, and I could no longer dream of my *derrière de gazelle*, for I was lacking some good, old-fashioned fat where needed. Instead, I had to content myself with a goose-stuffing feeling, as if I were always struggling against the need to push the food further down my throat until it would eventually be 'accepted' by the body, although 'acceptance' be the wrong word. The body too felt that this was wrong or somewhat counterproductive, and, soon, the energy intake would be stolen by the despotic mind to fuel even more these torturous thoughts and to trigger another series of panic attacks, or even to impose worse stress peaks onto the already-frail and shattered *physique*. Fuel through food was wasted on marching enemy soldiers of the mind, when it ought to have been stockpiled by the surviving platoon so that the latter could win its first victory on hostile territory.

So be it, when the flame went out on December 14th, 2017, I could no longer be saved by a changing food pattern, for I was already living thanks to the great nutritional advice and scheme drawn by my family doctor. He has thus saved me twice already from my despotic mind and good-hearted ambition. Even though the second time is happening *now*, I still need to prove that I will survive. To this, I shall reply: knowing how to survive is one thing, but living and existing is a totally different feeling. It means you have finally found your happiness.

Meet Cute

With the self. Burned as I am, the ravage is full-scale. The body alone is wrecked; the soul is wandering, lost, and scared. The mind keeps going strong, congratulating itself of the levels of destruction reached so far. But what for? Or, better put, what does it want to prove, *really*? Possibly that I have become a master in self-effacement, until it did not matter anymore who would take care of me.

In order to come back to life and let the spirit shine, one must ignite one's inner light, but only after the meet cute has happened. How odd though, that some words are instinctively associated to a certain experience, a lost memory, a saved-for-later moment to remember. To me, 'meet cute' travels all the way back to the many nights that I spent watching the movie *The Holiday* with the incredible Iris Simpkins and kind-hearted Arthur Abbot. For years, I could binge-watch the scene, taking notes and mental pictures of the homey and comforting *décor*, the corny-yet-romantic gestures, the haircuts of both Iris and Amanda; I would dream of Iris's job and writing myself a chronicle before melting for the obvious loving hearts of the male actors, both of whom made me believe that true love does exist, somewhere, sometime, and that it can be found, at last.

Nevertheless, the other meet cute that I wish to refer to ought to happen at least someday to all of us. It is the life-changing encounter between the body and the self; a balance so pure and so quiet that the light automatically shines, spreads, and lasts in time. One will never be the same person again once he or she has reached pureness of the soul and has made peace with the body. As a teenage girl, I grew up believing that little bulges around our waist (or what I like to call baby-fat or muffin top) were to be hidden, especially when on holiday and wearing a bikini at the beach. Yet, miles away from Belgium, I would be spending the summer holidays in Italy at the beach, indeed, where I was confronted with chubby, Italian, popular girls, the Queens, proudly showing off an even larger muffin top than I had (meaning that I could have indulged in another *bombolone* for breakfast after all?!). The *bellas* were parading with their most handsome beau, not minding the transparency of their white bikini when they strolled *a orillas del mar*, as I'd say in Spanish. It all seemed like an open-air, wet T-shirt contest, whereas I just stood there with my shorts and tank top.

To my 14-year-old self, the only explanation as to why Italian girls were allowed their *gelato* curves was the summer beach tan which (let us be honest here) has always been an incredible boost for one's self-esteem. This is especially true when it comes to one's body image and self-assurance. No wonder spray tans are a girl's must-have to survive long winter months. The *bellas* at the beach were of a beautiful golden brown and, quite honestly, they 'owned the place.'

Only later would I understand that one can be as suntanned as humanly possible (making sure one does not trespass the lobster's red-burned stage or the Ross Geller tan, both being, in fact, utterly ridiculous, and, yes, I am allowed to laugh, for I was once severely violet-colored, itchy pink, and blistered after returning from a one-day-only outing at the Belgian seaside; ironic, is it not?). Anyways, I came to realize that being suntanned, like I said, is no guarantee for cross-checking the beauty standards of the fashion industry's diktat; quite the opposite actually, for it is confidence that is the key that rolls out the red carpet for everyone to watch; it is confidence that unlocks the door to self-love and indulgence. Trust me, the Italian beach dolls had plenty of it. I, on the other hand, would ask my sister to check whether my bikini bottom was still covering my *derrière* (ahem, I often felt I really had a wedgie when attempting a plunge into the sea or being slapped by a surprise wave), whereas Miss white bikini would not mind at all if her very-poorly covered breasts would dangerously play peek-a-boo to the delight of the other *ragazzi*.

So how does one attain even a spark of confidence, just enough to reach that sacred level of pureness that will eventually unlock the window to finding balance and harmony, peace and quiet, until, finally, it triggers the meet cute between body and self, that happy *beginning* of a deserved freedom of life worth living and existing for? Unfortunately, I have not found the answer to that question, at least just yet. I am still a shadow, and, to be honest, I have never felt as much of an outsider as these past few days. I have become too down-to-earth, and, consequently, I have stopped believing that the start of a new month would trigger the change I have desperately wanted to see, especially a change within myself. Little do I know about my own strength to make it happen or simply to break free. Oftentimes, I wish I could fast-forward to the future and see how I am living a life that I have chosen myself, regardless of the diktats and ukases that sadly exist and by which too many lost or burned souls abide.

However, I hereby pledge that whenever I find that little *je ne sais quoi*, I will come back to you with the secret untold. It is out there, I know it is. Everyone deserves a meet cute. Everyone needs freedom. But, most importantly, everyone needs a 'one' that renders the word 'every,' the most unique and beautiful of all. Hence *e pluribus unum*, out of many, one; one soul out of the many experiences past and yet to come, out of the many lessons learned, whether positive or not, out of the many teachings spread and shared. One person. One meet cute. Yet, every possibility within reach and safe from spray tan.

Saying Goodbye

And saying hello to one of my favorite activities when trying to conquer and beat down those torturous thoughts: commenting pictures of food.

Because food can also mean art, especially when one considers art as a means to bring comfort and warmth to the soul.

Today's mood is made of salmon, broccoli, and sweet potato. *Olio, aglio, prezzemolo* and a touch of *piment d'Espelette* make a hearty contribution to painting our skies happy-colored and flavored, no matter what. How is your art speaking to you?

Monday like no other. How strange a feeling when you start the day with a chilly breeze and a timid sun waiting for what seems like forever a time to come out of hiding. You, on the other hand, are desperate for the evening to come, because you loathe the stay-at-home reality, although it be only temporary. Until, finally, everyone is coming home from a busy day at work, and pasta time has arrived, only, tonight, with a rather luxurious twist. May I present the *spaghetti all'astice*, or not just another Monday night dinner. Cheers to a warm and cozy encounter of the heart and soul, to family love and togetherness thanks to the pasta, that is all.

Walls Crack

Frida Kahlo again, when she says, "Don't build a wall around your own suffering, or it may devour you from the inside."

Huh, that is convenient. What is more, I happen to read this while scrolling down my Facebook newsfeed, trying not to lift my left arm too high in the air, for I cracked a rib yesterday morning as I tried to take my bathrobe without opening the doors from the shower tub. Again, huh? What was that all about, one may wonder? It might seem a quite atypical morning routine, I shall admit, but since I do not want to be cold, especially at the start of the day and all naked and wet (might as well get the details), I follow a ritual as I get into the shower tub: I close both shower panels and make sure my towel and my robe are hanging right above these panels. This way, when I am done with the soap, the Venus Gillette, the arms stretching and the yawning (again, details), I can immediately fetch the towel without opening the doors which would bring only a shiver of cold. I know, I am quite a genius. *Qui plus est*, I have also found the perfect combo for the two-meter walk from the too-narrow-a-space-to-get-dressed-into the shower room to the somewhat bigger bathroom: being clean and dry, I simply cover myself with a white, sponge bathrobe, specifically used for my passing through the cold corridor from one room to the next. Once arrived safe and warm, I hang it up, until it be put back above the panels the next morning.

Pointless explanations aside, I yawned one time too many yesterday morning while struggling to keep my eyes open, suddenly thinking about how one of my cousins had cracked his jaw, indeed, in the mere act of yawning and who is now deprived of his favorite French baguette for lunch, having, thus, no alternative but to swap the golden and crunchy crust for a plain, white, mushy, Pullman loaf. That morning, I was still breathing in the soapy damp that was left hanging in the carefully stay-closed, warm environment as I tried to reach for the towel – check – and after drying myself off, I also wanted to pull at the sponge bathrobe too and disappear into its rough warmth. I, thus, lifted my left arm, and as I was pulling the robe down, possibly a little too enthusiastically, I felt a rib, the one right under my breast, go upward until what felt like a dislocation. Crack. Mind you, it is not broken, but I definitely struggled to wrap myself up into the robe, get dressed, comb my hair. It now aches when I breathe or whenever I blow my nose, although I thank the Lord that I have not had to sneeze so far. Great, just what I needed. Ah-choo!

Bless you. Sometimes, a 'boo-boo' like this reminds me of my physical frailty and the code-red alert(s) that, I shall admit, I still ignore too often. I hit snooze. Until now, I had not thought it be possible for the bones *themselves* to be hurt. Yet, one has indeed been injured. On May two, one rib had been wounded; one rib had rendered me gasping, leaving me no other choice but to fight for some spare room when I breathe in. And out. This hurts. In. And out again. Still hurting, but at least I managed to hold in the last wave of sneezing.

Despite this new disturbance, I shall not be vanquished! In order to prove it (mostly to myself), I went to the little Thursday market to fetch some fresh sea bream from my fishmonger's. Mou had a day off, and, after breakfast (and coffee, one only *encore* and because of the previous stomach-burning episode), we decided we would not drive to Leuven and go shopping because (let's be honest here) that is still too hectic an activity, still too exhausting, too much, too everything for the frail me. Instead, we would buy some fish, skin on (you know me), and maybe wander a bit in the little town of Hal (Flemish Region). It is tiny, yet there are several clothing stores worth a visit, although not being too big and not being too many of them. They are strategically scattered around the city. Moreover, we would not, of course, be shopping like addicts; we would just take a walk, mother and daughter, into the streets we know so well and let things come to us. I'm not even certain one might call it window-shopping. Perhaps let us refer to it as a nice stroll. Yes, that will do.

Actually, it did not. After leaving the little place where the market booths stood, we walked through the narrow (and student-free at this time of the day) streets of my mother's teenage years when she went to high school in Hal. Looking up at the typical, Flemish, crow-stepped gables, the typical step pattern in bricks of the Gothic and Renaissance roofing styles that one might still come across in Bruges or Ghent, we suddenly discovered a charming townhouse which secretly sheltered an even more ravishing interior with tiles *d'époque*, church-like Gothic arches, and stained-glass windows. How breathless was I, but, this time, not because of the breathing exercise through a painful rib. We thought we knew the city by heart, yet there seemed to be one store whose portal we had never crossed. We thus mounted the three stairs to the entrance and walked through the old wooden doors, giving a finishing touch to this *maison de maître*. The *boutique* itself harbored Belgian and Dutch prêt-à-porter, and I was soon warmly welcomed into the store manager's picks and favorite items. There was no music playing in the background, unlike other brands that bet on glitz, loud music, and overpowering store perfume that gives away your shopping itinerary while walking in and out of these Abercrombie-style ambiances.

The manager, a lady in her 50s with very small yet fashionable, retro, round-shaped glasses, was proud of the neatly displayed collections, although I sensed a certain shyness in her manner. I respected the fact that she was not too 'pushy,' unlike the rude kind of managers that make a customer ill at ease, driving him out of the store, at least implicitly, leaving him no other choice but to never set foot there ever again, for that is how uncomfortable they can make a customer feel. For the last six years, I did not even need the menacing glare of shop assistants to flee and keep out of clothing stores. I used to love shopping, scrolling down online clothing websites and turning pages of fashion magazines without reading the articles, save from my horoscope. I used to change outfits three or more times after breakfast at my *kot* or student's room before going to classes, just to make sure I had accessorized it correctly and matched the right pair of pants with either black or cognac boots, either a pair of heels. I used to wear high heels, all kinds of them. I remember the lightness I came to enjoy when on eight or ten-centimeter high wedges, ankle or high boots. Even though I have always been very insecure, the playing of mix and matching my outfits in the morning chinned up my walking to university or wherever I would be heading. It all seems like a very faraway memory now. I seem not to remember the pleasure of it, and I have definitely lost the sparkle that made life a game worth rolling the dice.

I have abandoned myself, my body, my soul. Very quickly I got used to the shadow I saw in the mirror, the dark rings under my eyes, the bony structure, the disappearance (and flatness) of my behind, the hair thinning out, the easy-come but not easy-go bruises, the cold deep within my bones, the dry skin, the cracking hands, the occasional itchiness and consequent dermatitis, the lack of care and benevolence toward myself, the emptying of emotions, and the forgetting about physical pain or complaints. Over the last couple of years, I have looked into the mirror, only to witness the disappearance of my soul while pressing the snooze button whenever noticing an increase in physical deterioration.

Back into the Renaissance *boutique*, I looked again into the mirror. This time, however, I was not seeing an upset or sorrowful self; I stood there, ready to cry. There were tears of surprise at the unexpected size-fitting of a pair of pants that I had spotted. I would not try them on normally, but, in this case…well, for one thing, there was a 'but.' The Belgian designer, Nathalie Vleeschouwer, made me smile with her fun, monkey-printed, crêpe trousers. The silk material did not scare me off from trying the pants on. She even hands me a sword of truce; an attempt to reach an armistice between the body and the mind after years of hiding and fighting in the trenches. This torturous war waged between the revolutionary fighter versus the despotic ruler must cease at once. I have been a soldier of shadow ranks, crawling, yet not advancing very far. However slow the pace, for the first time, I feel like I have nothing to be ashamed of. I am wearing these monkey pants, and I might not have the *gazelle* bottom, but I will not let this missing piece of my armor spoil my outfit fitting, thank you. I have other hard combat gear in stock. Period. Or is it 'fired and out'?

Finally, when I got back home from this one-store outing with Mou, which had left me exhausted and broke for the rest of the month, I came across a sign on social media, which proves that the latter is not *always* harmful in the trying to reach a 'normal' recovery process. I watched the minute-and-a-half YouTube video presented by Rabbi Dr. Abraham Twerski: "What we can learn from lobsters about stress." How curious a coincidence, for I had only eaten lobster pasta earlier in the week, on Monday night to be precise. Little did I know that my *spaghetti all'astice* would be an eye-opener. Walls do crack, indeed, and so I have found out with my bathrobe routine. Although I shall confess the rib scared the hell out of me, for I suddenly realized my bones were under attack, leaving me little room for action before the fall, before the darkest hour of the night. Did I really need this additional bruise?

In the video, we learn that lobsters are amongst those fascinating creatures of the sea. They face adversity and stress because as they grow, they are confined and soon trapped into their rigid shell, as explained by the rabbi. They need time to crack and shake off what has now become an uncomfortable and too small a shell for them, and they subsequently produce a new and better-fitting one. During this process, lobsters cannot venture to stay in the incredibly perilous depths of the ocean and face the possible risk to be devoured by predators. They thus hide under a rock until they are strong enough and brand-new-shell equipped. This process stretches throughout their life, for as many times as they feel uncomfortable and cramped in a certain shell. As Dr. T. says, "Times of stress are also times that are signals for growth. And if we use adversity properly, we can grow through adversity."

I will need some more time to recover from this rib crack, and truth be told, I am scared at how much more time it will take for the body to get fixed and the soul to be healed. Yet, I shall never forget the lessons while writing my journey down, nor shall I ignore the future impact of the mountain that I have been assigned to climb. Fortunately, I hang onto Maya Angelou's words: "The love of the family, the love of one person, can heal.

It heals the scars left by a larger society. A massive, powerful society." I too shall survive; I too shall find light through the cracks.

Fix Me

Like Pinocchio, but in reverse. Perhaps the key that would finally unlock the shutters only to reveal an azure view that overlooks a peaceful ocean of growth and benevolence toward myself is for Mr. Geppetto to dehumanize parts of me, even just for an insignificant period of time, just enough of the right amount, with his fitting tools, to let my body recover and for my soul to find its haven of wellbeing at last. I am asking a woodcarver to take care of me and fix the splits and scrapes that have been attacking the marionette structure until now. Mister Geppetto, would you help me?

Mischief and lies make Pinocchio's nose grow, but I myself would compete with the wooden boy in the boxing ring of nearly still life. The sole difference being that I would be fighting with massive-destruction weapons of my own making: stress and oblivion, the former fueling the engine of war, the latter encouraging total abandonment of the possible person I would have become, only to secretly pledge allegiance to the despotic regime of the mind.

Unfortunately, the spectators in the elevated bleachers want to 'get more bang for their buck' and follow the unquestionable social precepts. Society being made of spectators, it also seems to applaud the numerous efforts made to render people less human and more akin to wooden toys with which it can play to its heart's content. I believe, indeed, that we are the toys of a system that does not value personal growth, since the managing actors at its core highlight the importance of sacrifice in the name of a larger (corporate and economic) group. Hence the regrettable evolution from artisans and woodcarvers of our own lives and the importance of personal growth, to us being the soldiers and toys at the service of an untrustworthy society which has been acting as a dictator hidden behind what appears to be a deceptive décor instead of a welcoming virgin territory upon which each and every single marionette would be given the tools to grow into a pure and benevolent human being, reaching out to its peers and finally paving the way for a concrete project toward the achievement of (inner and outer) peace.

Out of the many marionettes, we shall raise the curtain onto one world, a tale like no other, removing the remnants of a lurking tragedy. I wish I had written that 'we all should know that diversity makes for a rich tapestry, and we must understand that all the threads of the tapestry are equal in value no matter what their color.' Sadly, I have not, and I cannot help but bow to Mrs. Maya Angelou. She knows the words.

Admiring her courage, I too shall make an effort and consider the different layers of pain of my own tapestry as being part of a more flamboyant gallery. But days go by, and my own downward spiral never seems to end. Am I allowed to be afraid? Am I allowed to talk nonsense and blurt out my secret fear that other ribs might crack or break? Is it even possible for a body to break, and if so, how can I prevent this from happening to me? I would lie if I told you I were not scared.

For the last couple of weeks, I have 'felt' my bones more than ever, as if I were suddenly aware of their poking through the surrounding organs, of their dislocating acrobatic feat, of their capacity to make the joints crack and leave me hurt, both physically and emotionally. Sometimes, I catch myself munching a handful of unsalted, raw, organic (Italian or Spanish) almonds, or I would force myself into eating a Taste of Nature Almond, Raisin, and Walnut bar just to make sure I get a little extra fat. There are times, however, when even these healthy snacks are impossible for me to eat. There is a mental blockage preventing me from taking care of my outside shell because the inside is still on fire. Fireworks are indeed going off in the long and dark corridors of my gut; the tension quickly becomes unbearable, and the bloating is soon waiting just around the corner to prepare its grand finale. Tears of incomprehension, sometimes even of pain, run quietly along my cheeks. Suddenly, I am lost again, and a burst of heat invades my head and reddens my ears while my hands and toes are starting to freeze. So, no treat for me. Not today, unless there is a soy yoghurt left in the fridge. That may do even, though I can already hear the army's cries of the bloated foe. "I come in peace," I want to whisper, but the body is wary, and I cannot blame it. So, whoever it be, fix me please.

Room for Color

Today is May sixth, and I smell like $C_4H_6N_4O_3$. Please do not run away from this new piece of reading, I myself did not know what this chemical compound stood for before looking it up on Wikipedia. Allantoin is used by the pharmaceutical and cosmetic industries for its moisturizing and wound-healing effects. By promoting cell proliferation, the allantoin contained in the skincare product that I have just bought at the local supermarket will prevent my dry hands from cracking always deeper, always more. It is said to be an odorless powder, yet the perfume is all but a very pleasant scent. It reminds me of jasmine or lily of the valley and, dear Reader, out of the many things you already know about me, here is a scoop: I loathe both these overpowering fragrances.

How fortunate am I for having bought the sole hand moisturizer that actually works on my ill-treated hands, yet makes me want to retch? I am, however, not surprised by this embarrassing side effect, since I read somewhere that this chemical compound is extracted by the cosmetic industries not from the comfrey plant, but (buckle up) from animal urine (at least for most of the commercialized personal-care products). No wonder then that it has been infesting my natural aura, given the least-appetizing scents. Is it me or does the French sensitive-skin expert collude with the devil of the fragrance industry by mixing the odorless $C_4H_6N_4O_3$ from animal urine with smelly and much-disliked plants? I do not understand the logic behind their move. If only they would launch an almond or cotton-fresh version of it, I would stockpile at once.

Apart from the now-smooth-yet-smelly hands, I seem to lack color here and there. Raw is how my sister describes my writing; raw is how my soul is trying to find its way back to my inner voice. Although the latter is still whispering in an almost-inaudible tone, it needs time to retrieve the way home and make itself heard. I cannot blame it, for the body is all but a safe haven. At least for the time being. I got carried away by the turbulences of life, and who better than my favorite artist to sketch my feelings? *Raw* left is what I see. *Raw* right is the artist speaking. My sister. She knows. Again.

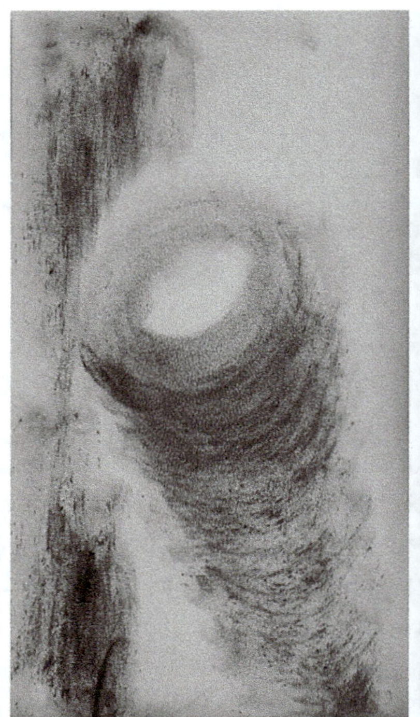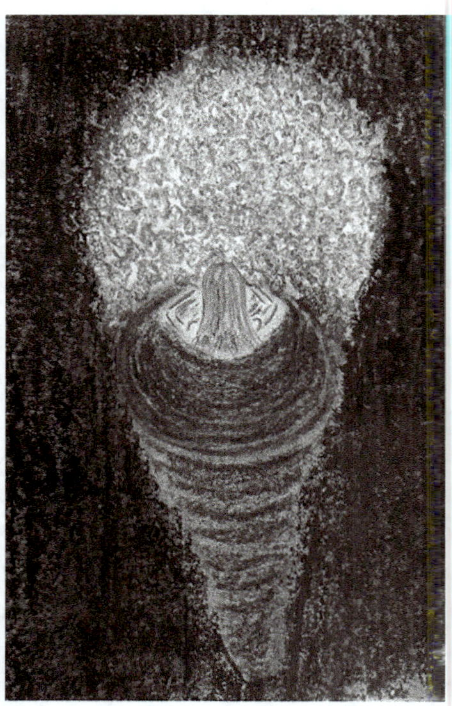

I wish I could see the colors of my soul instead of being blown further away from blossoming. However, I need to be strong, and instead of letting my mind paint me all blue and dark, I try to busy it with furniture I would like to buy for my future apartment, my *petit chez moi*. I imagine antique-white and floral, porcelain dinner plates to set the table with when my parents come over at *my* place to have dinner together – mind you, I do not talk about my sister's, for she is obviously going to hang around my place most of the time, if only to steal food. Moreover, I would like to choose a handmade Oriental rug, matching the vintage wooden closets and cabinets, although checking both traceability and transparency of the supply chain. Finally, I dream of a Lacanche 'Classic' range cooker, and although I am certain of the brass finishing for the knobs in the already-configured (and saved on my computer) Cluny 1000 design kitchen range, I still find it quite difficult to choose between the earthenware gray and armor colors. Oh, let us be spontaneous here: I will pick the latter, but if and only if it comes with a kitchen with a red-brick wall. Raw, here too.

These are only a few examples of how I keep my mind away from the otherwise-torturous thoughts and worries. The reason being that I am scared. I really am. The pain in my rib, the bloating, the itchy eyes and palms, the loss of emotions, the lack of flavor and taste during meals, and the clacking of joints have all responded present on this gray and winter-like morning. One detail though: we are in May.

Temperatures barely missed the freezing stage, and my mother had carefully covered the flat parsley with an old jute bag cloth to prevent it from dying at too early an age and before I could have used it to flavor the garlicky olive oil during a pasta-night meal prep. I wonder if such jute cloths also exist to warm up human bones. I regret to say that the cold has, again, taken root in all physical foundations, leaving them wobbling because of both exhaustion and hypothermia. Longtime exposure to sources of tension and fretting eventually erode the muscles and the brain, so much so that I am actually afraid to loose even more bits and pieces of teeth because of the additional (unseasonal and out-of-fashion, let us be honest) gritting and grinding, or sexy bruxism.

Wait. Freeze. Do not let your mind take over the little space you have left for colors. Go away. Hide in the woods. Even just for a while. Shoo! So I did. As I am writing these lines, it is ten to five in the afternoon, and the weather conditions have little but changed from earlier today. An owl has begun its night hooting as I wait to take my homeopathic dietary supplements. By the time Mou comes home from work, it will be over half past five, and I will count the minutes down before it be reasonable enough a time for me to start the zucchini and yellow bell pepper pasta sauce. With parsley, of course. Dinner will not be ready before 7:30, which leaves me enough time to drop a few lines.

While the sauce is simmering, I think of Mou and how she has always been there for me and still is. She is my traveling companion throughout this whole journey, perhaps even a fellow inmate of my captivity, for there is little she can do. She is the spectator of her daughter's years of personal struggle. I understand that it is I who need to change; I who need to learn; I who need to live rather than survive. I alone possess the only key that will eventually open the padlock to a tranquil, secret garden where self-acceptance and indulgence will grow along with care and love.

However, until I have found the long-awaited secret combination of this padlock, I might use a pencil sharpener to cast away the horrible spells of my mind in its attempt to push me back into serfdom. How I wish the tip would be sharp enough to pierce through and flatten the blue and dark bubbles. They have been too invasive. The pencil sharpener has that typical wooden scent that one would also come across when walking in a forest; the smell of it impregnates so deep into the soul that the mind is bound to give in and succumb to a state of absolute, although ephemeral, letting go.

So, sometimes, during weekends, Mou and I drive the five kilometers it takes to reach that pencil-sharpener tranquility of mind. Up and down the forest trail we stroll, but only upward do we look. Breathing in the fresh and still-humid air from the drizzle earlier in the day, I fight hard to shake off the shudder I feel deep into my spine. My hands get wet from the rapid cooling off and the reawakening of the much-appreciated fragrance of that skincare product I had applied before we left. The pencil sharpener has opened my eyes to see a sparkle behind the misty horizons; to witness how the lively greenness grows alongside darker paths and how the soothing silence of nature's colorful voices augur a metamorphosis from winter's sleep to summer shine. And guess what: we are nature too.

It only took a 30-minute stroll into the woods to free my mind and listen to my body, perhaps for the first time since what has seemed like forever. Upon my return and after what looked like the closest thing to a 'heavy-eyed interlude,' (I am no siesta sleeping beauty) I tried to listen to the echo of my soul. I have been searching for it for a long time, but I have been unable to hear its voice; unless it was I who had simply decided to ignore its desperate crying and calling for help.

In order to prevent future cracks, I have decided that from now on, I shall indeed make an effort and listen to my body's needs. I am scared, but who isn't? I shall try to remember that the fear of change cannot match the possible loss of life because of mere abandonment dictated by the mind. Fear, therefore, must not be considered a brake; more often than not, it ought to be regarded as a springboard to something (unexpectedly) greater. My head has started to tilt from side to side now, and I am sure that the chamomile herbal tea would not even out the balance of colors in my mind. I needed something stronger, but no, thank you, no brandy. I will pass. Instead, I welcomed a tiny cup of unsalted, organic almonds. Italian, just to cheer up the crowd. They are packed with magnesium, fiber, and protein. It feels like fueling up your car with the best gas available. I now thank the pencil sharpener and its bring-me-back-to-life scent, for it has opened a world of greater possibilities.

Cold Fabric

The clock strikes 9:18 this morning, and I still recover from having lifted my left arm a little too high while shampooing my shoulder-length hair. One would think I have now quit the habit of hanging my bathrobe upon the window doors of the shower tub. Well, I have not. I struggled too much last night to be warm at last under the covers, putting not one, not two, but, yes, indeed, three extra layers (!), so please excuse me when I do not wish to spoil the now-reached, desired comfort and warmth levels of the body's thermostat. Hence the bathrobe routine, despite it being hazardous for the ribcage.

Earlier in this memoir (should I call it that?), I stressed the importance of quality food to keep the most basic organs functioning. The kettle is not considered one of those organs. Perhaps I ought to have signed up for knitting classes in order to make my own woolen socks, garments, and sweaters. I was, however, quite surprised at the totally unexpected expensiveness of knit material, yarn and inspiration, the latter because I will honestly admit that the most beautiful patterns for cardigans, dresses, or scarves need the most exclusive yarns available on a website – yes, a website, for we live in a 2.0 tech society in which nobody (save our ancestors) heads to the fabric store; preferring the picking of colors and styles directly by clicking on a virtual pad in the left corner of a connected 'mouse,' to the actual touching of the desired fabric and the bonus advice of an expert (perhaps a former knitting world champion). *Bref*, even for matters of keeping warm, one must rely to the freezing atmosphere of virtual interaction.

The high cost of these yarns and the learning process of the most in vogue patterns would inevitably fast-forward me to the next summer holiday when, quite embarrassingly dressed for the season, I would be able to show off my personal knitting skills by parading in a full-fat, alpaca, woolen, turtleneck sweater. By the time I get my handmade cardigan ready-wear and think of making the Christmas-red and Rudolph-green socks for the chimney decorations, I ought to have asked one of my two best friends to trade the extra wool she gets from the shaving off of her three sheep. I would gladly trade for takeaway meal prep, for that is my kind of currency, my specialty. More than knitting actually.

All jokes aside, I value genuine and authentic arts and crafts. I wish I could make my own mittens and socks, thus being able to choose the thickness of the layers of wool contouring my frozen fingertips and toes. Just a safety precaution to keep me warm, even on the hottest summer days, because my heating system has long been on the blink. This morning, I have decided I shall not mind putting an extra turtleneck tee under my green it-says-cotton/wool-but-feels-like-polyester Swedish-brand sweater. It is May seventh, and if the outside temperatures do not get higher than a meagre ten degrees (Celsius, I am in luck), then I do not see how the many layers I am wearing are embarrassingly out of fashion. Farewell Mrs. Wintour, I have spotted you wearing fur at the 2019 MET Gala. And if it were not for fur, then your outfit was certainly made out of feathers, sprayed in a sorrowful Barbie rose what's more. I bet you like it warm.

Talking of the most-awaited event of New York's high (posh and gossipy) society, I let my eyes scroll down the pictures taken only couple of hours ago at the other side of the ocean, where the night was young while I lay wide awake, tossing and turning in my *baldaquin* bed. I do not know whether I am most struck by the Kardashian Klan carnivalesque outfits or the poor costume choices of the other guests. To my great sorrow, I must admit that the Wintour faux pas is the least mind-blowing of all. This year, all have but honored fashion; this year, the consensus seems to have been to commit the most hard-to-believe fashion serial-killer crimes. Can we now get this over with and start dressing up *chic* and elegant again instead of mocking what ought to be considered art?

Struck by my laptop's low-battery level, I have but no other option than to call in Mou's help to plug the cable in. Only when cracking a rib does one realize how the daily planning gets out of gear, especially when cleaning the copper pan I use to cook my pear-and-cinnamon oatmeal in the morning.

With a now-brighter screen from charging, the computer has proven a faithful companion for me through this somewhat life-changing experience. Earlier in this manuscript, I had talked about the rebirth of the phoenix from its ashes, but, lately, I have come to realize that the most resembling metaphor I can rely on is the caterpillar's metamorphosis into a ready-to-fly-away butterfly. I shall learn how to fly once I have let go of my hampering vulnerability. I wait for the day that I too shall fly away and into a secret garden.

In the meantime, I will share with you, dear Reader, my hold-onto. I hear the first cracking sounds of sizzling garlic in extra virgin olive oil (Italian, are you surprised?), mixed with the finely chopped, fresh, flat parsley (please do not keep it in your freezer, for it will lose all its flavor, and trust me when I tell you that a chef is better off leaving it out of a pasta dish rather than letting the extra defrosting water ruin the sauce). And here comes the grand finale or the *sardinelle,* two/three fillets, for they are bigger than their anchovy peers and perhaps less sharp in taste, at least to some, but still making all the difference between a bland and refined basic sauce. I did not add the peperoncino, for I was looking for a pure and genuine zucchini and bell-pepper match. For the anchovy haters, do not worry, they will disappear into the sauce, but elegance in taste has saved even the most basic pasta plate. Cooking simple and authentic meals has been saving me from inner dying.

Unpinned

It was Tuesday, and for the ninth time this year, Mou was driving me to the therapist's. Yes, the purple circles. If we were not in the year 2019, I would think she were a sorceress, a respected-though-feared medicine woman of ancient times. Her knowledge never ceases to surprise me, and her hands have healing powers, of that I am sure of.

Adding to the mystery around her is the fact that she lives in the countryside. Her house stands as the highest on the hill and mounting to it is not without travail. Mou makes sure our Fiat is all geared up when she drives the sharp bend in the road to the front porch. We would not want the engine to stall while engaging in the tight, ascending turn. The effort is laudable, and the view is definitely worth the stalling risk taken. The white façade reveals a cottage-like haven of peace and tranquility. So much so that the only way to announce one's presence is to ring the bell, although the door remains unlocked at all times by way of welcoming the lost and kind hearts coming to see her in the hope to find some comfort. Crossing the front door, visitors are soon wrapped with great care in a fresh and fragrant, 48 essential-oil scent. This is no intrusive malodorous jasmine or lily of the valley smell; quite the opposite actually, it is a soothing breeze that unveils care and compassion while appeasing the soul.

I climbed the stairs to the mezzanine whereas Mou took a seat in the downstairs lounge which I believe was a former bathroom (the pipework hidden behind one of the two accent chairs gives the room makeover away). Upstairs, I find myself in a peculiar artist's atelier. The varnished parquet floor feels warm and secure until my feet meet the faded blue-colored Oriental rug decorating the room. This time, I would not sit on the low wicker bench; I have been talking too much during my previous meetings with the therapist, so she immediately leads me to lie down on the wooden table. Yes, the one with the books as headrest. Believe it or not, these pocket editions guarantee optimal comfort and lightness for the head and the neck. I am not ashamed to tell you that I would most definitely swap my pillows at home for a couple of good reads cushions.

As I lighten up my heart and free my soul from the unceasing overthinking, I am suddenly oblivious of the table upon which I lie down. I continued to talk at first, but I soon gave up, as I felt my muscles relax. It is so unusual for them not to feel stiff and tense. There were no purple circles this time as the therapist positioned her hands on my head before relieving the tension in my neck and freeing my spine from the cold that had lodged itself in since however long, I do not know for sure. I felt safe there.

Safe enough at least to close my eyes and cast away this overthinking habit of mine, even just for a while. I let myself be transported away to a place which I know well. I could not spot myself standing in the picture, yet I knew exactly where I was: one of my happy places, the kind of souvenir you indulge in to let steam off before an important meeting, when trying to fall asleep, when daydreaming while riding the subway, or freezing at a red light when traffic is too dense for your nerves to bear.

I was looking at the sea. A rosy horizon betrayed the dusk as it was near closing time at the beach. The sand was all thick and wet, rougher than the usual fine crystals of sand after a heavy rainstorm. I knew this place; I have memory-traveled to this *lido* beach on more frequent occasions during the previous years. That sea. The sense of freedom. Broken shells and miniature, dark-brown jellyfish beach on the shore. Perhaps not the most translucid waters of all, but I do not mind the absence of the clear-blue coloring and idyllic beaches. I feel comfortable watching these tranquil waters I am so familiar with, since I have spent the summer holidays here since I was only nine months old. This time, however, there are no waves; there is no movement, nor is there any disturbance save the seagulls' flapping and the calm waves peacefully nearing the shore. I observe from (not so) dry land; I think of how peaceful the sea can be no matter how troubled its waters. Life does not give up. The waves come and go. And there will always be life because the current never ceases to ebb and flow.

This picturesque souvenir has brought a new lightness to my body. I have now reached slow breathings and inner quiescence. I have let myself be carried away, for I felt safe, even just this while. I wish it would last more than the last ten minutes of our one-hour Tuesday session.

Shaken

I left the house at 9:29 the next morning, off to Mamie Rose's. After a quick check for gas levels, I could not help but notice the 28.777 kilometers traveled by Choupette, the Fiat 500 car first owned by Mou, now used by one of its former passengers: me. Perhaps this is only a random and irrelevant piece of information, but I like to think of it more as a milestone. I just wonder when the time will come that I will drive this car to real-life purposes, instead of doctor meetings and short-distance-radius local-grocery shopping. I wonder when the time will come that I will walk into that car and proudly start the engine and gear up toward a new transformed me. In heels.

Proud, however, I have felt, as recently as yesterday, when, after hearing me out, Mamie Rose came back with a poorly closed box of natural organic Medjool dates, directly imported by a friend of hers from Israel. Only months ago, I would have freaked out at the thought of improvised 'snacking,' especially when you do not get to choose neither the time nor the treat. Yet, this time, it was different. Gone was the tension that would have shaken my bowels; gone was the fear that would have prevented me from breathing normally and consequently lead up to throat thickening, heart palpitations, and bloating, all the usual symptoms associated with guilt.

None of these discomforts had awakened though, and to my great surprise, I was indulging myself in picking the *biggest* date I could spot. I was struck by curiosity, for I already knew what dried prunes tasted like (they had been a loyal breakfast companion to my yoghurt and muesli for a couple of years before I eventually switched to oatmeal, the toppings of which I have changed a couple of times since starting this casserole-morning routine). I had, however, never taken a bite of a date, preferring to ignore the Deglet variety of dates imported straight from Algeria, and that I remember my parents both purchased and ate every once in a while when I was little. The North-African variety of dried fruits was usually soaking in some gluey syrup and did not look appetizing for the least. When these dates were left on a white plate at our kitchen table, my parents would take a bite along with some stinky, yellowy margarine and white bread (there was less fuss about the gluten-free diet back then). So, no thank you, I will pass.

Nevertheless, I shall not decline the second offering by Mamie Rose. The Israeli dates are simply exquisite. Dry yet packed with flavors. How blessed I am, for I will always think of her while indulging in (quality only!) dates. This is one more souvenir to which I can travel back to whenever I need some comfort (food). In the end, I did cross an important milestone that day: I parked the car in the driveway when I got back home, and on the dashboard, I read 28.804, yet my soul whispered that I got one step closer to real-life confidence and pride, for it was not about kilometers, it was about dealing with inner guilt.

Tightrope

I have been walking for some time, and I have always been afraid of the fall. I was an acrobat performing before an empty audience, for one's life is a never-ending grand finale that is not supposed to be applauded by anyone but yourself. One is not to live only to please and serve others; one is to embrace life and welcome both change or routine, criticism or kindhearted words, reason or a touch of *folie*.

Although the acrobat might not see the high wire's ending while walking in the air, it will not prevent him from performing his best act, one foot at a time, without ever looking down. Why would he? No need to be tempted, for the grounds do not harbor courage and adrenaline but only fear and defiance; so, the only way to look is forward, always.

Up and down, left to right, the tightrope has been wobbling, and I have lost my balance somehow. I have experienced the fall, and I am trying to get back on my feet and climb that rope again, only, this time, I shall be better prepared. I am still too stiff and tense to perform my act, but an acrobat is like an artist; he does not give up, for in the battles that he has fought, he finds inspiration, and in his art, he will embrace peace of the heart.

I fell once, but how many tightrope walkers have not touched the ground only to get back on their feet and attempt to walk even higher up in the skies? Perhaps the very imperfection of one's performance is what keeps our inner light burning and our heart going. If we were to know beforehand how smooth and perfect the act would be performed, would we really put as much heart into keeping our balance, into looking forward, into searching for yet another light to illuminate our walking along the rope? One foot at the time is all we ever need to continue, slowly but steadily through life. One at the time.

After the fall, it took me quite some time to realize that my anger at my body was irrelevant and preposterous. Until now, I had always seen this body as frail and disappointing, for it did not grow stronger by the day no matter how hard the efforts to nourish it properly. I realize now that what the body needs most is for me to cherish it. But I shall first need to free myself from both shame and guilt. How could I have looked over something as important as the very fact that this body I have been complaining about, especially because of its too-long recovery process, is also the body that has kept me alive through my falling? It held together…somehow. So, rather than feeling guilty, I ought to feel proud. And, yes, it might not recover completely. Actually, it will not look like the body I had in my teens and early 20s (mind you, I am only 26, and I have trouble thinking of my early 20s…). Still, a body changes. Every single body is bound to change in the course of one's life. Everyone's does. How great is this body for being able to adapt itself to our changing environment, to our personal growing, to our…living our lives? We ought to be more thankful. I need to, at least.

So away with the body shaming; away with the guilt. True, the body might not recover completely, but it does not mean that it will stop supporting you and caring for you, because, as a matter of fact, it has, until now. My body has known hell, and I am sorry for having neglected and ill-treated it. I ask for forgiveness. I have only just realized this and I think I owe my body an apology. I am sorry that my stress levels have torn you down. Almost torn you down, because here you are, still holding the pieces together. I feel proud that you are still willing to support me, to carry me. I thank you for protecting me from the devious mind. When we are little, we are told not to trust strangers, but we are not warned about our own thinking. It is time we climb back up again and continue our walk along the tightrope. One foot at the time, bearing in mind that the only way is forward.

Mother's Day 2019

We have started early, only to watch,
At first, with innocent eyes,
Before you taught us to look closer with our hearts.

We have learned how to touch and feel,
First with the hands,
Then standing upon our feet,
Whether well-balanced or staggering,
With you always standing there, next to us,
To support our ups, yet sometimes to soften our falls.

We have grown now,
But we still watch, touch, and feel,
The comfort and the love,
That only you can bring.
Happy Mother's Day.

Perception Takes the Plural Form

This morning is May 12th, and the sun is trying to win the battle up above in the air while flocks of gray and threats of darker skies make for quite a peculiar resonance in the 11-o'clock landscape. The shaving-foam-resembling clouds seem to be swept away by too strong a wind for the time of year. I cannot recall a tempest was forecast or that one was on its way. Nevertheless, only when opposites meet, is the contrast worth the wait, for it might just illustrate what one has long buried too deep away.

Sunday morning breakfasts are perhaps the most looked-forward to at our house. My sister is back from what has come to look more like a failed attempt at co-living than a genuine and respectful house share. The housemates seem to be very in favor of a restricted and military-driven community regime in which the players are all on the same foolproof team, only letting the ball roll in their camp and among players that they only have previously approved of. Much to their astonishment, they did not count on the plurality of actors and the open-mindedness of one of their 'mates' of their selective team, a.k.a. my sister.

She was perhaps the very one from whom they had least expected to hold such a colorfully rich-in-friends address book. Whether with bulging or pinching eyes; whether dark, yellow, pink, or green (the elves), my sister is proud of her creative recital of *connaissances* (acquaintances), for she has an always open window to multiculturality and embraces more than anyone the melting-pot metaphor.

All this to say that Sunday breakfasts always promise to be rich in colors and anecdotes. Whenever she drops by at the family home, I make sure I have two ripe bananas ready, of which I will only use one-and-a-half to bake fresh oatmeal pancakes for breakfast. I have tried to stress the importance of this first meal of the day, hence my efforts to satisfy her taste buds at the start of the day, even though she has never really been a breakfast person. The traditional *crêpes* or the American pancakes would not do, nor would the kids' favorite Nutella with white bread – never her favorite match, save on our Italian summer holidays where the nutty chocolate texture does taste differently, as if the flavor has been enhanced and improved to please the Italian children, big and small, and saving other adaptations of the recipe for export breakfasts of the children worldwide. Until that one morning when she had sure been pleased with the banana-and-oatmeal pancakes, chomping on them with satisfactorily enthusiasm. I believe this happened two years ago. I had 'invented' a morning routine that would please her taste buds, and since I have been concerned about her having a healthy yet fulling breakfast, I always keep a too-ripe-to-eat banana which I mix together with one egg, a couple of tablespoons of oatmeal flakes, and a bit of vanilla sugar. A pinch of salt, and ready it is. Bake and flip until golden brown and until the batter is used up.

Now that I think of it, our breakfast table is incredibly varied and rich. Our family is what I would, from now on, call a typical hotel-buffet representation with the choices being displayed at a one and only wooden table, perhaps deprived of the plain white tablecloth and napkins but soberly dressed with table runners or placemats or both. And candles. Enough chit chat already, I present to you our breakfast buffet. Mother is of the salty type and indulges in a soft-boiled egg (five minutes), a slice of ham (could be smoked salmon or bacon when *really* in a hotel breakfast lounge). A Medjool date or two with butter and multigrain leaven bread make do for her happy day and glorious smile. My sister's menu preferences have already been described earlier, yet she is perhaps the easiest mouth to please: apple cake, banana pancakes, gingerbread, banana bread, and the many variations of it, peanut butter with bread while at work only, a chocolate puff pastry or yoghurt and muesli she will have but only if in a hurry. I will not go into great details when it comes to my plate, or shall I say 'bowl,' since it has already been stated that I am mostly pleased with fruit and porridge now. Last but not least is my father, who has probably the sweetest tooth of us all and the worst possible combination (when talking in terms of digestibility): French croissants or raisin pastry puffs are among his favorites during weekends, while, on weekdays, he will have two to three slices of preferably white and mushy bread, topped with industrial (fake) honey, apricot jam (homemade, bonus point) and ending with either Nutella or a piece of *speculoos* with a thick layer of butter, but the latter option is only reserved for the December holiday season. *Bref*, the four of us do make for a quite peculiar, melting-pot picture and are glad to represent the multiculturality of breakfasts, all colors and sizes welcome and embraced. Great tolerance here. No, I am not being sarcastic.

I wish I could say the same of our Mother's Day dinner-party conversation. What an antagonistic view of society and life my grandmother from my father's side provides. Especially to the human rights' activist (and feminist) that was sitting next to her that Saturday night: my sister of course. I might be exaggerating, perhaps just a tad, but as a spectator of yesterday night's paella dinner party – we celebrated Mother's Day a little earlier with both our grannies – I can assure you, dear Reader, that the conversation between the two of them is one day bound to end up in a warzone conflict, for neither the grandmother nor the granddaughter would give up their stance. No need for them to keep up appearances and save face. Neither will give in, of that I am absolutely sure.

Yet, I secretly feel that Mamiche has more than once called my sister a rebellious soul. Just like a cookie that, even though prepared following the exact steps of the sacred recipe, tastes a little different, not odd but not quite right. Only connoisseurs will appreciate the enhanced *saveur*, for only they will acknowledge and acquiesce the improvement from basic baking to fine and refined *haute patisserie*. I do not believe that in today's society, there is room for discrimination and hauteur. My sister's views are different than the baby-boomers', and perhaps this is for the best; it means that change is about to happen. Sadly, there is not much to do or say to change an ancient bourgeois' opinion on life. Mamiche has developed her viewpoint over the years based on her experience and sometimes on rather old-fashioned social codes. We cannot expect Mamiche to simply give her blessing after the (in her opinion) too-long academic career. Six years and two diplomas have inevitably delayed our debutante's life into stereotypical society. To tell the truth, I believe that neither my sister nor I are meant for the quiet suburbs reality with the perfectly mowed grass, the leased cars, the kids, and the inevitable debts. We are misfits. Brainy misfits, perhaps even too idealistic a sort. But we have each other's back and shoulder to cry on. She is my person. I am hers. We are lobsters.

So, as I was sitting on the opposite side of the table, I could not help but observe the candid narrow-mindedness of Mamiche who would rather see us happily married with children and hence puppets of a society we do not understand, rather than single and strong-opinionated, halfway through a process of personal development including the finding of our inner voice and peace. I regret to tell her that some of us need a little more time to find their place into a society they can no longer relate to. Unfortunately (for me), defending our position is both time and energy consuming, the latter I lack of. I have emptied out and tore down my armies by wanting to prove myself to others, always and endlessly more; by striving hard to be the perfect girl, daughter, student, the perfect selfless person everyone could rely on, everyone but her own body and soul. I have lost my self and seem to have buried my soul too deep for me to call it back. I need now to get back my artillery and shovel up the pieces, wherever I can find them, until the day I too shall rise again.

Back, Yet Unwelcome

Yesterday night was a roasted fennel and Scottish salmon Sunday night, but, more importantly, the end of the Mother's Day weekend festivities. We had celebrated the occasion on Saturday with both our grandmothers for a dinner party and had then spoiled our own mother on Sunday morning, handing her a new pair of gabardine pants of her favorite designer and, obviously, the matching salmon-colored (no joking) knitted top. Actually, when I come to think of it now, it was more of a *vieux rose* color rather than a rich, fat, omega-three-fishy one (no offense to salmons). But none of this really matters, for she absolutely adored her outfit and would have too if it had been shrimp-colored, so much so that she even could not help but shed a little tear, *tradition oblige*. Or was it the text on the card? I guess that is a secret that she will never tell.

The official celebrations being over and done with, the weather also started to change, as was forecast by the Royal Meteorological Institute of Belgium – I just checked that out on the official Belgian website for weather and climate because, *obviously*, I would never have guessed what I.R.M. stood for but wished to boast a bit as well. Most of us are used to accessorizing our work outfits with either a hooded parka/raincoat or, as is more convenient for perm-hairstyle ladies, an umbrella. Better to be safe than sorry. What's more, ladies save 80 bucks for not having their perm go fuzzy electric like. Moving on.

Sometimes, as happens when your hair is inexplicably untidy, messy, and hopeless at being tamed, one can also be astounded by the quick turn of events and their intricate modus operandi. Okay, be honest now, your hair looks quite like Einstein's. So Mother's Day had been windy and gray, not leaving a single opening of light in this gray, cotton, woolen sky, although not a sufficiently gloomy-painted landscape to keep Mou from settling in her deep-forest-green sun lounger on the terrace. Yes, indeed, she did venture in a mid-morning tanning session. With something of a ski-season scarf (ahem, neckband or neck warmer if you like) and a sleeveless vest, zipped all the way up, she let the wind attack her face now and then, always hoping the sun would take a sneak peek and add a little color to her face. It did not. And it would not until Monday, at least according to the I.R.M. Despite the puddles and cold, the happy festive time was warm enough in our hearts to bring all of us comfort and sun in both our home and all the way to our seafood-paella party. Who needs a dollop of sunshine anyways? Luckily, dessert on Saturday night involved a lighter version of homemade apple cake and vanilla ice cream so as to even better juxtapose warmth and cold, the pole's opposites, yin and yang – dualism, let us say.

Yet, we did not sulk when the capricious weather got cast away on a desert island at the start of the week, to our great surprise. Well, not so desert at all, for it only went a thousand kilometers south, to little Italy, poor *them*. I am as delighted as a Seattle resident when reading in the morning newspaper that it has been raining in California; it is a once-in-a-while dose of fun, or just plain 'weather' justice.

This mid-May depression hit hard the usually sun-stealing countries of the Mediterranean, even leaving flocks and a white rug of fresh snow in Corsica (not that Corsica be a country, at least not yet to some people's great displeasure, but that is a debate I do not wish to stir nor conduct – good job showing yourself out of this tricky situation, fool *me*!). To cut a long (and boring) meteorological story short, that Monday meant more than the start of a new week; it officially welcomed the spring season we had all long been waiting for, at least in Belgium. The temperatures would even rise a bit to a nice and pleasant 18 degrees until Friday of the same week (four days of weather justice, not too bad I ought to say). This meant it was the perfect mix of sun and warmth for anyone (Mou, are you reading this?) to lie down and enjoy a tingling of sun along with a refreshing breeze that keeps the sweating away. Very little does Mou need indeed to get tanned; I, on the contrary, choose not to be facing the sun directly or else I will make a funny lobster of myself. Hence the reading and the chamomile beneath a sunshade. Reading in the outside heals the soul, or so I like to think. Truth is, I could not wait to end Vladimir Nabokov's *Lolita* to get my next book started: Sebastian Faulks's *A Possible Life*. Faulks again, guilty as ever.

Sadly, I could not keep still. Nor could I disturb Mou's half-snoring tanning session with what felt to me like the comeback of heart palpitations and a curious, if not stressful, headache. It did not feel like a 'traditional' pain that invites itself into your head because of lack of sleep or plain tiredness, or any of these routine pains I can identify as fast as the first symptoms show. I feared I was soon to experience the second migraine I have had in the course of my life. And, believe me, *this* sort of headache is absolutely *hors catégorie*. Perhaps half unconsciously, half apprehensively, I was starting to feel the presence of an unwelcome and not-seen-since-long fiend. That peculiar headache. A dark flash crossed my head, and, soon, I would feel the tension and weight invade my skull, all of it, but more specifically center stage until it explodes and contaminates all the other parts of the head, the left side always being more painful, especially behind the eye. That headache is like a leading actor who knows his spotlight place. I was acquainted with fellows of his for months, the supporting headaches I shall say, but I also got rapidly used to and relieved by their absence. Until that clear-blue-sky Monday after Mother's Day, upon our return from a little walk into the woods, for Mou thought it would do me good. I understood the origin of this ache: stress had returned to my body, and it started to show. The next day, I was to meet the psychiatrist for a *mise à jour*, a reporting meeting. How odd that after all these months, my mind still retains command and control of bodily aches, preventing the soldiers to emancipate and be set free. If I worry, my body suffers the consequences. If only I could tear down the whole command post and claim victory upon the despotic ruler.

This migraine-esque episode was the *mise en bouche* for the next course. I had been harvesting too much tension and apprehension; I had been running silly like a headless chicken, worrying sick unbeknownst me, yet annoyed with the bodily repercussions. That night, at 0:47 a.m., a blowtorch was lit to heat up and make a decent caramel crispy crust *crème brûlée* out of my bowels. I wish I were talking about the French dessert here. Burns. The torch was only the reflux which caught me off guard; surprise-attacking my inner defensive walls that had been destabilized and undermined already once before. I was burned again. This time, however, the trigger had not been a certain type of food pertaining to a too-acidic terrain; instead, the catalyst was my own excessive and exhausting stress. My mind was playing tricks on me with burning consequences. The flames kept ravaging me from the inside, doubling me up and keeping me pain-awake among the untidy and too warm bed sheets. Until, at last, I was freed at exactly 1:58 a.m. when most of the fire was put out, although the damage had been done, and the tears had started to dry. If I had known this beforehand, I might as well have savored a piece of grapefruit. Or the whole thing. I could have blamed the fruit. In this case, I knew I was becoming a danger to myself.

Nuts Are Hard to Crack

About last night. While my father was away, dropping my sister off at the house she shares with some *huis clos* good society people (according to them at least), I was watching an episode of the 1970s British series *Fawlty Towers* with Mou, sipping tea and treating myself to one of the last Milka Easter eggs left on the low-standing coffee table in our sitting room. These leftover chocolate eggs are quite uncommonly put in a vintage (although poor quality) miniature, copper, frying pan, and since there is no matching lid, it has proven far too easy for us to fetch and eat them (almost all). I had put the television on and had chosen this sitcom – if choice there was, for there are not many interesting things to watch or worth watching lately. It was the least bad option of all if we did not want to fall asleep before a too-serious wildlife documentary whose end-of-the-world background music does not match the live image of a still-life bug species or whatever this was.

All seemed quiet, perhaps too quiet. How was I to guess that a tempest was coming? My father had been harvesting crops of frustration, haste, incomprehension for too long since his last growl. He 'does not mean' to be hurtful in any way, or so he says. But how can he expect me to distinguish the humor behind a knife-cut wound of his uttered words? Although I have had my share of *coup bas* or low blows in the past, always trying to save face and defend my condition (I really am burned both outside and within, please can we drop this now?), last night was particularly hurtful, since I am now empty and too tired to argue even more. I cannot keep having this argument. Yes, I am aware that this 'situation' must be tough on his side too. What father would not want to boast about 'his girl' living the life of her dreams and making heads turn? Well, I am sorry I have left a sour or disappointing opinion about my falling and burying deeper into the grounds. I need time – possibly too much according to some, I agree – yes, I need time to bounce back. First, I need to stand upon my feet. It might be useful to find those feet back. It just might. Only then will I try to find the balance to stand upright and move. Forward. I seem to have lost my way.

To my utmost surprise, some will state that it is better to recover at home while being married with kids, divorced but still with children of your own, even unmarried or something in between, but always with little ones running around. When you are sick or suffering from an illness or a certain condition, you are most likely to be respected when you have already proven to society that you have, indeed, check-crossed the first moral codes expected from women. I think it would have been easier for me to have a house and a family of my own, for then at least people would have 'given me a break' from recovering at my own (snail's) pace. Actually, now that I come to think of it, this is all very utopian. People will always judge you based on what they believe is good for you.

I find comfort in the thoughts that love is free and that love is all; it is untraditional and unconventional, since the lover picks his or her own palette to add some coloring to his or her life. The recipient shall be blessed, and he shall spread his gratitude to the world around him. Acts of kindness tend to respond to a snowball effect; the more love you give, the faster it reaches other hearts and encourages them to do follow the tracks.

Yet, one must also set some boundaries, for you cannot lead the way without securing your own path. The act of giving must not prevent yourself from hearing your own voice, especially not when it has been desperately crying for help. I understand the importance of this statement now, but I wish I would not have snoozed the alarms because here I am, wandering in the family house corridors, devoid of myself, completely lost and physically (and emotionally) wounded, trying to recover from my deepest fall. Nevertheless, it does not matter how many times you travel back to nostalgia in search of a clue, a hint of where and when it might have gone wrong; you get hit in the back every single time, and not once has this knife been less sharp-edged. The scars it has left, whether seen or unseen, cannot be healed completely, so I shall better ask for forgiveness to myself. Forgotten, however, they shall never be.

Oftentimes, the wounds remain unknown variables of some intricate mathematical problem. When facing the subject's impossibility to solve that problem on his own, it is common for the entourage to start meddling in the calculus. Unfortunately, my recent experience has made the cut go deeper. Only last night, my father started to speak about my need to find a project 'soon enough,' otherwise… He did not finish his sentence. I know it does not sound like he is going to get me banned from anything; he is merely preoccupied. He wants me to get a grip on my life, although he lacks tactfulness. According to him, I ought to sit an exam and start as an administrative worker for the federal government. I have no idea what he thinks federal workers' life and work styles are (actually, I do, and it is far from being laudable or enviable), but all of a sudden, my throat was thickening as he was making his point clear, and I could barely prevent my tears from caressing slowly my now-red and warm cheeks. My voice got hoarser as I tried to argue, yet quickly it turned out to be pointless, for the harm was done no matter what. I knew he would say that 'he did not mean it *that* way,' but I did not see *any other way* to interpret the message, and it certainly was not humorous at all, regardless what he told me later on.

Yet, I cannot blame him. It must be tough on his side too: how come his daughter cannot live her life? I can relate to his despair at the sight of his 26-year-old *girl* wandering at home like a phantom would wander through the walls of the remains of a cold sand castle on a desert island. Why has time stopped for me? And where is the drawbridge that is expected to lead to the hopefully happy and favorable exit?

I decided that, this time, I would investigate into my father's reaction. Why had he suddenly made all sorts of plans, whereas he knew I still lacked the energy to carry them out? I suddenly realized that he too had been wounded by a sharpened knife, during the Easter family reunion some weeks ago. My father had suffered the attacks of his own mother and the dire comments of his aunts regarding my 'condition' or the burnout reality that is still very complex to understand (at least when you do not experience it). Trapped between all the tarts and pies, he was under siege during that reunion, which I did not attend, since I could not stand on my feet that day. It was the weekend before the Easter holiday. On April sixth, most brothers and sisters of Mamiche gathered together to, *ahem*, celebrate the New Year (better late than never). The first generation of cousins was also invited as long as they brought tarts and drinks to cheer the ranks. Like in most cases, the host ends up with a Mount Everest of pies and oceans of soda to drink, at least until next year's reunion. I wonder if they will end up celebrating the previous New Year on Christmas Day of the present year. It might be a grand première; the start of a new tradition.

Bref, that day of early April, my father was surrounded or trapped, it all depends on the terminology one wishes to use to describe this surprise field attack or fire-meddling questioning that lasted half an hour or so. "She should go back to work, the sooner the better," or, "It cannot be good for her to stay at home for so long a time," were among the projectiles launched by both aunts and cousins. Although I know they mean well, they lack to understand that my body has been through *a lot*, too much actually to handle. Whatever injustice there must be felt, it ought to be on my side of the battlefield; how unfair this all seems, being trapped with clear physical aches and brakes that hinder the projects that the soul has on the wake. "I still *dream*, you know," I want to shout. I still *want* a go-back to a balanced (this time), busy-bee life, but if busy it shall be, it ought to be chosen by who else than…me? I like to remember what Sebastian Faulks says in *A Possible Life*: "The project of my life is to make the most of what I have." So it shall be.

Dear Reader, you will have grasped, indeed, that I have finished Vladimir Nabokov's *Lolita*. The author has brought a welcomed and much-needed turn of events at just about the right time, for I was starting to feel bored by the journeying and motel lodgings while on the road with his little girl protégée. Though the language used was outstanding, and I do appreciate a bit of French and German once in a while in the text, I had started to get bored with the action. It was time for a change, and whenever I feel the need for the language to be absolutely brilliant in a reading, I must admit that I tend to turn to Sebastian Faulks; he is my favorite rescue reading.

I needed to be rescued. Still do. I shall be honest, for the last couple of days, I have been feeling a little shaky, unstable even. My head started to spin, for I was thinking too much again, and I feel like there is too much pressure on my brain. Especially when considering that these sources of stress ought not to be triggered by family chit-chat, regardless of their thoughtful nature. I could not help but feel deeply sorry for my father; that he be disarmed on his own (family) terrain; that he be forced to deploy his artillery at the most unlikely moment: a late New Year's gathering. He did not tell me the exact projectiles that had been launched, but he need not to: his silence suffices to translate the destabilization and bewilderment he was put up with.

I am sorry, Dad, I really am. I wish you could boast about me leading a V.I.P. life somewhere in New York or elsewhere, anywhere, just as I had once dreamed of. I too wished I could leave some apartment I would be renting in a Brooklyn townhouse (the Upper East or West, Soho, and others might be a little too expensive), stopping at the local coffeehouse and ordering a double black, no sugar, and making sure to repeat the exact same phrase every day, although the barista would know it by heart, given my frequent in-and-out on my way to work. Work. And what might that be? Writing? I wish I could write and revise, proofread and express my own creativity as to nurture my soul and take care of it being lit and staying alive after this destructive episode. Office work? I try not to think of it too much. It is still too soon; it is still too easy to fall into the trap again and erase myself further.

Instead, for months now, I have been trying my best not to stagger. I try not to think too much of how perverted this world is and how I do not fit into a twisted, rather unfair, society. This nut is hard to crack, I tell myself. Over the years, I have not only blown out my inner light and silenced my soul; I also seem to have built a shell aimed to protect myself from disappointment and distrust, a shell that ended up squeezing me always tighter into a safe and solitary comfort zone. I trusted no one and only relied on myself. Too much for a person to handle in this ever-growing society that prioritizes, on the one hand, the delegation of tasks, while on the other hand, stressing the importance of multitasking and know-it-all. Ironic, is it not?

Sebastian Faulks seems to share my thinking and also points to "how financial institutions had all but bankrupted the developed world". One of his characters, Elena, "couldn't see what she was meant to do about it. She had one life to live. And surely every human being in history had been born into a world that was in some way peculiar: blown out of shape by cataclysm." While this behavior and way of looking at life must be shared by scores of people who are deeply rooted in their daily routine and following like sheep a leader they see in 'society at large,' I, however, find myself holding onto a piece of wreck left floating onto a sea whose current I do not follow, given my inability to just pretend. Neither will I use a subterfuge to fit in; I would rather live the way I find decent, honest, and respectful. Faulks is right when he says, "We are like home computers." Well, most of us are. He refers to the point-and-click theory in which "the self is like the icon of the trash can – a false cartoon representation of the real work done on the hard drive". He cannot be more accurate. And that is the very reason why I admire his writings so much, for I seem to find myself little by little as I list the last books I have yet to read by him. Hence my need to be rescued by reading.

Blank Sheet of Paper

That is what I am and what I am most good at: a blank sheet of paper waiting for the first drops of ink to be written; it will only take the first droplet for the rest of the story to reveal itself. One. Yet, the ink reservoir is as dry as my skin. The latter I try to keep moisturized with this deliciously fragrant, jasmine, hand-care tube – I do, I promise, I do…at least one time out of four when I think about it, perhaps a little more often, but who does use these skincare products anyway? If I am willing to admit that the one I (seldom) use is not greasy at all, I am still a little skeptical about the use of it just before lunch or dinner time: I just cannot imagine a jasmine taste to be added against my will into a simple yet authentically flavorsome and exquisite *piatto di pasta*. Hold it, no. And may I add, "Not gonna happen, there, nope." This is finished, kaput. End of discussion. Or wear kitchen gloves.

Why do I always end up drifting off course when I try to end a paragraph with at least *some* complementary information about the opening sentence? So, about the sheet of paper, I do recognize that it has been blank and empty for some time now, possibly forever. It is up to me to fill the words and give a voice to a story yet to be unleashed, a tale *en devenir*.

Ever since growing up, I have always wanted to follow the right path, to be the perfect everything; and this meant that I also wished the ink reservoir to be filled right up to the brim before, well, I guess, starting to *live* really. This behavior has unfortunately proven to be self-destructive and adventure-killing, for no one waits until full as ever as it might get, not even a car. Do you know any car that constantly runs on a full tank? I thought so. Yet, it does not hinder one's coming into and getting out of the car, nor does it put a stop to any trip one wishes to embark on; quite the opposite actually, and who am I to judge after driving all the way to my sister's previous *kot* in Louvain-la-Neuve on an almost-empty tank? I was literally driven by the adrenaline, for I knew I could still travel as many as 50 kilometers and the trip to and back would take at most 45. I was safe enough, and so shall I be now.

In hindsight, I believe I have always wanted the inkpot to be filled up to the brim before I started *real life*, almost as if the running up to that very moment – life – was only practice. The equipment I thought I needed would guide my 'choices' over the years: homework, studies, work, benevolence, empathy, care, perfectionism leading to the controlling of absolutely every detail. I seemed to be filling the pot with an ocean of waves; the very ones I wanted for the current to flow without ever thinking about the intrinsic nature of it; thus forgetting about emotions and personal preferences/choices.

Unfortunately, I had also forgotten about the most important element of it all: water or simply ink. I had been filling a pot up to its brim without ever noticing that I was doing so with only 'constituents of' rather than the raw material it needed most. Where was I to find ink? Where does one find the essence of life, the water to nurture the heart, make the body grow and let the light shine on one's very soul? I had missed something. I had missed what the sunlight is for flowers, what the sky is for the ocean, and what the wind is to silence: all these years, while taking care of everyone and everything, I had forgotten to care for and love myself first.

Nevertheless, I do like the blank sheet of paper challenge, for that was something I was good at. Ask me anything, and I will gladly do the research; I will find the information, and I will take care of a project until you are completely satisfied with its (successful) outcome. If it were not for my father to coin this metaphor, I would not have thought about it that way, but he was right when he told me that 'I can always start from scratch and put all the pieces I find together.' There are scores of illustrations.

At work, for instance, I was 'dropped' in a couple of square meters of what seemed to be an old storage room turned into an office with only a tiny window to let the light in. I was early (of course, I was) and had been waiting for over 30 minutes with an empty Starbucks coffee carton-mug to go that I had picked up at the Brussels Central Station. I had carefully drunk the black magic potion while on the subway, facing the occasional spill of coffee while bringing the cup to my mouth just when the driver hits the brakes. Thank you for that and all the times it may have happened to me. Check. This was my first day at work, it was a cold mid-December day in 2016.

I arrived before nine that morning, and as my hands started to freeze, I spotted the embassy's accountant walking on the pavement to meet me. He had started two weeks earlier and did not know much more about the managing of such an honorable workplace. So when I discovered my desk and the poor half-broken chair (although it did have wheels, so what am I complaining about, *really?*), I was told to start right away. Noted. But with what exactly? Among the heap of copies of contracts (that ought to be in the accountant's office, *I'm just saying*), I managed to turn on the computer and read my predecessor's emails in order to get an idea of her daily tasks and duties. I quickly found out that I was to manage the embassy and take care of external relations with our providers, help out the diplomats with the understanding of Belgian traditions and work/life balance, with the occasional translation. I am grateful for all I have learned, on my own. I was given a chance, and I will forever be thankful for their trust, their confidence, their care, even though I put perhaps a little too much heart and soul into the managing and running tasks. Somewhere, I knew I was not in good shape physically; the academic career had left me paralyzed with a fear I could not understand at the time. I feared the mere fact of living my life, of being a leading lady. Until then, I had only lived through definitions of efficiency and performance, perfectionism and self-effacement. I had started with a blank sheet of paper at the embassy, but I did not change; my mind was even stricter and I emptied myself from whatever left there was of my being. When the first pages were filled with enough words for the rest of the story to be written, *i.e.* when I got used to the workplace and the wonderful people I had found my body and myself burned out, devoid of light, but not because of work, simply because of me. I had failed my own body, and it got scared that I would go too far into self-oblivion and mistreatment.

Hence my question: how does one live? How does one follow the stream and go about the day? How are you the leading lady or actor of your own life? If I am well-aware of the fact that I will never blend right in, I would like to know, however, how to wake up and live *for me*, although this sounds quite selfish to me when I think about writing this down.

I shall admit that my body is still frail and perhaps not in the best of shapes, but I long for gumption; I wish I were not so hesitant, indecisive, and, yes indeed, broken. The burnout reality has struck twice, for both the body and the soul, the mind and the self, have suffered severe and extensive damage. Perhaps the filling of the inkpot was not so much a first draft to my storytelling; but rather the destruction of both the author and its sharpened feather-quill pen. I needed this burnout to save myself.

Fortunately for me then that my inner light whispered sweet words to the soul in order to keep it alive. For the last 15 months, I have been trying to shake this self and give it a new *élan*, a new inspiration. Only this time, there is no room for mistakes – or 'mis-fills' in the ink reservoir – the body would not take it, the soul even less. I wonder what the first word of this story shall be, yet I feel blessed that I was given another chance as its author, and I shall write with even just droplets of the ink I have saved up. There is always a new beginning, always a new chapter to be written.

Translucent

What if there is no getting out of this? What if I do not find the exit of this labyrinth I have been roaming into for the last couple of years? I wish I could see what more there is behind the hedges, above the bushes, but I still have not found yet the central place where all passages lead to, a place I imagine to be decorated only by a weeping willow tree under which one would be able to sit on a wooden bench to read a book, enjoy the view, and contemplate life as it is. Once arrived at the center, I believe it is easier to picture one's way out. After some time spent wandering about, sometimes crawling, sometimes running, other times just walking and getting lost, one is happy to find the tranquility of a willow tree, the breath of fresh air brought by the wind passing through the green leaves of the tree to find the inner peace of the traveler's soul, for the latter already knows that once it has reached this center-stage *étape* of the journey, the road ahead lays wide open, and it is only a matter of making the first step for the others to quickly follow suit. I remember a Grandmother Willow telling a famous Disney character that, "Sometimes, the right path is not the easiest one," and I could not agree more. So, when will I finally reach center-stage?

The passages seem to become only narrower with the days. Perhaps my heart is being crushed, perhaps my very hopes are shrinking. And these last two or three weeks, I have felt transparent, translucent even, more than ever. I had never really imagined this were possible. I had not, until now, realized that there was a slight possibility for the outcome to be *triste*. It has been four nights in a row since a different kind of fear has settled in my soul, making the heart cry a little bit more, well more than it used to. I need to see what my life *could* look like. I need to see the *future* me. I wish I could see a *possible* me. What does she look like? Will she ever shine, not for others but for herself? Will she be kind not only to others (well, that too, of course), but, more specifically, will she have learned by then to be kind to herself?

Since I am no clairvoyant and have no intention to going and consult one, I merely have to make peace with time, for only time will bring the answers to these questions; only time will tell when it is right for me to shine and walk through the exit of this labyrinth. Please let it be soon, although I can already sense that there is more than one possible exit.

The sooner the better, some say. In my case, however, I believe I need a little help, for I still struggle every day. It has become common knowledge that I overthink everything, that I erase myself for others, that I do everything to please everyone as long as I am not required to think about and take care of myself. I have no idea where to start, and for the last 15 months, I had first wanted to recover physically before embarking on the 'learn to live your life' journey. Unfortunately, since the body is still locked down, I need to shake this destructive mind of mine once and for all. People need to find a balance between the body and the soul. So do I. I need to find a way to manage both issues at the same time. Women are said to be good at multitasking, and I am a queen in this field, save when it comes to my person: I then let myself, my soul, and my body down.

At first – and this was a couple of months ago – I thought I needed to go away for a while, to take some time away from everyone and everything I know. It had become too comfortable a home for my mind to keep destroying the body and crushing the soul. I believed that getting away would force me to start over and learn how to live *really*, or at least in a more realistic way, without being overwhelmed by all these thoughts, questions, and fears that have been harassing me for too long. I realize now that this loophole would only have made matters worse, for I would have been weaker physically (and there is no room for more frailty; I am already afraid that my body is going to break anytime) and run over emotionally. I need to be honest; I have been severely burned twice, both physically and emotionally. If the fire is under control for the time being, my dearest wish, however, is for the fighters to extinguish the flames and let the cool rivulet flow until it finds the heart all the way to the soul. Only then will it come out and start to shine, the sunrays of which mirroring in the tranquil stream.

The fact is, I did not go anywhere. Well, I did not get an extra stamp on my passport, which I do not have, by the way, since one's identity card is enough to travel between European boundaries, or so we will see after the Brexit, or not. I sometimes wonder though, what it would have been like if I had had the guts, if I had decided to leave everything behind and start afresh. I admire the people who do, and I would be happy to know their secret recipe for gumption and daring. While daydreaming of New York, San Francisco, Italy, and the many places I wish to discover, I wonder where my heart will settle…eventually. Will it? Ever?

Being ready for takeoff means that I first need to break free from this destructive pattern I am imprisoned in. And I, myself, am the prison guard. I, myself, have the key. Only, I seem unable to unlock the door. I am running through the dark, sometimes bright, corridors of incomprehension, overthinking, sorrow (sadly, there are those days too). I suppose I *did* get away in a sense. Staying at home and trying to reach center-stage has made me realize that I had been effacing myself even more because the thought of getting worse instead of getting better during this not-yet-physical recovery process made me scared to the point of oblivion. I preferred to *forget* about myself, to *taking care* of myself. Instead, I only tightened the screw and got tougher on my daily routine until the need to control things got me emotionally burned out too.

Truth be told, perfectionism and despotism upon the self and the body were only signs of love and care toward the others and a means *for me* to silence (even just for a while) the fears that were devastating me from the inside. Until it showed outside. So, please, meet me, the paradox in itself: the one who embarks on a kilometer zero getaway route, for she had found a better loophole which led to her (almost-achieved) own destruction. Do find that key, silly. Hurry.

Dame Blanche

It has been over a week since I have last put something on paper. Rather than an inspiration standstill, I merely could not seem to find the time to write. The last week has, indeed, been very busy, perhaps too hectic even, especially since I still cannot recover with 'a good night's sleep.'

I know better now than complain about it. I ought to consider myself 'happy' with the couple of hours of rest that I could bring together at night. Unfortunately, since everything works frighteningly backward with my body, whenever it gets too exhausted, it just switches to some automatic response that I call 'the invisible filter.' From then on, everything that happens and everything that is being said or done just passes right through me. I have become the invisible filter. I feel no pain, no emotion whatsoever. I do, however, feel a bit irritable at times, and to be honest, when I wake up in one of 'those mornings' with a heavy and swollen head, with empty and sunken eyes, the least smack or slurp gets on my nerves, and the baby lamb turns into a porcupine: I seem unable to stop hurling barbs at the people near me. Poor them, it is not their fault. If only they knew. This is another person. This is not me. It is the lack-of-sleep side effect speaking.

I am, thus, this piece of transparent cloth through which everything seems to pass. During the day, I try to keep busy in order to forget about my own limitations; it has been over 15 months now, and I find it hard to fuel up some new hopes. At night, I stand guard and keep watch. I wander somewhere in a foggy *entre-deux*, the name of which I do not know. Between heaven and Earth, a soul wanders through Purgatory, but I lack both the psycho-philosophical and medical backgrounds to explain (rationally?) the intermediary state one wanders through before reaching sound sleep, daring to dream even of 'beauty' sleep, meaning a restorative rest for both the body and the soul that prevents one from waking up looking haggard and gaunt, feeling filter-like, or phantom indeed.

These past few nights, I have stood guard more often than ever before, and to make matters worse, I have also found the time to be too bungee stretch, too long. I am against the very fact of getting out of bed before seven in the morning, first because I believe it is unfair for the other sleeping beauties at home (their rest ought not to be disturbed by my morning shower, although I am no singing contestant, but, still, one never knows: how often does it happen that your shower-gel bottle falls into the tub, making a loud noise, hence waking everyone up and making *you* out of all people miserably guilty and sorry?); second, because I still hope I can get my body and my mind accustomed to a 'normal' morning routine, but, again, "Who am I kidding?" as I like to say.

Perhaps, the very reason I strictly forbid myself from getting up before the clock strikes seven is that I am afraid the morning will last too long and that I, incidentally, will go round in circles, brooding over what *the everyones* in this society would be doing and what great lives they can lead while I (and by this, I do not mean to be the ugly duckling) am stuck and unable to gear up. I cannot even engage first gear, and this while I have had my driving license for almost eight years – ironic, is it not?

Perhaps, I ought to explain why I have been feeling haggard and gaunt for these past few days: I have been too busy for a suffering body and soul like mine, both subjects still fighting to merely 'make it through the day' without too many additional scattering. The underlying reason would be the two-day city break our family had, but, in this case, I would like to stress the importance of what I call 'healthy burning out.' Sometimes, indeed, I too wish to feel alive and well, as if nothing were wrong and I were in the prime of my life. Enters Bruges and the *dame blanche*; enters the fantastic four and the celebration of our mother's birthday.

After breakfast on May 29th and the quickly drying off tears left by the surprise effect and the discovery of the birthday present (happy tears though, at least on Mou's side), the four of us shut the car doors, and off to Bruges we were! We had chosen this medieval city for its grandeur in its ironically small circumference. Mother had it all: the Dukes' Palace (a 15th-century palace now turned into a five-star hotel, booked with a huge discount, just saying), the upper-standard yet not too posh restaurant, the picturesque townhouses, the Holy Blood blessing, for we did, indeed, pray and laid our hands above the relic of the Holy Blood that is safely guarded under lock and key in the Basilica of Bruges, yet shown to the public only once a year during the procession on Ascension-day.

Upon arrival, the clock struck midday (well, a quarter to, but this is less fun to tell). We were welcomed by two young hostesses and their famous Bruges Flemish accent. Although I am no supporter of stereotypes of any kind, I must admit that accents in the Dutch language vary depending on the geographic location rather than the social ladder (the latter – and please excuse the homonymous fortuitous pronunciation – only dividing the register used in the language: slang, coarse, posh, grotesque?)

Actually, when I come to think of it, neither does social class have something to do with the register of the language one uses; my best guess now is personality-based. I believe, indeed, that regardless of the social class, the level of education and the environment you live in, one can choose between this or that word, slang or upper posh, and I have more than one example of rich (parents-savings-account-safe) presumptuous 'chicks' that talk until my ears fall off from both horror and shock. I feel panic-stricken at the record-breaking amount of swearwords they can put in one sentence only. Yet, this being said, let us get back to the main point: the hotel welcoming and our first get-to-know in the lovely city that is being referred to more than one time as the Little Venice of the North.

The City Hall (the 'Burg'), the main square or market square (*Markt* in Dutch), and the 88-meter-tall belfry were our first (picture) stops. We later walked through narrow streets and passed not twice but thrice in the same cobbled street, always missing our lunch spot, a tapas bar I had found on a lifestyle blog but which failed to print out its name on the front window, leaving the (absent-minded) tourist a little disoriented. In a certain way, this made the shrimp ceviche, ham *croquetas*, fried oregano-flavored potatoes, mini-hamburgers, and salmon/asparagus tapas even tastier; we had deserved the right to enjoy this savory feast. Oh, and it was Mou's birthday after all, so I guess we were allowed the extra green beans salad and the rest, and by 'rest,' I really mean the fact of putting our feet under the table and letting ourselves being served and pampered until dessert.

Belly-fueled to the top, we continued our tour. Next, were the Basilica of the Holy Blood (you know the story), the Old St. John's Hospital (and pharmacy), the Saint Salvator's Cathedral, and exhausted we were, our legs staggering and happy to head back to the hotel for a hot shower and some more cosseting, this time at the hotel's restaurant. It all happened after 9:14 p.m. when my father had just started on the dessert, the Belgian classic, the *dame blanche* or a vanilla ice-cream (homemade, obviously) traditionally served with hot, dark chocolate (probably melted with a teensy bit of butter to make it shine even more and add some calories to the not-yet-overloaded levels of sugar), and a dollop of *chantilly* (whipped cream, with a whisk, not store-bought, again…obvious). Enters the magic.

I still cannot quite explain its source or its origin, but after a ten-minute tough debate (with my mind), I decided to order one as well. Panic-stricken. Not me, but my family. It had been years since I had last ordered dessert, many more since I had last enjoyed a sweet 'closing' of dinner. Mou got surprised, two times even, for the *garçon de salle* had lit a firework-like candle for my mother to blow out and make a wish among a dollop of dark chocolate mousse with some notes of fresh red berries here and there and a chocolate coulis. This unordered dessert was the happy ending to a fantastic, although exhausting, first day. Out, I was. Physically, I mean. Blacked out, exhausted, yet extremely happy to crawl under the sheets; the extra eiderdown being asked for at the lobby, because I knew I would be chilly after so many adventures. This is the kind of fatigue that is worth experiencing.

On the way back home on the second day, I fell asleep in the car. Still, I had found the time to look back on the morning activities and the closing lunch at the Dukes' Palace hotel. After a gargantuan breakfast and the absolute opposite of a strong espresso (the coffee aroma was, indeed, too poor too common, I am afraid), we headed to the deep south of the city and walked silently through the gardens of the Béguinage/Begijnhof, a typical green central yard surrounded by white houses that once were the homes of the *béguines*, pious women that, in the 16th, 17th, and 18th centuries, lived as a semi-monastic community in this domain founded by Margaret of Constantinople in the 13th century. We paid our museum fee and visited one of these typical houses from the kitchen to the living room, then walked outside along a patio to reach what must have been a cold and lonesome bedroom. The *béguines* did, however, sleep in a *baldaquin*, a too small canopy bed, so I guess their dreams were safely kept under the veils. An old press reminded us of how their uniforms and linen were ironed and neatly folded. The open fireplace was supposed to be lit back in the olden days, although I do not believe they could use the logs whenever they wanted or felt the first chills in their bones. Out in the central yard, I was surprised to see the grasses left untamed, growing wild and free. Perhaps this is how we best let nature have its way and find tranquility while silently admiring the surroundings and counting the white swans that invade Bruges's canals. A 120 or 200 of them, was it? I seem not to remember the number that the captain had told us earlier in the morning while we were on a 30-minute (tourist, but needed) boat tour.

The final attraction before lunch time would be the Diamond Museum with its twice-a-day polishing show. I was not aware of the fact that the polishing technique had been invented in Bruges by Lodewijk van Berquen more than 500 years ago. I had always thought Antwerp were the city of diamonds and shine; but, apparently, the art of cutting and polishing was discovered by a Bruges-native goldsmith when the dukes of Burgundy reigned over the Flanders's territories.

The show had begun a little earlier than our coming into the museum, yet we could sneak into the back chairs and attend the live demonstration.

Unfortunately, the host had chosen a somewhat sluggish question-and-answer teaching mode; his wish to keep the audience listening and enthralled was rather met by disorder and noise. On top of it all was the incessant crying of an eight or nine-year-old whose mother had simply decided to ignore the nuisance, hoping her delightful daughter would grow tired of her own annoyance. She did not. And neither did she for the entire time of the upstairs exhibition.

Reaching the last floor and tired of the one of too many reading boards, I started to stagger. My legs were abandoning me, and I was afraid my body would not support me much longer. Why now? I knew we still had to walk all the way back to the hotel for lunch, and this would take another 30 minutes, by foot. Moreover, we would need to fight our way through the overcrowded streets, spotting the first spectators, taking their reserved and front-row seats for the annual procession of the Holy Blood of Jesus Christ. (Who else, really?) Fortunately, for me, my sister walked next to me, sometimes lending me her arm so that I could lean on it and think less of the strength I had to find to take one step after another without tripping over my own feet. Lunch would be *petit* but chic, and, soon, I would doze off, absolutely weary but happy in my heart that Mother had been blessed for her birthday. Happy birthday, Mou. Picturesque Bruges was all for you. And us. Spending time together. Putting on hold the hectic hustle and bustle, the burning out and the void. Bruges filled our hearts with new hopes and a renaissance for family love.

Reconciliation

The Bruges getaway and the discovering, the tasting, the savoring, the fears of out-of-routine meal plans has proven to be a first step toward a long-awaited-for reconciliation between the mind, the body, and the soul. I feel no guilt nor do I feel shame when replaying the *dame blanche* souvenir and the licking off dark hot chocolate right out from the milk churn. I know I should not, from a start, feel guilty about 'food.' How many a man wish not to lecture me 'it is just food.' I have heard this countless of times, yet I cannot trigger any rational relationship with food. Not since the high-school girls society, nor since the Salamanca deprivations and frustrations, and, finally, not ever since the *kot* years and the fear of 'not having enough of something,' because one might think students are blessed with Mommy's meal-prep containers and microwave-friendly healthy dinners lasting up to four days, but once you have had your first mouthful of Mommy's best, it always tastes like, "I wish there were some more leftovers," for the food is no more, as empty as the dishwasher-safe Tupperware could be. This is when you leave it on the counter somewhere in your room, to be washed later on in the week, for university students do not have dishwashers, obviously, nor do they share the adults' spontaneous and logical post-dinner reaction of doing the dishes right away.

As I write these lines, I cannot help but notice the empty tea mug standing on the left of the living-room table and facing an also-empty soy-yoghurt pot with a 20-year-old spoon still from the very first cutlery set my parents had bought after moving into this house. This spoon is the last one of a surviving set of two forks, one (unsharpened) knife, and one bigger spoon, the latter being left somewhere deep down a cooking pan and kitchen utensils drawer which I do not wish to tidy up, for that would take a considerable amount of time and energy. This being said, I solemnly swear that I will do my dishes; I shall not leave any proof behind of the chamomile afternoon treat. But I shall first write.

It is almost four o'clock on this sultry and quite oppressive (weather-like) Tuesday. I have met earlier in the day with Mamie Rose who sparkled in a blue-jeans-colored linen dress. Her heart is so rich, her soul so generous, and her trust and care so paramount to me that I feel blessed only to know her. Unafraid was I as I unfolded the events and anecdotes of the past couple of weeks. We had skipped three weeks since our last chat, and meeting with her again rejuvenated my soul.

"How are you?" she asked me when sitting down and adjusting her hearing device. Her eyes gave away both her concern and compassion. "Actually…" I started, "I have been feeling different, not better physically, although I am half a kilo heavier than before, and, mind you, it is not only the *dame blanche* effect, this is a lasting change. I can feel it. So, indeed, I feel *different*. Positively different, and I have been feeling more tranquil as if I have, at last, found a way to put things into perspective."

Her smile at that very moment is one I will always remember. I think we both were relieved in a way that some green shoots have finally found a way to grow in this very damaged and burned soil. Perhaps this fallow land left uncultivated for more than 15 months now is just what I needed to sort things out. I know I still have to be patient and water the plants, but this is a first step toward the building up of the self, the development of my soul, and the taking care of my body. I was given a second chance, and just like the fields that have been depleted and wrecked, life will grow strong again after some rest. Until then, I still need to learn how to enhance self-care and, what is more, self-love. Until then, I shall need to learn to 'give some time to Time.'

Gift

I have just wrapped up the last Amazon package delivery received earlier this week (in two shifts) for this coming Sunday, two days from now, we will celebrate Father's Day. As you might expect from me, I do not believe in quick, unsymbolic, and unthought-about presents. Nor do I believe in writing simple and obvious wishes like 'Happy Father's Day to you. Love. X and Y.'

Unfortunately, the impersonal chop-chop gifts have increasingly become in fashion these days, acquiring a full-spotlight front-row coverage with traditional date-set celebrations such as Christmas, Mother and Father's Day, even birthdays are not exempt from this general rule/trend. How often do we find ourselves in a difficult and quite-embarrassing situation of being empty-handed the day before some important event? It is Saturday, late in the afternoon, and you walk through the aisles of the local supermarket, aware of the fact that, exactly tomorrow, this or that takes place, and you still have not decided what you will bring or give to the host or birthday boy or the very someone this whole thing is about. The cashier is looking at you, as if he knows. On the left, luckily, you spot some ornamental flowers on sale next to a shopping cart full of articles on discount, which, let us be honest, you cannot imagine buying as a present. Oh look, your favorite soap gets the 'buy one get one for free' stamp! Saving this for later, your mind is driving you crazy, for you still do not have a present, a little something at least to bring for the next day. Until, at last, on the shelf, just before checkout, you see a cactus and some orchids for sale. Done with overthinking it, you end up buying a white orchid (pink if for a girl), thinking this is better than nothing. And, quite unconsciously, you have been yet another victim of the quick and easy, unthought-about gift.

Waiting until the last moment to buy someone a gift might not be the best and most considerate option. At least for the recipient of it. The giver, instead, will only shrink more into embarrassment, making up excuses for his lack of time, sharing some common general knowledge (garbage) about 'the week's gone by before we knew it' or 'well, you know how kids are, you drive them everywhere and you're unable to go about your own shopping,' are among a few examples. But why is it, really, that we forbid ourselves to be honest? Who is ever going to frown when you tell them you needed the extra time during lunch to clear your head in the bookshop next to your office or the little walk you took to digest the morning's meeting that had sucked the last energy out of your body, or even the little blouse you bought for yourself, not because you were window shopping but because it happened to be on the way to the deli where you go buy that special sandwich they do not have anywhere else in the office neighborhood. No one. Like I said, no one is ever going to be mad at you for swapping the gift shopping for some needed and deserved 'you' time. You earned it. So, just be honest and get a good laugh about the situation. It is not about the gift, it is about the genuine talk.

There is no need to buy expensive gifts, nor should you go for too much extravaganza. Be your own self and sit down, take a pen, and write something out of the ordinary to fill the card (that is, if you bought one). Something as classic as 'Happy Birthday' can be turned into a more original 'Happy You Today,' although everyone seems to use it nowadays. Why not go for 'Get spoiled rotten with love and care' or the traditional joking opening, 'Don't choke while blowing that one additional candle.' Finally, 'save some cake for me' would be quite challenging and perhaps the inauguration of some sort of pie contest. All this to say that when it comes to surprising someone, the best way is to make sure they feel loved and cared about. And one does not need a gift to accomplish that goal. One solely needs a warm true hug, a deep look in the eye, and an authentic smile. Genuine thoughtfulness beats materialism.

I do like, however, the happy thoughts that are linked to the anticipation of giving someone something, even if this be the tiniest little something. This Sunday, as I said, is Father's Day, and I cannot help but smile at the thought of my father unwrapping the presents we got him this year. You see, my father is one very complicated person, for he can never be surprised or taken aback. Never as in, not ever. You might remember him as a victim of consumerism and the need-to-have-it-all society pawn. He would always end up buying everything before we even got the time to secure the rights to buy it first. I know it is not a competition. Still. We wanted something more than a card and box of chocolates. Well, we are kind of famous in Belgium for our chocolate, I must admit. But still.

If he had already repeated many times in a row that 'tomorrow is the second Sunday of June,' hinting to the Father's Day celebration, I believe he had ended up giving up on reminding us of it. He did believe we had forgotten about him, and the child in his heart could not help but feel disappointed or hurt, upset perhaps. His reaction, however, was priceless and one to recount. That Sunday morning, indeed, my mother and I were having our usual breakfasts, sitting at the table in our living room and waiting for Father Bear to come out of his grotto. As soon as he opened the glass door between the staircase in the entrance hall and the living room, his sleepy eyes disappeared behind a broad smile at the sight of the little presents that were displayed on the table. With the sister coming downstairs and unready for the not one, not two, but, yes indeed, three rounds of 'thank you' kisses and the additional dose of too-much aftershave that, to our great pleasure and quite unwillingly, got glued upon our cheeks, our father could finally notice that his child's content had been satisfied, for gifts there were indeed. A knitted, English-made, dark-blue knit sweater, two crime books by a to-him-unknown Italian author, an Italian comedy on D.V.D. (one he could not find in Belgium and that I had to order online via Amazon), and another book, history this time, about the Roman Empire, by one of his favorite television figures. All presents had been carefully chosen for him and according to what we know he likes most.

The joy of seeing my father speechless, even just this one time, hid back another reality I wished to crush a little longer. I was not, again, feeling that well. I recalled the conversation I had had with Mamie Rose or Marraine la Fée only a couple of days ago, stating quite proudly that I did feel different *now*. What can I say? It was not meant to last for long.

One more time I would be torn by abdominal cramps and bloating, then the breathing was getting harder, until, finally, my tongue got cut, for I do not know how many times, only because my teeth are on edge, like spikes, preventing the peace and tranquility to enter the castle. I am surrounded. By pain. Quite frankly, the aches I feel in my legs, in my bowels, the dry skin, the nocturnal wakeups, all are still bearable to me; what is not is the trying to figure out why it takes so much time for the body to follow on the mind's evolution. I feel like I have made such progress; I can now rationalize more; I have not had any panic-attacks for a while, and I no longer fear the doorbell whenever someone is waiting outside, for I used to think that somebody from the embassy or some kind of social inspector would be standing there, wanting to turn me in and make me go back to work again.

So, no, I am not doing better. I wish I could wake up one morning and see past this whole experience. I have grown. I have learned. Yet, sadly, I am not ready. For some reason, I still need to fix some unfinished business. I still need to develop a healthy relationship with myself and provide for a safe haven for the body and the soul, safe enough at least to recover from this fall and build a person strong enough to get that morning coffee on the corner of the street, book under her arm, purse in the other, and the élan to get going, never to stop again. Gumption. So much of it.

The book in question would always be the result of an in-depth research that I would have done previously before buying it (ordering it online would be last resort, only and if only I would not find any other bookstore where to purchase it within a reasonable time lapse). Some upper corners of these books will be folded here and there, highlighting a must-stop, an insightful pause, a quote, an inspiring message, anything at all worth notifying and saving for later. Last in line was that "while pain is universal, it is also utterly private" by Viet Thanh Nguyen in the absolute masterpiece, *The Sympathizer*. I like the subsequent realization that "we cannot know whether our pain is like anybody else's pain until we talk about it. Once we do that, we speak and think in ways cultural and individual." This is the goal I have set myself to achieve. I wish, through my writing, to share my own story in the hope it can help others to never fall that hard and break into pieces, ever.

The Candle Wick

"How do you feel today?" whisper some people, whereas they really wish to know whether I have not capsized yet into some sort of depression or mental illness. "The intellectual faculties are intact and will stay so, thank you," is my ready-to-go answer before I pinch my lips, take the big puppy dog eyes and shyly admit, "The body, however, is still a wreck." Even after 15 months-and-a-half. Mind you.

It was only last week that my father had come up with a metaphor I had not thought of yet. As he was having lunch with one of his close colleagues (the wife of whom also struggling with some health issues), he was asked how I was doing and, not wanting to lie, he said the recovery process was very slow. Too slow perhaps. If I shall admit that the mindset has already made some noticeable progress, the body, on the other hand, does not seem to follow suit. The colleague seemed to understand this. Instead of nodding along and hearing only half of the story, he was (according to my father saying) genuinely worried and very compassionate. "She is like a candlewick that is struggling to keep upright, waiting for the flame to be lit again," or so he said.

I have indeed gone too far, I have indeed asked too much, and I have indeed won a war that was not meant to be fought: the destruction of the armed forces, my own body's reserves. We are almost halfway through the month of June, and I was again struck by how slow the recovery of a body can take. "Be kind to your body, give it time," said the therapist when I went to see her yesterday after a two-week break for her to fly off to Greece and discover an island unknown to me, except for *The Sisterhood of the Traveling Pants* movie (I have only seen number one of the series). Santorini, if memory serves me well. The body, despite me considering it frail, weak, or disappointing, does not forget a trauma, hence its caution in delivering too much energy at the same time or too much joy to share at once. How could I blame it? It cannot be fooled, for the slightest indication of the least sparkle will be absorbed right away by the mind who, in turn, will slip back into conflict and fight for perfection, control, and restriction. All the battles and the arguing, until now, would have been useless, so the body protects itself by prohibiting too much energy from running through my veins. Or so it shows. I really feel like a beached whale though.

The Last Straw

The vertical blinds are shut to protect against the coming heat wave that will hit Europe this second-to-last week of June. I have stockpiled on bottles of water, and I am the proud owner of at least 12 of them, each of one-point-five liter, this leaving out the 20 bottles of mixed-brand sparkling water, cola or soda cans, cartons of almond, cashew, and soy milk, and bottles of alcohol that we no longer use but keep in store (in our cellar) just in case somebody who we might invite over might fancy a sip of (before noticing that the bottles have been stored for more than a decade). The two Lipton Ice Tea bottles we had bought around Christmas time for when our cousins were coming over are now challenging the Italian counterpart, the 50-ml San Benedetto's Thè alla Pesca, bought for the same purpose but neglected at the time for being too healthy to them. Actually, the former is a full sugar treat, whereas the latter's flavor is only best appreciated when served with ice on hot days spent at the beach along with a Mulino Bianco cookie (Pan di Stelle being our favorites when my sister and I were kids) or the more traditional and cross-generation ones, the *plumcake*.

Proof being given of the refrigerator's excess body mass index (we will be safe from drying out or dehydration), I wished to share a recollection of the events that have taken place only this week, ending today, a Sunday. The bottle of water will empty as I will guide you through the hectic week I leave behind.

I was walking in the woods last Sunday with Mou, enjoying the at-the-time still-refreshing air and the chilly humid wind blowing in our necks. It was a first since long, but I could not quite understand how my legs did not keep pace. They somehow felt heavier, as if I were carrying leaden chains on both feet. My belly was at war too; fighting some spasms traveling from left to right like those little marble balls that kids play with, going crazily in all directions. The head, well, it was looking down, thinking hard, struggling not to let the dark flashes come back. In vain.

After our 30-minute escapade, Mou and I headed back to the car, sipped from the lukewarm bottle of water that had been left behind, and we drove back home, only to dread the upcoming pressure of the following day, a Monday.

There are two ways of reacting to any kind of hustle and bustle or to a rough-and-tumble life situation: either you fret about it, either you belong to the stress-resistant people who take the current when it serves. If I am a first-class hopeless nerve-wrecking chicken, my sister, however, is already miles ahead of me, at the most antagonizing pole on the tension ladder, for she has already learned to shake things off her shoulders, especially when they hold a destructive power and have a potentially mind-killing factor. Okay, too much. I am overthinking this. Again. Truth be told, I do pressure myself, for I want everything to be perfect all the time, while this is almost unachievable.

That Monday, however, the symptoms that had awoken during the Sunday walk into the woods grew stronger and more acute. There was little I could do but to fret. I wish people would understand that a burned-out body and soul is locked inside his or her home, as if grounded, but for their own best. I suffer from peaks of little energy during which I try to write or cook, but then, all of a sudden, I can feel my body collapse and give up on me, as if quitting in supporting me. Those are the times when I know that almonds won't do the trick, nor will chamomile herbal tea or any other magic trick to fuel up on. Those are the times I need to be patient and wait until the dizziness is over, until it is safe again to venture out on both my legs, to put one foot after the other. So, meet me, after 16 months of combat, still fighting for the light to ignite again and to shine my way through life.

I am not on some sort of vacation. I am burned. Deeply burned. The road to recovery is long, and, sometimes, I feel like I was given 'free tickets' to kick-start my life. But the flight got delayed, and I seem to miss every departure. For now. I need more time…and I will earn that one-way ticket that will take me directly to the deserved destination of inner peace and tranquility, confidence (some at least), hope, and love. For now, again, as I am unable to cope with the hustle and bustle, I need to protect my body, myself, from the mind that still rushes me through the dark corridors of perfection, control, restriction, and servitude. Why do I have so much trouble with taking care of myself, especially since I am a first-class passenger when it comes to helping out and reaching out to others? I wish I knew the answer, for it would give me back 16 months of fretting and years of self-destruction.

That walk into the woods was different than the other times we had gone out. I could not enjoy it for the least. The symptoms had had three full days to ripen and burst at the most inconvenient time: a get-together family dinner date. Waking up on Wednesday morning, I knew something was wrong. It took me a lot to manage myself out of bed before it hit me: I could not stand up in the shower, so painful and torn was the lower part of my belly. Cramps and spasms were challenging the already-concrete feeling just below the explosive limit of the organs. And there I was, looking like the Hunchback of Notre-Dame. For the remainder of the morning, I was very still. Not that I am a loud type of person, but *come on*, let us be honest, even though I am severely burned from within, I tend to keep myself (too) busy (given the circumstances), and I still cannot shake off the guilty feeling that eats me up.

On Wednesday morning, I was dead silent, slumped on the couch, the V-shaped abdominal cramps having me left doubled over. It was only 10:37 when I checked my cellphone and there were no messages other than the usual Facebook and email notifications, mostly spam, uninteresting stuff.

The original plan for that night was for my mother and me to meet with the rest of the family sometime later so that we could all have dinner at Ellis Gourmet Burger in Brussels. Our American family would be there, Mamiche would be too, the cousins. All of us, reunited. Now, that can be turned round any way one likes, but the truth is that *this* is a night out. And *I* am a wreck. Meaning, in burnout language, that *if* I take the train, walk all the way up to the chic burger tent, meet with them and find myself in a quite noisy or hectic (and probably too-hot) environment, *I* will most definitely drown. And I can't, for I have lost my last paddles to swim my way up to the shore. More than ever, I need to keep my head above water because I have already taken too many hurtful plunges. My body, clearly, can take no more.

I knew this all too well during the Sunday walk into the woods. How naïve can I be for thinking that I could go out in the city center without suffering the consequences? I was grieving silently, biting my lips not to call the doctor, but, in the end, I gave in, for the pain had already triggered some tearful episodes that had rendered me red and puffy. There would be no family dinner in a fancy restaurant. Even *this* is too much for me to take. I need the peace and quiet.

This was the last straw. Those cramps, those spasms and the cystitis, the burns, the near-fever *slash* cold sweats, the gritting teeth, the fretting were one time too many. This was my body's last rebellion, and I knew nobody anymore ought to expect from me to turn up at any out-of-the-ordinary-routine event. I just can't. I need the peace and quiet. I need the time. So, please, would you let me take the time I need to heal?

All my life, and this being especially true during the last 16 months, I have kept telling myself to be the perfect girl, the perfect student, the perfect everything, reaching out and helping any time I could. Until, sadly, the 'what others think about me' got completely out of hands and crushed me; it destroyed me. How counter-intuitive this is to me: I need to *learn* how to be self-protective in order to reach self-care and benevolence – love – toward my own body and self, as much as I care for the *everythings* of the *everyones* around me. And this in a world that has increasingly become more self-centered and narcissist, a society that pushes the lost or burned souls off the cliff; those genuine caregivers that are trying to make up for the collapse of solidarity and human interaction; the backers of love and peace.

We just cannot *let it be*. Even if we pay with our bodies and souls. But the key is you. Us. The self. To find this key, I shall remember Donna Tart's words in *The Goldfinch*: "You'd be surprised what small, everyday things can lift us out of despair. But nobody can do it for you. You're the one who has to watch for the open door." Until then, I will sort out the way to lift me up and grab that doorknob. Knock, knock. Am I there yet?

Prelude to Life

'You need the hurt,' for that is when you know 'you are out of that cave.' Wise words coming from a Netflix series, but it has never been more accurate. Trust me when I tell you that the cave might seem a secure or safe place to crawl or hide into when everything seems wrong around you while, in fact, that cave is but a dangerous and hazardous place to retire to. You do not live there; you are merely a shadow. You survive. But only for a while.

After the fire has gone out, and the remains are burning ashes and coals, one finds a haven in the comfort and sometimes in the solitude of that cave. One discovers a refuge in the time passing by, in the settling routines, until these too become the steel bars of your own imprisonment. Crawling out means finding oneself at the surface of the ravage, in a landscape still damp from the fire that has been blown out, some charcoals scarlet red only to remind you that the burn and the scar are deeply impregnated indeed.

First, I shall need to overcome the fear that still runs through my veins and thickens as soon as defiance and stress are plotting against my already-battlefield-looking recovering. Second, I shall admit that the burnout, no matter how unfair and difficult an experience, has, in fact, saved me. The 16-month period of time until now is but the tip of the iceberg; the hidden part, however, has grown bigger and stronger over the years because of the destructive lifestyle I had imposed on my body and myself (although unbeknownst me). My mind was steering a tight ship, an Iron Lady of the seas, until it became untamed and destructive, with goals only set higher, with standards only pushed further up a ladder toward perfection and a sure cloak of invisibility.

As it becomes impossible to meet these stringent and authoritarian requirements, the self and the soul vanish in their own cave, leaving the host to its own devices, completely emptied of its soldiers, nude in a battlefield, deprived of its rightful weaponry. This captain has deserted and fled away.

Lastly, I shall merely accept that only time will help me toward self-acceptance, self-care, and self-love, in such a way that these values can coexist with the benevolence and care I feel toward *the everythings of everyone*. Good deeds, whether big or small, contribute to the human nature of reaching out, to greater understanding and being understood in a respectful and tolerant manner. Hoist the flag, for the ship of peace is ready to set sail. Let us find out how many will embark on this voyage and dare the adventure.

So, dear Reader, look out there. Look out at the world. It may not be perfect, but if it were, would it not bore you out? Let your self be surprised, let your self be spoiled, not with presents, but with life. Breathe in the life, and you will be spoiled with its wonder and love. Because it comes out, eventually. Until then, walk…with eyes sparkling and set toward the future, the next second already belonging to the past too soon. I will try to meet with you along the way. However, in order to do so, I cannot skip any step, nor can I fool time. The hurt has been done, the scars remain, yet there is beauty and strength in your suffering, for it simply means that life is burgeoning and that your time will come for blossoming out. It will. Eventually. It will.

*

The sequel of this story shall depend on the soul coming out of its cave and shining light upon the ashes, in such a way that the same colors that have been used for destruction can now be transformed to paint the sky pastel tranquil and love plentiful. A *bientôt*, along the way.